D1180826

Trincomalee

TRINCOMALEE

The Last of Nelson's Frigates

Andrew Lambert

Foreword by HRH The Duke of Edinburgh

CHATHAM PUBLISHING
LONDON

FRONTISPIECE: The *Trincomalee* as currently (2002) displayed in Hartlepool's Historic Quay. The restoration is complete and the ship is afloat, but because of limited depth at the entrance to the dock she is not ballasted down to her seagoing marks. This reduces the ship's stability, so as a safety measure the upper yards will not be fitted until the ship is alongside her permanent home in the larger basin of the Jackson Dock – the site is out of the picture to the right. (All illustrations by courtesy of the HMS *Trincomalee* Trust, unless otherwise credited)

First published in Great Britain in 2002
by Chatham Publishing,
99 High Street, Rochester, Kent ME1 1LX

Distributed by Gerald Duckworth & Co Ltd,
61 Frith Street, London W1D 3JL

British Library Cataloguing in Publication Data
A catalogue record for this book is available from the British Library

ISBN 1 86176 186 4

Typeset and designed by Tony Hart, Isle of Wight
Printed and bound in Great Britain by
Bookcraft (Bath) Ltd

This book is dedicated to the memory of the men who built this ship in Bombay close on two hundred years ago, and to their modern counterparts who restored her to life in Hartlepool.

Contents

Acknowledgements

This book could not have been written without the unwavering support of all those concerned in the *Trincomalee* project, my fellow authors, and a host of friends and colleagues around the world. While such a well-travelled ship will always take her biographer on many new voyages, the excellent new charts of her great Pacific voyage were produced by Roma Beaumont not twenty yards from my office! Less obvious, but equally essential support has come from Zohra, Tama-Sophie and my parents.

Andrew Lambert

BUCKINGHAM PALACE.

British sea power in the 18th and 19th centuries was the basis on which the British Empire was founded and maintained. Whatever shortcomings modern historians may discover, it will always remain one of the great events in world history.

There are many tangible reminders of the Empire, but there is little to illustrate how that overwhelming sea power was achieved and maintained for over two centuries. The brilliantly reconstructed *'Trincomalee'* provides an invaluable clue to the practical exercise of sea power in the days of sail. Her story is the story of the naval and mercantile contribution to the development of the Empire and she brings vividly to mind the conditions under which the seamen of the period lived, fought and worked.

Captain David Smith and the HMS *'Trincomalee'* Trust, together with all the craftsmen, deserve great credit for the highly successful restoration of this historic ship. I am quite sure that this excellent account of the restoration, which includes a detailed history of the ship herself, will be of great interest to all maritime enthusiasts and historians.

Philip

Introduction

The Worlds of HMS *Trincomalee*

THIS BOOK is the story of a ship and the many worlds she has touched, but it is also the story of the men who built her, who sailed in her, and used her as a drill ship. The story continues with war service, and the young people who came aboard for holidays afloat, before her most recent occupants restored her and gave her back to the many worlds in which she belongs. She is now afloat, fully restored, and to all intents and purposes, ready for sea.

The frigate was the workhorse of the Royal Navy in Nelson's day. Used for reconnaissance, scouting, convoy escort, coastal operations, and occasionally to support the line of battle, they were involved in every significant action of the long wars with France. There were never enough of them, and Nelson once famously declared, 'Was I to die this moment, "Want of Frigates" would be found stamped on my heart.'

After two decades of experience the design of the frigate had been improved and refined, creating something close to the ideal. Ordered in 1812 HMS *Trincomalee* is one such frigate; she would be instantly recognisable to Nelson, and most welcome in his fleet. Although her form had

An inter-war view of the *Trincomalee* when she was known as TS *Foudroyant*. A cabin was built on the quarterdeck, producing a second tier of stern windows, but otherwise the main features of a standard frigate hull are still apparent.

been copied from a French ship, captured in battle, the structure of the new design was entirely British. The first ship of her design was already in service by 1805, and many more would follow, including HMS *Shannon*, victor in the greatest single-ship action of all time.

Unlike the great majority of British warships, HMS *Trincomalee* was constructed in the Indian port city of Bombay (modern Mumbai) by a powerful trading and administrative body, the Honourable East India Company, that combined the government of Indian territory with a monopoly over the trade of the East, especially the tea trade with China. She was built in the Company dockyard, of Indian materials, by Indian craftsmen, under the direction of the great Parsi shipbuilder Jamsetjee Bomanjee. As such she symbolised the unity of the global empire of trade, linked by the oceans, and dominated by the chain of naval bases around the world that enabled British fleets to sustain operations in all seas. She was named for the great anchorage on the coast of Ceylon (modern Sri Lanka) that had been taken from the Dutch in 1795 to complete British control of the Indian Ocean.

Built at the end of the Napoleonic wars, *Trincomalee* spent her first twenty-five years in the reserve fleet as part of the deterrent force that secured the Empire without the need to fight. Over time she became obsolescent; her guns were now too small, and her type had been replaced by steamships in the main fleets. However, her solid construction ensured that further uses were found for the ship. In the mid-1840s she was modernised, with a new, more powerful armament, but a smaller crew, to serve on the distant peripheries of an empire which made incessant demands for naval force to resist American expansion, uphold law and order, support British commerce, and influence local rulers. Her two commissions as an imperial cruiser, on the North America and West Indies station, and then in the Pacific saw her involved in anti-slavery patrols, fishery protection, disaster relief, protecting British interests in war-torn countries, Arctic exploration, native American issues, and scientific research.

At the same time *Trincomalee* witnessed a remarkable transformation in the nature of naval life to meet the new industrial society: continuous service for ratings, the effective end of corporal punishment, new disciplinary codes, improved food and medicine. The ship felt the impact of the industrial revolution, with iron cables, water tanks, canned food, and so on.

Although the transitional Royal Navy did not inspire any major literary assessment of the changing worlds of seafaring life, another frigate cruise from the Pacific to the Atlantic, that of the USS *United States* in 1843-4, formed the basis for the only mid-century naval literary masterpiece, Herman Melville's *White Jacket, or The World in a Man-of-War* of

1850. Although the core theme is a denunciation of corporal punishment, Melville was too acute an observer to miss the wider movements that were transforming naval life as he wrote, from the impact of technology and the nature of warship society.

By the time *Trincomalee* paid off in 1857 the sailing warship was effectively obsolete, a point brought home even in the seemingly trackless wastes of the Pacific. However, while the ship had finished exploring new worlds abroad, there remained many new worlds at home. Her solid teak hull and quality construction led to a new career as a drill ship, along with many of her contemporaries. The new technical navy of trained and skilled ratings, many in the reserve, needed training ships to hone and refresh the skills that would be required should a major war break out, and it was thought that this work would be most effectively done afloat. While her Bombay contemporary HMS *Ganges* achieved immortality by giving her name to the Boy Seamen's Training Establishment at Shotley near Ipswich, *Trincomalee* suffered the indignity of being renamed. At the turn of the century the eccentric ship preserver and training ship enthusiast Geoffrey Wheatley Cobb had saved Nelson's *Foudroyant* from the breakers and restored her, only to see her wrecked on Blackpool beach. With no more old battleships to hand Wheatley Cobb bought the *Trincomalee*, and renamed her *Foudroyant*, and as such she masqueraded under false colours for close on a century. At least she was preserved, and for this Cobb deserves great credit. After years at Falmouth she spent the Second World War in Portsmouth, and felt the wrath of the enemy – although only slightly, unlike the Bombay-built *Wellesley*, which was sunk by a dive-bombing attack.

After the war *Trincomalee*'s stout build kept her going, while her companion, the French-built *Implacable* was taken out and ceremonially scuttled, being reckoned beyond economic repair. Her Bombay contemporary HMS *Cornwallis* lasted until the late 1950s, before being broken up and turned into garden furniture at Queenborough. Finally, having provided generations of budding Nelsons with the chance to 'serve' afloat, she was in need of a major rebuild if she was going to enter a third century.

Fortunately ship restoration on the necessary scale was already being undertaken at Hartlepool, in the North East of England, now eclipsed as a traditional shipbuilding centre. The successful restoration of the great ironclad HMS *Warrior* had demonstrated the depth of talent available locally, and *Trincomalee* arrived, somewhat ignominiously, aboard a barge in 1987. Although her restorers were men of iron and steel, they quickly reversed two hundred years of shipwright development to master the art of wooden construction, while developing innovative methods to address the major problems of the ship and the available infrastructure, all within the context of a major conservation project.

The combination of a skilled workforce, sound management, careful research and the generous support of major donors, including the Heritage Lottery Fund (conceived and established just as the earlier sources of income had been exhausted) enabled this complex and costly process to be completed in 2000, when the ship was formally opened to the public. She had been a major attraction for many years, providing new generations with the opportunity to see large scale shipwright work on all aspects of the ship, from keel to mast head. At the same time television has shown her to a wider audience, opening new worlds for the last classic frigate of Nelson's day.

Such is the enduring fascination of Nelson's Navy that the fictional genre of naval novels has grown to become a major publishing phenomenon. The first master of the format, Captain Frederick Marryat was a veteran of the era, and started writing fictionalised accounts of his own experience serving under Captain Lord Cochrane, one of the greatest frigate captains. Other landmarks of this genre have been C S Forester's Hornblower series, and more recently Patrick O'Brian's Aubrey/Maturin novels. To all these stories, and the many others that have joined the genre, the *Trincomalee* is the ultimate companion, a real life, full-sized frigate of the type that features in almost every book, prepared for sea and ready for action.

The *Trincomalee* has touched on many different worlds, worlds that she, and perhaps she alone, can connect. In the twenty-first century her story needs to be told and retold, for it is both unique, and all-embracing, a testament to the innate talent and perseverance of the human spirit in all conditions.

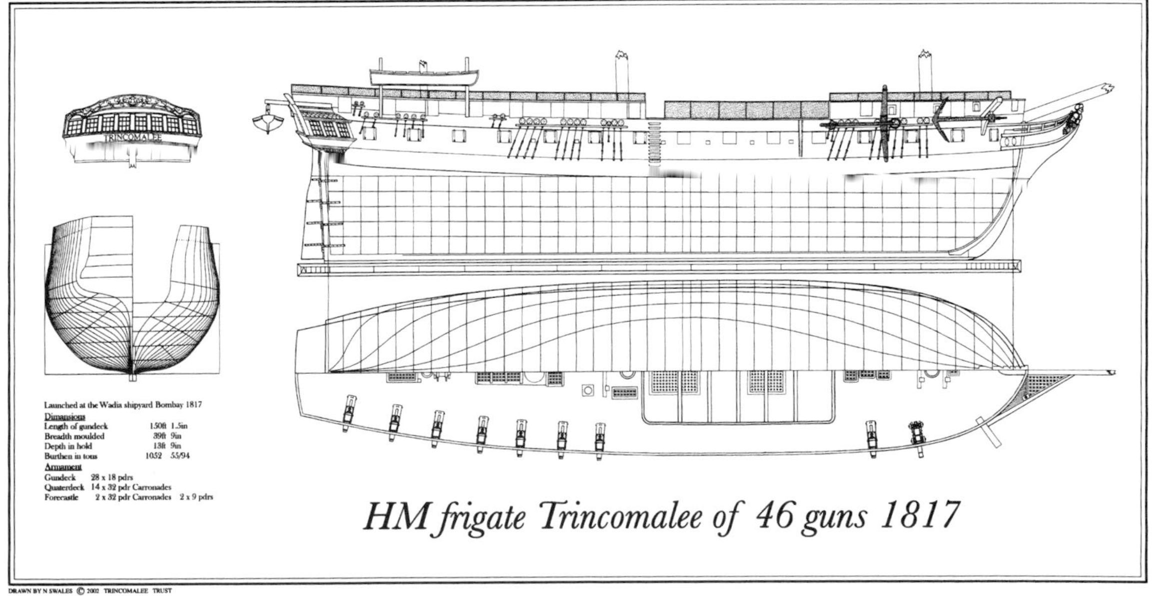

A modern drawing by Norman Swales of the *Leda* class as fitted out at the end of the Napoleonic Wars. This is the configuration most likely to have been followed for *Trincomalee* had she been commissioned for operational service when first built in 1817.

Chapter One | # The Frigate in 1815

What is a frigate?

THE ORIGIN of the word 'frigate' is lost in antiquity. Over the centuries variations of the word, in many languages, have been applied to vessels ranging from small oared galleys to ships of the line which were the ancestors of twentieth-century battleships. But if the ship types differed enormously, they all had one thing in common: speed. However and wherever the term was used, it carried the connotations of a vessel that was lighter, more nimble and faster than the norm.

This was still true in Nelson's day, but the definition had become more precise and more generally accepted by all the maritime powers. In essence a frigate was a ship of moderate size designed to operate outside the line of battle. Whereas a ship of the line carried at least 64 guns, and anything up to 120 on two or three gundecks, the frigate was restricted to around 28 to 44 guns, with a single main battery (although, like line-of-battle ships, the quarterdeck and forecastle also mounted guns or the lightweight large-calibre weapons called carronades).

The frigate was a multi-purpose ship, capable of scouting for the battlefleet, or operating independently in trade defence, commerce destruction or patrol – the ancestor of the twentieth-century cruiser. In fleet actions their role was secondary – repeating the admiral's flag signals so they could be read elsewhere in the line, towing damaged ships out of harm's way, and occasionally acting as a decoy to draw fire from hard-pressed ships of the line. They were neither powerfully enough armed nor strongly enough built to take a place in the slugging match that was the usual sea-fight of the time, and by convention frigates were not fired

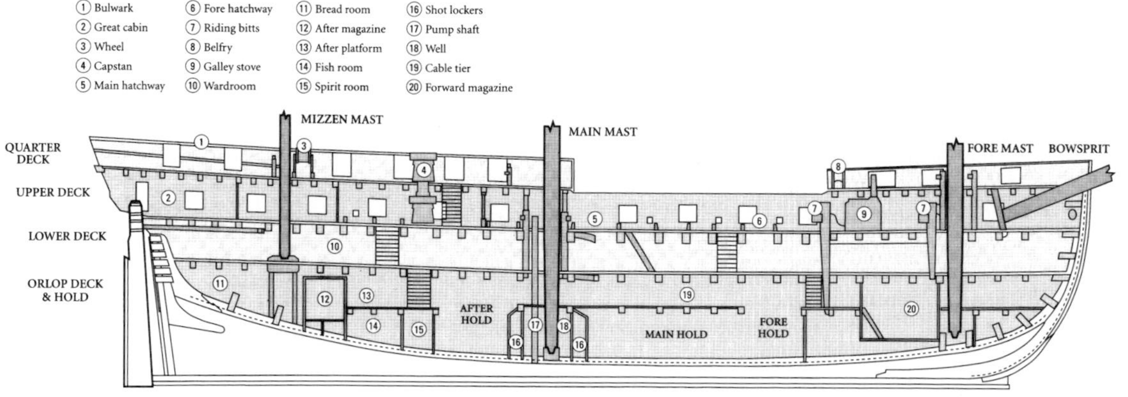

Profile showing the layout of a standard British 38-gun frigate of about 1815. The basic arrangement had been established over half a century earlier, and was subject to only detailed changes in fitting-out, although frigates grew substantially in size and firepower during that period.

on by battleships unless they fired first. However, they were generally faster and more manoeuvrable than ships of the line so could be used for reconnaissance, tailing an enemy fleet or tracking it down and bringing their own fleet into contact. These same qualities made the individual frigate a very powerful weapon for the attack on trade, and conversely as a convoy escort; but they were also deployed in squadrons - by Britain's enemies largely to enhance the commerce-destruction effort, but by Britain as hunting groups to track and destroy enemy raiders.

As the Napoleonic War progressed and the demoralised French fleet became ever less willing to engage the Royal Navy, the main task of the battlefleets became confined to close blockade. However, while the main fleets were involved in this tactical stalemate, the frigate came into its own. After the crushing victory over the French and Spanish fleets at Trafalgar in 1805, the frigate was the principal weapon by which the Royal Navy controlled the world's sea-lanes. Although some enemy frigates and even the occasional battle squadron might escape the blockade, in general British frigates were freed from the likelihood of encountering a more powerful opponent. This made it possible to deploy frigates, on their own and in squadrons, to exert the kind of sea power previously the monopoly of battleships. From the Caribbean, via the Mediterranean, to the Indian Ocean, frigates were used in coastal attacks, sometimes in support of armies ashore (as in Spain during the Peninsular campaign), but also in self-contained amphibious operations that ended in the capture of enemy territory. Their boats, armed with a small carronade and manned by both marines and seamen, extended the reach of their parent ships into any shallow water or poorly defended port where a target of opportunity might present itself.[1]

Perhaps most importantly, frigates led the fight against Napoleon's Continental System. This was an attempt at economic embargo to which the British replied with a very effective blockade, stopping and searching all merchantmen that might be carrying goods to or for the French empire. At sea French resistance was largely a matter of sorties by frigates, and single-ship engagements continued right down until 1815, although they were very one-sided: during all the wars of 1793-1815 for 17 British frigates lost in action (9 of which were recaptured), 229 enemy frigates were taken or destroyed, from virtually every maritime power of note. More damaging in the long run was the resentment among neutrals that this blockading policy provoked, eventually leading to the United States declaring war on Britain, supposedly in defence of 'Free Trade and Sailors' Rights'.[2] Although something of a sideshow, this War of 1812 was important in drawing the world's attention to a new style of frigate, for the US Navy had a class of ships so big that many refused to regard them as frigates at all.

1 This theme is expanded in Ch 12 of Gardiner, R, *Frigates of the Napoleonic Wars* (London 2000)

2 Lewis, M, *Social History of the Royal Navy* (London 1960), pp346-50

Design of the frigate

The frigate of the Nelsonic era was unique in being the only standard type of warship with a complete structural deck that carried no guns. This was neither a trivial design feature, not was it accidental. The unarmed lower deck – appropriately known as the berth deck in the American navy – allowed the crew greater space per man than on any other class of ship. Not quite so crowded and unsanitary as the gundeck of a battleship, the frigate's berth deck made the crew less susceptible to ill-health, and made it easier to stand up to the rigours of long cruising that was often the frigate's lot.

More importantly, with the main battery mounted over this deck, the guns were carried high enough above the waterline (freeboard, as it was known) to be fought in any weather. Ships of the line had their lower deck gunports only a few feet above the sea, so when rolling or heeled or in rough weather they could not run the risk of opening their ports without flooding the deck and eventually causing the ship to founder. Frigates on the other hand might have 6-8 feet of gunport freeboard, which was enough to fight the guns safely in most conditions. These were not usually guns of the heaviest calibres in any case, so they could be handled more easily on a moving deck than the huge 32- or 36-pounders to be found on the lowest gundeck of ships of the line. In certain circumstances, therefore, a frigate might take on a ship of the line which could not open its lower-deck ports, the most famous example being the January 1797 combat between the 74-gun *Droits de l'Homme* and the *Indefatigable* commanded by Sir Edward Pellew. Pressing the attack in a full gale, Pellew's powerful frigate harried the unfortunate 74 until she was driven ashore and wrecked.

Assuming the unarmed lower deck to be the defining feature of the frigate as understood in the Nelsonic period, then its ancestry can be traced to the late seventeenth century. The Anglo-Dutch Wars of the 1650s-1670s saw the development of formal line-of-battle tactics, and from this was derived a concept of a ship specifically fitted for that role: the ship of the line, or line-of-battle ship, from which we get the modern term battleship. In the early years, warships of almost any size – and even hired merchantmen – had taken part in fleet battles, sometimes seeking out opponents of similar power. However, in the formal line there was little freedom of manoeuvre, and the weakest suffered most, so it encouraged larger and more standard ships of two gundecks and above.

The Dutch Wars saw the emergence of the battleship, but as yet there was no specialist cruiser. Fleets had small craft to carry messages, to intercept or support fireship attacks, and to tow becalmed or damaged ships, but they were not fit for the open ocean. Most of the battles between

Britain and the Netherlands took place in sheltered coastal waters, and the more distant duties like commerce protection and colonial warfare were deputed to the warships now regarded as too small for the line of battle. Many were very small two-deckers, with little freeboard to their lowest ports and ill-suited to oceanic cruising. The major strategic change came in 1688 when the Protestant William and Mary came over from Holland to replace the Catholic James II on the throne of Britain, thus making the Netherlands an ally and, more significantly, France an enemy. For the first time the Royal Navy would have to fight regularly on the wilder and more distant Biscay coasts of France rather than in the

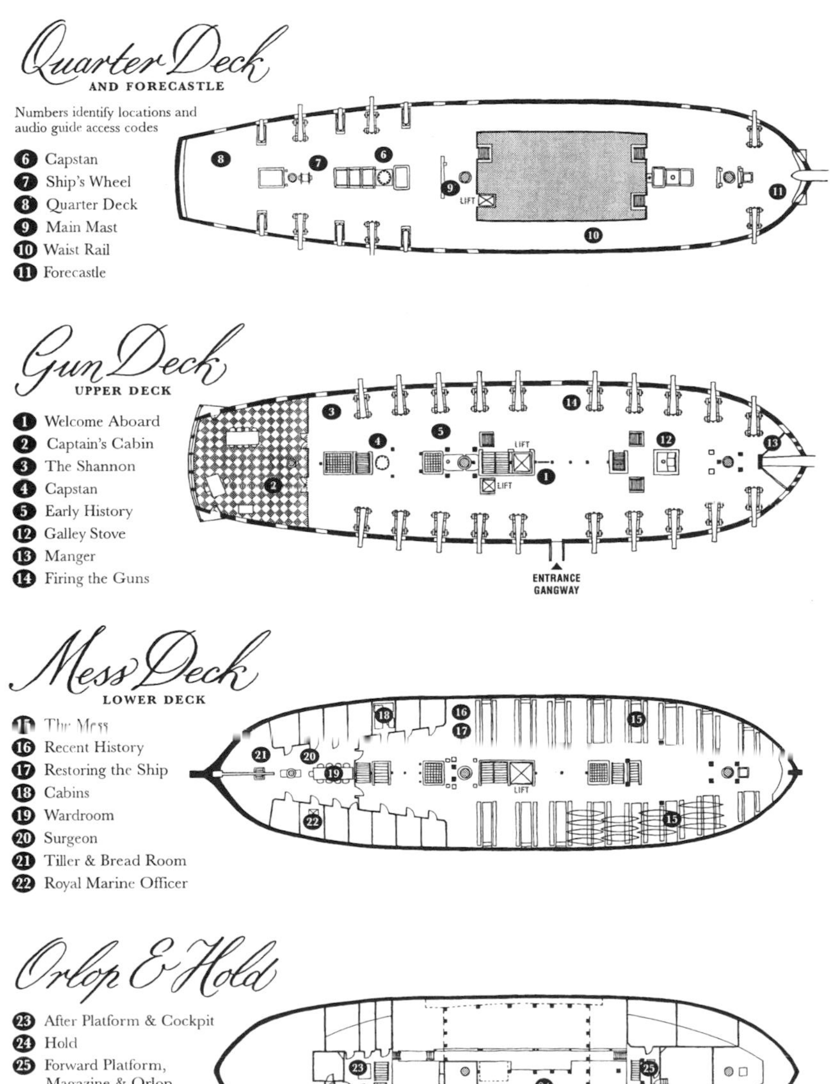

The main features of the frigate as displayed aboard the *Trincomalee*. In order to make it easier for visitors to move around the ship, some of the guns and carronades have been omitted.

Channel and North Sea. Furthermore, France had a powerful navy, but nothing like the merchant marines of Britain and the Netherlands, so would be very likely to launch an all-out assault on her enemies' trade.

Britain's naval leaders understood the novel nature of the challenge, and Lord Torrington produced a specification for a new sort of cruiser.[3] They should have only one battery, on a flush upper deck, so the guns could be fought in all weathers (up to 7 feet of freeboard); the lightly built lower deck, used to berth the crew, was unarmed but had a row of oar-ports for the large sweeps used to manoeuvre the ship in a calm, and it was at the level of the waterline when the ship was fully stored. It is an almost perfect description of a Nelsonic frigate (some even had a row of oar-ports, but they were moved to the upper deck after experiments in the 1760s).

As built, the ships were not quite as Torrington envisaged. They tended to mount a few heavier guns right forward and right aft on the lower deck – the rise of the decks fore and aft (called the sheer) allowed a little more freeboard than amidships, but these guns were never very useful. This basic concept – and, at around 400 tons, the size – remained almost unaltered for the next fifty years. In 1719 an attempt was made to return to Torrington's pristine concept, with no lower-deck ports and much reduced topsides, but in the 1730s and '40s a few guns began to creep back on to the lower deck, and the ships developed larger quarterdecks and more elaborate officers' accommodation, features typical of any long period without the acid test of war.[4] The traditional shipwright's temptation to add guns wherever feasible underlines one salient feature of the frigate proper: because of its unarmed deck, it was a relatively expensive ship for its firepower, and some authorities were advocating small two-deckers as late as the 1770s in preference. However, the frigate repaid its greater cost with better seakeeping and superior performance under sail, both prime qualities in a cruising ship.

British versus French design principles

After a generation without a major naval war, in 1744 Britain once again found itself in conflict with France. At sea the latest French frigates proved to be superior under sail, being generally faster and more weatherly. The latter is an important characteristic of a sailing ship and needs some explanation for the non-sailor.

With the wind from anywhere except directly aft, a sailing ship is blown both forward and to some degree sideways: the closer the ship attempts to point towards the direction of the wind, the greater the element of crabbing sideways, which is called 'leeway'. But design factors also affect the amount of leeway a ship will make: shallow draught increases it (which is why modern sailing dinghies have centreboards), as do high topsides which catch the wind. A ship which makes relatively little leeway is said to be 'weatherly', the opposite being 'leewardly'. This is highly significant because a square-rigged ship like a frigate could not point within about 70 degrees of the direction of the wind, and made progress to windward in a series of zig-zags called 'tacks'. Leeway made each leg of the tack longer, so taking more time to cover the same distance forward. Therefore it was quite possible in chase situations for a leewardly ship which could go faster through the water to be overtaken by one which, although slower, was more weatherly.[5]

The French had achieved speed by building longer hulls (all other things being equal, a longer ship will be faster), and superiority to windward by lowering the height of the side. This was done by reducing the headroom of the berth deck (and positioning it lower in the hull), as well as cutting back on bulwarks and rails along the quarterdeck and forecastle. The credit for this advance belongs to Blaise Ollivier, an innovative French constructor, who first applied the principles to the *Medée* of 30 guns, built at Brest in 1741. This ship carried French 8-pounders, equivalent to the 9-pounders of its British opponents, but from 1748 France began to build far larger ships with a similar layout and armed with a 12-pounder main battery.[6] For these there was no British answer.

In the Royal Navy this provoked some radical rethinking about the nature of cruiser design, which had altered in little but details for half a century. The standard British 24-gun ships retained their full height between decks and the deck itself was positioned higher above the water because they carried a few guns there. The height and windage of the topsides was also increased by the 'big-ship' features of long quarterdecks and quarter galleries, substantial forecastles and beakhead bulkheads. By comparison with the latest French frigates, these ships, in the phrase of the time, sailed like haystacks. As was often the case, the British responded initially by copying the French designs, the first being the *Unicorn* and *Lyme*, launched in 1748 and given the new rating of 28-gun ships.

Experience with frigates either captured or copied from the French soon proved that they were not ideal for British tactical and operational requirements. This was largely because strength had been sacrificed for speed, and the French structural style would not stand up to the more rigorous cruising in all-weathers implied in British naval strategy. French ships were usually sent to sea only on specific missions, but the Royal Navy expected to 'keep the seas', blockading the enemy's main fleet and giving battle whenever opportunity presented itself. The weakness of French hulls was further exacerbated by some elements of their design style: the long low hulls, optimised for speed, were more prone to flex, causing an increased maintenance requirement and, some believed, reducing that speed as the hulls became older and more distorted.

3 Fuller details can be found in Lavery, B (ed), *The Line of Battle* (London 1992), Ch 2

4 Goodwin, P, *The 20-Gun Ship Blandford* (London 1988), pp7-8.

5 Harland, J, *Seamanship in the Age of Sail* (London 1984) elaborates on the concept; see Ch 4.

6 Boudriot, J, *The History of the French Frigate* (Rotherfield 1993), pp68ff

As a result, when the British began to build 12-pounder armed frigates at the beginning of the next war in the mid-1750s, they followed their own design principles. These ships were more robustly built, with shorter, deeper hulls. These stowed their provisions better, so were more suited to extended operations, and turned more quickly, so were often handier in a single-ship fight. Oddly, although very low, French frigates proved less weatherly than they might have been because of their shallow draught, and the deeper British ships were often superior to windward. On the whole British vessels were better sea-boats and handled rough weather with greater ease, but there was no denying that in the right conditions French frigates were faster. This dichotomy of approach, which persisted for the rest of the eighteenth century, could be summarised as the firm belief that French hull forms were superior but British ships were better built.[7]

From time to time the Royal Navy attempted to have the best of both worlds by copying the underwater form of French ships but building them to British standards. Being smaller, the French navy always strove to offset its numerical inferiority with better ships, which generally meant increasing their size. Bigger ships for a set rating of guns gave the designer more scope, and often an Admiralty order to copy a French ship was a way of justifying a politically undesirable increase in size, and cost – numbers was always a greater concern than individual quality to the dominant navy, but there was inevitably a point at which the disparity became too great for operational effectiveness. This was usually when a French design was copied.

Hébé and the *Leda* class

Such was the situation in the mid-1790s. The Admiralty under the direction of Earl Spencer was determined to end the traditional size disadvantage of British warships, and a string of new and larger designs of many rates of ship were put in hand. The usual principle was to order two or three vessels to the same specification: one or two plans would by drawn up by the Surveyors (the Navy's own designers, of whom there were usually two), while by way of comparison one would be based on a captured French ship. In theory this allowed the Navy to evaluate many designs simultaneously, but in practice it tended to produce a fleet of one-off ships whose design was never repeated.

One exception to this pattern was the *Leda* class of 38-gun frigates. The first was ordered in 1796 and used the hull form of the French *Hébé* captured in 1782. The all-round good qualities of this design gradually came to be appreciated through the fleet and eight more were ordered between 1802 and 1808. The French were no less appreciative of the qualities of

7 This subject is covered in great detail in the articles by Gardiner, R, 'Frigate Design in the 18th Century' in *Warship III* (London 1979)

8 Boudriot, *French Frigate*, p199

their design, and by an odd coincidence sisters of the *Hébé*–built in even larger numbers–were the nearest thing to a standard frigate in the navy of the French Empire. They were designed by Jacques-Noel Sané, the greatest French naval architect of the age, whose ideas dominated French naval construction, so although the design was already a generation old, frigates of this class were still being built when Napoleon was sent into exile.[8]

After 1801 the experimental approach of the Spencer administration had been replaced by a concentration on what might be called 'War Standard' designs, which were chosen as the best in each class and built in large numbers. With the exception of a handful of 'super-frigates', the largest regular ships of this type were rated as 38-gun ships (but usually carrying 46), with a main battery of 18-pounder guns and 32-pounder carronades on the upperworks. Built in parallel with the 150-foot long *Leda* class was the slightly larger (154-foot) all-British *Lively* class, which if anything enjoyed greater official favour, thirteen being ordered during the same period as the eight *Leda*s. However, the futures fortunes of both designs were to be radically affected by the War of 1812.

This magnificent lithograph by T G Dutton depicts HMS *Pomone*, the second ship of the *Leda* class, which was built alongside the *Shannon* in Brindley's yard at Frindsbury on the Medway river opposite Rochester.

War with America

Exasperated by the Royal Navy's stranglehold on seaborne commerce, the United States declared war on Britain in June 1812, and the new republic's tiny navy proceeded to amaze the world with a trio of victories in frigate actions. Two of the beaten British frigates, *Guerrière* and *Java*, were themselves prizes taken from the French and neither survived the fight–the former because she was in poor condition to start with, and the latter because she was so well defended that the wreck had to be burnt. However, the *Macedonian*, a relatively new *Lively* class frigate, was surrendered by Captain John Surman Carden and taken into the US Navy, a fact more galling than defeat.

The victorious American frigates, *Constitution* and *United States*, with their sister USS *President*, were the largest frigates in the world. Rated as 44s, they regularly carried over 50 guns, although their real superiority lay with a main armament of 24-pounder long guns. With a tiny navy the United States was also able to man these ships with a large complement of experienced seamen. Structurally, the upper deck comprised, not separate forecastle, gangways and quarterdeck, but a continuous spar deck, and as built the ships had carried guns in the waist. Based on these kind of technicalities, the British were keen to dismiss their pretensions to real frigate-hood, while conversely Americans exaggerated their originality.[9] In fact, they were just very large frigates: the layout of the upper deck of British frigates was approaching the 'spar deck' concept by 1812, while the 44s themselves fought the war with weather-deck batteries divided fore and aft, with an unarmed waist like any other frigate.

This comparison between a British frigate of the *Macedonian* class (top) and an American so-called '44' was produced just after the War of 1812 by William James, a British historian keen to explain why three British frigates had been lost in single-ship actions. Apart from the greater size of the US ship, James pointed to the wider gangways which were integrated into the quarterdeck and forecastle, making, in structural terms, a continuous deck, known in the US Navy as the 'spar deck'.

But to the British public, fed on a diet of almost uninterrupted British single-ship victories for two decades, the size, firepower and manning levels of the American ships did not matter. Revenge was required if the credit of the Royal Navy was to be restored. In any likely scenario, the defeat of a 24-pounder ship by one with 18-pounders was a fantasy; but luckily there were only three American 44s and US 18-pounder frigates were very similar to their British equivalents. Two of these were to take part in the only battle of the war between genuinely well-matched ships, fought off Boston on 1 June 1813: it was an amazing encounter that lasted less than a quarter of an hour, but was probably the most bloody single-ship engagement in history.

The protagonists were USS *Chesapeake*, under Captain James

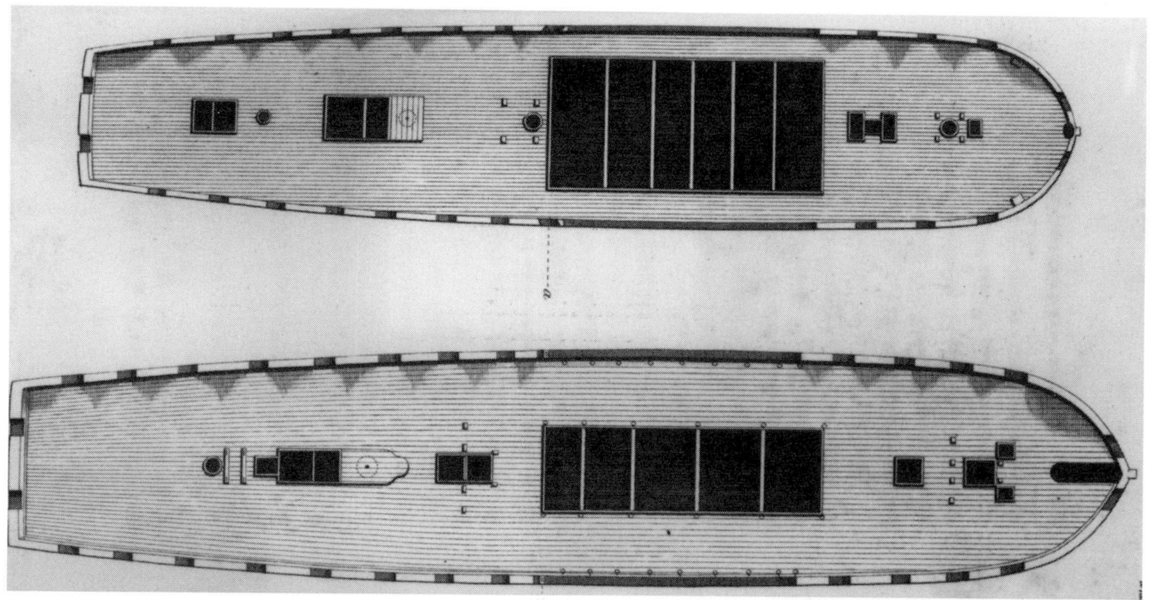

Lawrence, and HMS *Shannon*, a *Leda* class 38 captained by Philip Bowes Vere Broke. Lawrence's ship was newly commissioned, and although the crew was made up of experienced seaman, they had had no time to exercise as a team. Broke, on the other hand, had a crew that had been together for years, and since their captain was the Royal Navy's greatest advocate of scientific gunnery, they may well have been the most proficient gunners of their day.

The action would take longer to describe than it took to play out. In short, *Shannon* lay to, inviting attack, and Lawrence, possibly overconfident after the string of American single-ship victories, obliged by slowly ranging past the British ship. As she did so *Chesapeake* was systematically dismantled by aimed gunfire, her wheel and headsails were shot away by the chase guns specifically assigned to such duties, and when the uncontrollable American ship fell back against the *Shannon*, Broke saw his chance and led a boarding party himself. From the first shot to the striking of the Stars and Stripes, 11 minutes had elapsed.

Lawrence himself was mortally wounded, uttering his famous exhortation, 'Don't give up the ship' before expiring; Broke was struck down in his moment of triumph and, although he lived, he was never again fit enough for active service. Among both crews the casualties were truly terrible: of 395 in the American ship, 69 died and 77 were wounded; British losses were 34 killed or mortally wounded and 49 injured from a complement of 330. The ships themselves fared in similar proportions: *Shannon* was hit by 25 shot and 130 smaller rounds, but *Chesapeake* received 56 shot hits and 306 of the deadly man-killing grape. As Peter Padfield has calculated, on a casualty-per-minute basis it is probably the most deadly combat of the whole age of sail.[10]

An eyewitness described the state of the defeated *Chesapeake* when brought into Halifax as a prize:

> . . . internally the scene was one never to be forgotten by a landsman. The deck had not been cleaned, and the coils and folds of rope were steeped in gore as if in a slaughterhouse. She was a fir-built ship [not true, but some softwood had been used to repair the topsides] and her splinters had wounded nearly as many men as the *Shannon*'s shot. Pieces of skin with pendant hair were adhering to the sides of the ship, and in one place I saw portions of fingers protruding . . . Altogether it was a scene of devastation as difficult to forget as to describe.[11]

The Admiralty, the government and the country at large showered Broke with honours and rewards, greatly relieved that the American run of victories had been halted. There had been great concern that the Royal Navy's aura of invincibility might be destroyed and indeed that the US

9 The most virulent British reaction is represented by William James, whose *Naval Occurrences of the Late War between Great Britain and United States* (London 1817) may be regarded as the beginning of the post-war controversy. For a modern American overstatement of the case for the originality of the big frigates, see Martin, T G, *A Most Fortunate Ship: A Narrative History of Old Ironsides* (Annapolis, MD 1997)

10 Padfield, P, *Broke and the Shannon* (London 1968), Appendix A

11 Thomas Haliburton, quoted in Padfield, *Broke*, p188

The opening moments of the short but bloody battle between *Shannon* (left) and USS *Chesapeake* off Boston on 1 June 1813. Unlike the other frigate engagements of the war, the ships were well matched, but the new and undrilled American crew was beaten by what was probably the best-trained team in the Royal Navy. Although ship design had little to do with the outcome, the victory of Captain Broke's frigate made *Shannon* a household name, and no doubt contributed to the post-war popularity of the design.

Navy might acquire it for themselves. *Shannon* was proof that this was not so, and until the end of the wars in 1815 she was probably the most celebrated ship afloat. By sad contrast, the *Macedonian* now flew the Stars and Stripes, and after the war the Americans lost no opportunity to flaunt it in the face of Royal Navy squadrons.

The War of 1812 achieved little for either side, but in a conflict between peoples speaking the same language, propaganda had been a much-abused tool, and emotions continued to run high long after peace was agreed. In the continuing war of words, both ships were potent symbols.

Preparing for peace

Despite the distractions of the American war, from about 1813 the Admiralty began to consider the probable size and shape of the post-war Navy. One major area for concern was the frigate force: many of these ships were worn out by long and arduous service, while even the newer frigates had often been built too quickly of unseasoned timber, and some had been the subjects of experimental structural schemes designed to circumvent acute timber shortages. *Shannon* herself was built to a commercial shipbuilder's patented method that Broke thought so weak in heavy weather that his ship's sides 'worked like a basket'.

The answer was a large programme of new building, with all ships built in the royal dockyards to the highest standards of material and techniques to ensure the greatest possible longevity. This concern determined the post-war expansion in the teak building programme, and also led to the widespread adoption of the structural innovations of Sir Robert Seppings – diagonal bracing and round sterns which were economical of timber while at the same time producing greatly enhanced strength. Since little peacetime need for frigates was anticipated, they could be built slowly and carefully, and even when launched most were laid up in Ordinary (reserve) with a solid wooden roof built over each to preserve the hull. That the policy was effective is proved by the survival of two frigates from this era: the teak-built *Trincomalee*, but also a half-sister, the *Unicorn* at Dundee, which exhibits all the Seppings features and a wonderful example of the protective roof.

To decide *how* to construct ships was probably easier than determining *what* to build. The successes of the big American 44s meant that similar ships would be needed, although they were so costly that no navy would be able to afford more than a few. For the Royal Navy, with its worldwide commitments, the more difficult problem was to determine what would be the smallest effective frigate; it had to be a ship that was relatively cheap so it could be built in large numbers, but one that could still handle most of the varied roles expected of a frigate. The Admiralty decided that the 38-gun class would become the baseline frigate, but reclassified as 46s to reflect their real armament. No smaller frigates would be ordered, although some Sixth Rates of around 28 guns were built for peacetime imperial policing duties (or, as the cynics insisted, to give sprigs of the nobility a post command), but their usual appellation of 'jackass frigates' sums up the Navy's opinion of them.

The existing 38-gun classes, divided between 154-foot and 150-foot designs, would continue, but since nobody was going to advocate building more sisters for the disgraced *Macedonian*, a new draught was required for the larger type. Based on another captured French ship, the first of the new class, *Seringapatam*, was built of teak in Bombay; but the design was never entirely satisfactory and went through a number of modifications before cancellations curtailed the programme at nine ships. There was no controversy about the other design: it had to be a repeat *Shannon*. Four more had already been ordered in 1812 (including *Trincomalee*), and three more were added to the original draught by 1815.

However, after the war the design was modified to include Seppings' round stern, 'short-timber' framing and diagonal bracing, and employed for no less than twenty-eight ships. Two orders were cancelled and three were transferred to another design, but the *Leda*s and their post-war half-sisters comprise the largest class of sailing frigates ever built. If what might be considered their first-cousins in the French navy are included, the hull form is surely the most significant in the history of frigate design.

There could be no better representative of the Nelsonic frigate than a ship of this class, and with her traditional appearance and restored rig *Trincomalee* is perfect.

Details of *Leda* class 38-gun Fifth Rates

Specification

	Lower deck	*Keel*	*Breadth extreme*	*Depth in hold*	*Burthen*
	feet-inches	*feet-inches*	*feet-inches*	*feet-inches*	*Tons*
Design	150-1½	125-4⅞	39-11	12-9	1062⁷⁹⁄₉₄

The restored *Trincomalee* in dry-dock showing off the fine lines of a hull-form that found great favour in the navies of both Britain and France.

Designed Armament

Upper deck	28 x 18-pounder, 8ft 38cwt Blomefield pattern long guns
Forecastle	2 x 9-pounder, 7ft 6in 26cwt Blomefield pattern long guns 2 x 32-pounder, 4ft 17cwt carronades
Quarterdeck	2 x 9-pounder long guns (by 1815 usually replaced by 2 more 32-pounder carronades) 12 x 32-pounder, 4ft 17cwt carronades 1 x 12-pounder, 6cwt boat carronade on elevating carriage
Rating	38 guns (46 guns from February 1817)
Ammunition	round shot: 100 rounds per gun or carronade on Foreign Service, or 70 in Channel Service grape shot (all Service): 50 18-pounder rounds per gun; 5 9-pounder rounds per gun grape in tin cases for carronades (all Service): 4 32-pounder rounds per carronade case shot (all Service): 10 rounds per long gun; 4 rounds per carronade double-headed bar shot (all Service): 3 rounds per long gun, reduced to 1 round after 1811 powder: 170 whole barrels (90lbs each) on Foreign Service, or 156 in Channel Service
Men	284 (1806 Establishment), comprising: 12 officers 33 petty officers 58 able seamen 58 ordinary seamen 56 landmen 3 boys, first class 6 boys, second class 9 boys, third class 48 marines 3 widows' men [fictitious members of the crew whose wages were used to support naval widows' pensions] 320 from January 1813
Boats	1 x 32ft barge or 10-oared boat (or an 8-oared cutter, supplied on Captain's application) 1 x 26ft longboat or launch (replacing the Brenton's yawl by order of 15 March 1810) 2 x 25ft Deal cutters (or a yawl in lieu of one cutter, supplied on Captain's application) 1 x 18ft Deal cutter or jolly boat

Building data

Name	*Ordered*	*Builder*	*Launched*	*Fate*
Leda	27 Apr 1796	Chatham Dockyard	18 Nov 1800	Wrecked near Milford Haven 31 Jan 1808
Pomone	25 Nov 1802	Brindley, Frindsbury	17 Jan 1805	Wrecked on the Needles 14 Oct 1811
Shannon	24 Oct 1803	Brindley, Frindsbury	5 May 1806	Hulk 1831; renamed *St Lawrence* 11 Mar 1844; BU Nov 1859
Leonidas	19 Jul 1805	Pelham, Frindsbury	4 Sep 1807	Powder hulk 1872; sold 23 Nov 1894
Briton	28 Sep 1808	Chatham Dockyard	11 Apr 1812	Hulk 1841; target and then BU Sep 1860
Lacedaemonian	28 Sep 1808	Portsmouth Dockyard	21 Dec 1812	BU Nov 1822
Tenedos	28 Sep 1808	Chatham Dockyard	11 Apr 1812	Convict hulk 1843; BU Mar 1875
Lively, ex-*Scamander*	28 Sep 1808	Chatham Dockyard	14 Jul 1813	Hulk 1831; sold for BU 28 Apr 1862
Surprise	10 Apr 1809	Milford Dockyard	25 Jul 1812	Convict hulk 1822; sold Oct 1837
Diamond	30 Jun 1812	Chatham Dockyard	16 Jan 1816	Accidental fire 18 Feb 1827; wreck BU
Amphitrite	21 Oct 1812	Bombay Dockyard	14 Apr 1816	Rasée 26-gun corvette 1846; BU Jan 1875
Trincomalee	30 Oct 1812	Bombay Dockyard	12 Oct 1817	In Ord May 1819-Sep 1847; corvette 1845; restored, Hartlepool 1987-2001
Arethusa	18 Dec 1812	Pembroke Dockyard	29 Jul 1817	Hulk 1836; renamed *Bacchus* 12 Mar 1844; BU Aug 1883
Thetis	22 Nov 1814	Pembroke Dockyard	1 Feb 1817	Wrecked off Brazil 5 Dec 1830
Blanche	29 May 1815	Chatham Dockyard	26 May 1819	Hulk 1833; BU Oct 1865
Fisgard	24 Aug 1815	Pembroke Dockyard	8 Jul 1819	Hulk 1847; BU Oct 1879

Notes:
The Bombay-built ships were constructed of teak. The above were the only vessels completed to the original design, but post-war a further twenty-five were ordered to modified draughts with Seppings's circular stern and 'small-timber' system of construction: *Venus*, *Melampus*, *Amazon*, *Minerva*, *Nereus*, *Latona*, *Diana*, *Hamadryad*, *Aeolus*, *Thisbe*, *Hebe*, *Cerberus*, *Circe*, *Clyde*, *Thames*, *Fox*, *Unicorn*, *Daedalus*, *Proserpine*, *Mermaid*, *Mercury*, *Penelope*, *Thalia*, *Medusa*, *Pegasus* (the last two were cancelled in 1832); orders for a further three, *Jason*, *Nemesis* and *Statira*, were transferred to the *Druid* (Modified *Seringapatam*) class.

Sailing qualities

Very fast, particularly going large, when most recorded 13kts and *Lacedaemonian* even claimed '13½kts by repeated heaving of the log'; good but not exceptional close-hauled, 10kts being the usual figure. They stood to their canvas well and liked a stiff gale, but not heavy seas, because they were subject to deep pitching. With their French-derived proportions, they were not very weatherly compared with frigates of British origin, and all captains took steps to remedy this, usually by requesting additions to the false keel and gripe–although *Surprise* shipped additional ballast until the captain decided that whatever the ship gained to windward she more than lost in fore-reaching.

All captains complained of poor capacity, barely 4 months provisions going under hatches, and this needed careful stowage. In fact, they seem to have required a good shiphandler to get the most out of them. Broke of the *Shannon* noted that his ship was 'delicate in trim' and he made a habit of sailing with the bow- and stern-chase guns amidships, and the shot and hammocks struck below. The same care needed to be exercised in tacking and wearing, when *Shannon* was slow but sure; however, some captains were not impressed with their ships' handling. The other common criticism was of their light structure, which combined with their lively rolling and pitching in a seaway to make them work and strain constantly. This made them wet and *Leonidas*, for example, regularly needed the waterways recaulked and damaged scuppers replaced. This was a particular problem with the early ships constructed with Brindley's 'bolt-and-carling' substitute for knees, but even the Dockyard-built ships appear to have been weak. One captain felt that the design was at fault in combining the fine underwater lines of a French ship with the wall-sided upperworks of British practice. There are no such complaints about the ships completed post-war, where the problem of strength had been addressed by the far superior diagonal structure of Sir Robert Seppings. Stowage was also made more efficient by the adoption of iron water tanks.

Based on reports of: *Shannon* (17 Jun 1812); *Leonidas* (5 Feb 1812, 1 Jan 1814, 1 Jan 1815, 16 Jun 1815); *Briton* (27 Apr 1830); *Lacedaemonian* (undated, but under the command of Samuel Jackson, so probably Jun 1815 when the ship returned to England); *Tenedos* (24 Aug 1815); *Lively* (31 Oct 1825, 4 Dec 1826); *Surprise* (31 Aug 1815); *Diamond* (1 Dec 1826); *Amphitrite* (6 Jan 1817, 10 Jan 1817, 18 Jan 1817); *Trincomalee* (4 Apr 1819); *Thetis* (28 Oct 1826); *Blanche* (25 Oct 1827, 1 Jan 1831).

Typical draughts of water

	Draught	*(ft-ins)*	*Freeboard (ft-ins)*	*Ballast*	*(tons)*		*Victualled*
	fwd	*aft*	*midships port*	*iron*	*shingle*	*water*	*for months*
Lacedaemonian, 1813	17-10	18-8	6-3	90	52	88	Foreign Service
Leonidas, 1808	15-6	18-5	7-10	90	77	96	Channel Service
Leonidas, 1812	16-8	18-4	6-11	90	120	95	Channel Service
Diamond, 1824	17-5	18-9	7-5	105	0	132	Foreign Service
Thetis, 1826	16-4	18-1	7-6	141	0	115	Channel Service

These figures demonstrate the beneficial effects of iron water tanks (in the last two ships), which allowed more water to be stowed while at the same time improving the average height of the midships gunport. Tanks also permitted the abolition of shingle ballast, which had been a breeding ground for disease.

Chapter Two | Building a Frigate

HMS *Trincomalee* was built by an Indian workforce, under the direction of Jamsetjee Bomanjee, (1754-1821) the great Parsi master shipbuilder of the Wadia dynasty. In this portrait he wears a Silver Rule, awarded to him by the East India Company for his outstanding contribution to the warship building project. He received similar commendations from the Admiralty.

ALTHOUGH *Trincomalee* is a typical example of the Nelsonic frigate, with many sisters, she was not built in Britain. Unlike th great majority of British warships she was constructed in the Indian port city of Bombay (modern Mumbai) by the Honourable East India Company. The Company, a powerful trading and administrative body combined governing much of India with a monopoly on the trade of the east, especially the tea trade with China. She was built in the Company dockyard, of Indian materials, by Indian craftsmen, under the direction of the great Parsi[1] master shipbuilder Jamsetjee Bomanjee (1754-1821). A truly imperial warship, *Trincomalee* represented the two forms of power that made Britain the superpower of the age – commerce and warships. Britain had built a unique global empire of trade, linked by oceans and protected by the Royal Navy, which used a chain of naval bases around the world to protect maritime enterprise at any point on the globe. She was named for the great anchorage on the coast of Ceylon (Tricomali in modern Sri Lanka) that had been taken from the Dutch in 1795, to complete British control of the Indian Ocean. Other 'Indian' warships[2] were also given names that demonstrated Britain's dominion over the eastern arc of empire, starting with the frigates *Salsette* and *Malacca*, which were somewhat parochial, but rising to the imperial theme with the names of great servants of empire, like Wellesley, Cornwallis and Melville, the great rivers Ganges, Indus and Tigris, the Presidencies of Bombay and Calcutta, Hindostan and ultimately the entire continent of Asia.

The construction of teak ships at Bombay by the East India Company for the Royal Navy was part of the process whereby the Company was transformed from a commercial power into an imperial agency, running India under the general control of the British government. This process began after the loss of America, when the British government adopted a more imperial perspective. India was to be more closely integrated into the empire. In January 1784 Prime Minister William Pitt the Younger told the House of Commons that India should be 'the source of infinite benefit to the empire at large', and framed his India Bill accordingly.[3] This concept was at variance with the commercial priorities of the Company directors, and implied national access to Company assets. This clash of interests took fifty years to resolve, transforming the Company into a purely politico-military agency. Having set the broad lines of policy Pitt left the implementation to Henry Dundas, later Lord Melville. From the beginning Dundas favoured the imperial exploitation of Indian resources, and he was among the first to take a truly global view of empire. Advised by leading naval, scientific and commercial figures, notably Sir Joseph Banks, President of the Royal Society, he tried to create a maritime strategic/economic unit that could defy the world.[4]

Bombay and shipbuilding

Bombay was the key to British strategy in the East. No other navy had access to a naval base in the region that offered a secure island location, strategic position, a small fleet of warships, and a dockyard, which included the only dry-docks in those seas, a burgeoning shipbuilding industry, and access to skilled labour and materials.[5] Landlocked by powerful neighbours, the development of Bombay relied on increased maritime activity,[6] in large measure reflecting the protection of locally based Company and imperial naval forces.

The combination of a British fleet and Bombay dockyard would keep the French out of India, and deny the Indian powers access to French support. In 1788 Dundas stressed the strategic importance of Bombay, and proposed building 64-gun ships to carry the China trade in peacetime, and be ready to secure command of the Eastern seas in war.[7] The biggest problem remained the timber supply, which was only secured with the defeat of Tipu Sultan of Mysore in 1799.

In 1801 Dundas resolved that the Company should build warships for the Royal Navy, and only Bombay had the necessary combination of infrastructure, artisans, docks and facilities to carry out the task. Unfortunately the Company, fighting for its independence from the same government that now wanted ships built, exploited the badly drawn contract to overcharge for the work. The first warship, the frigate *Salsette*, was laid down in 1803. She was followed by other frigates and, once the new double dry-dock was completed, ships of the line. The frigates were built in the Upper Old Dock, the innermost of three docks initially built back in the 1750s. As the docks, the shipyard and the timber being used

1 The tightly-knit Parsi community of merchants and shipbuilders were descended from eighth-century Persian refugees who had fled Muslim persecution. Their religion, Zoroastrianism, places a high value on the purifying effect of fire. The silver nail ceremony used to name ships was part of their tradition

2 These included ships built in British dockyards from Indian materials sent home on board the Bombay ships. See Appendix 1

3 Frost, A J, *Convicts and Empire: A Naval Question, 1776-1811* (Oxford 1980), pp81-3

4 Gascoigne, J, *Science in the Service of the Empire: Joseph Banks, the British State and the Uses of Science in the Age of Revolution* (Cambridge 1998), chs 1-2 & 7.
Kennedy, P M, *The Rise and Fall of British Naval Mastery* (London 1976), pp128-9

5 Ingram, E (ed), *Two Views of British India: the Private Correspondence of Mr Dundas and Lord Wellesley: 1798-1801* (London 1969), pp167, 183, 251

6 Nightingale, P, *Trade and Empire in Western India 1784-1806* (Cambridge 1970), pp12-13

7 ibid, p5

The Bombay workforce was both numerous and highly skilled. While British observers were struck by the quantity of men at work, and the rather perilous staging employed, they had nothing but praise for the quality of the work carried out under Jamsetjee's control. Ample evidence of their skill can be seen on board the *Trincomalee*. This contemporary drawing of Parsi carpenters is from a manuscript in the British Library, WD315 70(74).

were all Company assets the directors saw no reason why they should not receive a healthy profit on their investment, to the extent that the Bombay ships were invariably more expensive than those built in Britain.

However, the cost was largely offset by the superior quality and durability of teak (*tectona grandis*), among the finest of all shipbuilding timbers. The modern classification considers it very durable, the highest grade of timber, and unusually resistant to marine borers such as the dread *teredo navalis*, although only suitable for moderate bends, and possessing a severe blunting effect on tools.[8] The tree is native to much of India, Burma, Thailand and Indonesia, and matures after between 95 and 140 years of growth. Felling was normally preceded by girdling, which kills the tree, and allows the sap to drain away, so that the felled timber is light enough to float.[9] Forest-grown trees produced straight trunks up to thirty feet long, while mountain-grown trees, as with oak, produce the natural bends needed for shipbuilding. After clear felling seeds that have lain dormant will germinate, once the sun and rain can reach them. The importance of a sustained supply inspired the introduction of serious forestry in India, starting with the establishment of the Botanic Gardens at Calcutta in 1786 and continuing down to the end of the wooden shipbuilding period. The Calcutta Garden was founded by Lieutenant Colonel Robert Kyd (1746-1793), the Superintendent of the East India Company's dockyard at Calcutta, with the support of Sir Joseph Banks, the botanical imperialist at the head of the Royal Society. Kyd's successors in India and Burma down to the 1860s shared the teak imperative.[10] Despite this, demand quickly outstripped supply once the merchant building boom began at Bombay, leading to careless exploitation and ill-conceived conservation efforts at Bombay between 1805 and 1822.[11]

The reasons for teak's superiority over all other timbers for naval purposes were obvious. More than a century later experts concluded: 'Compared with other Industrial hardwoods of the world, teak is a medium weight, strong wood of average hardness and of outstanding merit in retention of shape and durability.' This only applies to the heartwood, the sapwood being perishable, while the heartwood can be affected by fungal decay in extreme conditions. 'In shipbuilding it is in a class by itself. Its popularity is due to its relatively small coefficient of expansion and contraction, and its durability'.[12] When dried and ready for use teak weighs about the same as oak, but possesses 10-20 per cent greater resistance to bending strains.

Teak requires only the most brief period of seasoning, normally less than a year stacked in open piles under a roof. In addition the natural oil, in sharp contrast to the tannic (gallic) acid of oak sap, acts as a preservative of ferrous metals. As a consequence Indian shipbuilders had always fastened their vessels with iron spikes, and had no experience of boring and fitting treenails on the European pattern. Using teak Bombay could deliver fully seasoned ships in little more than a year from laying the keel, ships that could be used in hot, humid climates of the Indian Ocean and China Seas when new, something that was considered unwise for English-built oak ships.

Shipbuilding around Bombay underwent a remarkable growth in the late eighteenth century. Large 'European' ships were built at Bombay and other ports on the west coast of India before 1800 for the 'Country Trade' carrying cotton to China. These vessels, which integrated British designs with Indian labour and materials, were built by Parsi builders, and owned by various combinations of Parsi and British merchants. Commanded by Europeans, crewed by Indians, they operated under the protection of the Royal Navy and the Company's Bombay Marine.[13] These ships provided the resources for ever larger construction projects, starting with ships to trade with Britain, and then ships of the line for the imperial fleet. With the increasing cost of constructing large Indiamen on the Thames in the traditional Blackwall yards–both timber and labour costs rocketed during the French Revolutionary War–large Indiamen were built at Bombay, beginning with the *Scaleby Castle* of 1798.[14] Increasing the tempo, and size of shipbuilding at Bombay created concern for the timber supply. Previous rulers of the teak forests had obtained a revenue from the sale of the trees, while Tipu had established teak as a 'royal' tree,

8 Farmer, R H, *The Handbook of Hardwoods* (2nd edn London 1972), pp201-3

9 Gamble, J S, *A Manual of Indian Timbers* (London 1922), p528

10 Chandra, S, 'The Profiles of the Founders of Indian Forestry' in Rawat, A S (ed), *History of Forestry in India* (New Delhi 1991), pp337 & 362

11 ibid, p29

12 Trotter, H, *The Common Commercial Timbers of India and their Uses* (2nd edn New Delhi 1941), pp163-4

13 Bulley, A, *The Bombay Country Ships, 1790-1833* (London 2000), pp11-37

14 Lubbock, B, in Parkinson, C N (ed), *The Trade Winds* (London 1948), p89

which belonged to the Sultan, a regulation the Company continued. In 1800 the felling of trees over 21 inches in girth was prohibited.[15]

In Britain the apparent failure of native oak to supply the needs of the Royal Navy had become a source of concern by 1802. This forced the Admiralty to permit increased prices, and reduce contract specification. The First Lord, Admiral the Earl of St Vincent, also threatened to limit the East India Company to 800-ton ships, in place of the normal 1200 tons, while expressing his desire that the Company should build one ship of the line and one frigate at Bombay every year. These, he concluded: 'would be of great importance to the support of the naval strength of the Empire'.[16] By an order for a 74 and a frigate sent out in 1803, the Company would build the ships at Bombay, under the supervision of naval constructors, being paid for the hire of the dock while the ship was building, the cost of construction, plus 20 per cent. The Navy would also provide a large quantity of tools, including axes and adzes, rope and blocks for hoisting up the frames, along with iron bolts, nails and weights. This arrangement, entered into in time of war and emergency, proved to be a charter for Company to exploit naval funds.

This completed the long term initiatives of Henry Dundas, who returned to office in 1804.[17] Dundas continued the Indian project, developing Indian resources and pushing forward the boundaries of British control.[18] Dundas had many contacts in India, the most important of whom was the Governor-General, Lord Wellesley. Dundas sent out fresh orders to Wellesley with Admiral Sir Edward Pellew, the new Commander-in-Chief on the East Indies Station, who proved to be a powerful advocate.[19] Pellew persuaded Jonathan Duncan, the Governor of Bombay, to build new dry-docks, capable of holding large battleships. When the cost overrun on the docks reached 50 per cent Duncan, nervous that he might be held responsible, claimed that Pellew had over-persuaded him of the importance of the docks for naval service.[20] This may explain why he proved ruthless in squeezing the Navy for every rupee of dock hire. In addition there was a concerted effort to build a naval arsenal at Trincomalee in Ceylon (Sri Lanka) to avoid becoming completely dependent on the Company. Relations between the sea officers, the naval commissioners and the Bombay administration remained poor throughout the war period, and coloured the decision to move to Trincomalee, which was fated to fail for want of commitment post-war.[21]

In Britain the Board of Control saw the latest series of forest reports as indicating 'a permanent and valuable supply of large ship timber', which they wanted to exploit to repay the cost of the surveys and, rather more significantly, of the new docks. To this end they hoped to build two 74s per year.[22] Negotiations with the Admiralty indicated that both parties were anxious to contract for a second 74.[23]

15 Stebbings, E P, *The Forests of India* (London 1922), Vol 1, p63

16 Navy Board–Admiralty 5 May 1802: Adm 106/2229: in Morriss, R *The Royal Dockyards during the Revolutionary and Napoleonic Wars* (Leicester 1983), at p82. Earl St Vincent–Deputy Chairman of the EIC 31 March 1802 & 17 April 1802: in D B Smith (ed), *The Letters of Lord St Vincent 1801-04*, Navy Records Society, 2 vols (London 1921 & 1926), Vol II, pp238 & 241-3

17 East India Company–Navy Board 3 April 1805 encl Deptford Dockyard to Navy Board 22 January 1805: Adm 87/1. St Vincent - Dundas 14 July 1801: in Smith, *Letters of Lord St Vincent*, Vol I, p301

18 Furber, H, *Henry Dundas* (London 1931), pp126-141

19 Dundas–Wellesley 4 July 1804: Add 37,275, ff260-387

20 Duncan–Dundas 14 October 1808 & 16 April 1809: Scottish Record Office (SRO) GD 51/3/158 1 & 2

21 Graham, G S, *Great Britain and the Indian Ocean: 1810–1850* (Oxford 1967), pp305-28. The yard was closed down in 1821, still incomplete

22 Board of Control–Bombay 27 June 1810 & 18 December 1812: F/4/429

23 Admiralty–Sir William Ramsay (Chairman of the EIC) 9 November 1811: MEL/103 National Maritime Museum (NMM)

24 Johnstone–Navy Board 2 January 1815, rec 20 January 1816; 24 April 1815, rec 14 November 1815; 20 May 1815; 26 January 1816, rec 15 August 1816: Adm 106/2012-3

The classic image of a British frigate as it appeared about 1815. The white stripe along the hull emphasises the single tier of main-battery guns that characterised the frigate, although there are also gunports along the quarterdeck and forecastle for the secondary armament of carronades.

The original Bombay Dock, seen here in a painting by Francis Swain Ward (fl 1734-1794). In this view two ships are in dock, while the dock is positioned at the corner of the island fortifications. HMS *Trincomalee* was built in the Inner Dock, by then one of three docks comprising the Old Dock. (By courtesy of the Martyn Gregory Gallery, London)

For much of the long peace between 1815 and 1854 the main strength of the Royal Navy was laid up, a strategic reserve in case of war, and a standing warning to any hostile powers that Britain, despite her tiny active fleet, still had the power to control the oceans. Here the *Trincomalee* is seen at Portsmouth, in a painting by E W Cooke. The roof keeps rainwater out of the hull and was essential to her long term survival. The curious structures above the ridge-line are ventilators, that allow the interior to be dried by the tiny maintenance party.

The midshipman's berth on a frigate, about 1830, an oil painting by Augustus Earle (fl 1806-38). There was little space, and fewer comforts, with anchor chains, and vital vertical and horizontal access routes running through an area that modern visitors would find claustrophobic, but few complained at the time. (National Maritime Museum, London)

On 23 September 1854 *Trincomalee* and her sister ship the *Amphitrite* (left) beat out of San Francisco, with the French Frigate *Artemise* in company. They were heading for Hawaii, where an Anglo-French force was gathering to preserve the independence of the islands, before sailing off to attack the Russians at Petropavlovsk. The *Trincomalee* has just loosened her jib sheets ready to tack through the wind. Losing contact in a fog soon afterwards, she easily outran her two consorts. The small craft in the foreground is an American pilot schooner. (National Maritime Museum, London)

The *Foudroyant* in Portsmouth harbour during her last days as a youth training ship. This aerial view shows her final state before restoration began, built up, with only a stump mast, and some incongruous structures on deck.

'Foudroyant' lying alongside at Hartlepool, awaiting a decision on her future. The damaged and patched port quarter is very evident, as is the cabin built on the quarterdeck during the ship's training days. The scale of the task facing her restorers is clear.

The lower deck of the restored *Trincomalee* displaying the messing arrangements in a frigate. The absence of guns on this deck – where the crew both ate and slept – was a feature unique to frigates and meant that they were more spacious and habitable than any other class of the Navy's warships.

The main armament of a frigate was carried on what was formally the 'upper deck', although it was covered by another, almost continuous structure of quarterdeck, waist gangways and forecastle, which in action protected the main battery from falling spars and rigging. This is the restored gundeck of the *Trincomalee*, showing the 18-pounders and their equipment.

The Ward Room (as here reconstructed in the *Trincomalee*) was the centre of social life for all commissioned officers other than the captain. Here the lieutenants and Marine officers lived and ate, separated from the crew by a flimsy partition, designed to be cleared away in battle. While the physical separation was slight, it marked a clear social division.

Trincomalee's galley range. With 240 officers and men to feed, and only one stove, the ship's cooks needed both skill and strength. There were few luxuries for the men, and little choice of cooking method other than boiling and roasting. However, food was a vital element in the success of a ship; hungry or dissatisfied men always grumbled, so a good captain ensured they had enough to eat, and tried to provide hot food and drink in the worst weather. While naval rations could be dull, they were always ample.

The sensitively lit gundeck with its battery of 18-pounders gives the visitor to the *Trincomalee* a strong impression of the conditions of life at sea in a sailing warship.

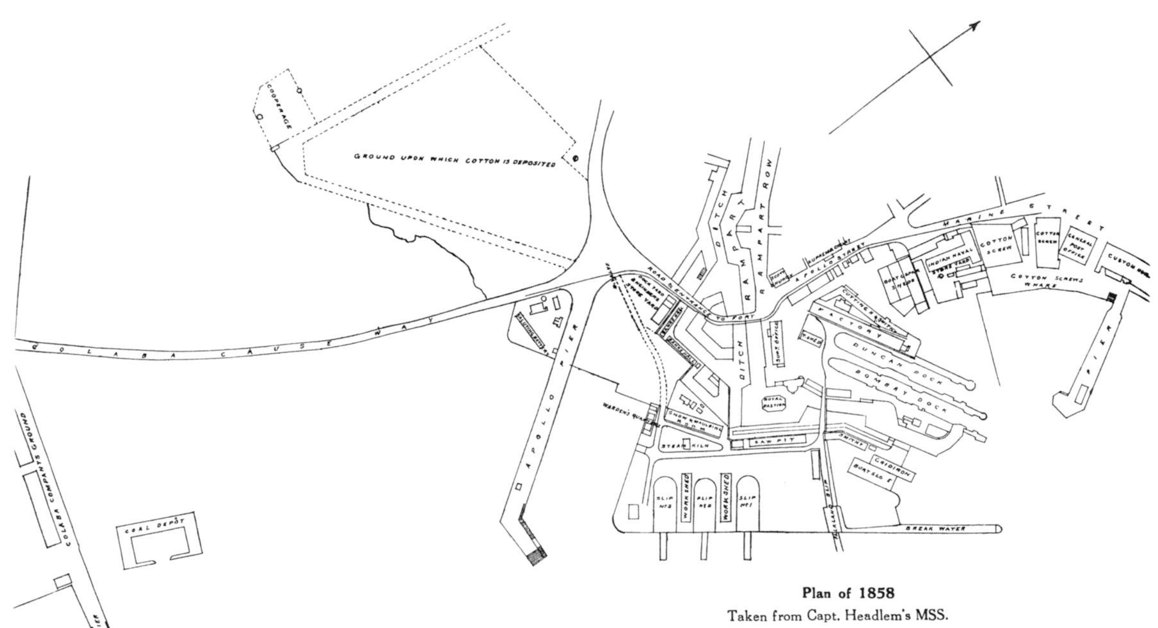

Plan of 1858
Taken from Capt. Headlem's MSS.

This plan of 1858 shows both main docks at Bombay, together with the three new slipways built on the glacis of the fort in the 1830s when the Royal Navy briefly renewed the construction project. In addition to the shipbuilding projects for the Admiralty this yard had also built and maintained the Bombay Marine for over one hundred years.

Within a year the local supervisor reported that Governor Duncan appeared to be intent on a little sharp practice at the Admiralty's expense. He charged the Navy for the use of a dock in which a merchant ship was being built, and deliberately delayed work on timbers for warships. It seems Duncan wanted to ensure more work had to be done after the keel was laid, from which point dock hire was charged. Even so, the Admiralty was content to keep ordering ships while the war continued.

At the end of the war the Admiralty reviewed the arrangements for building in India. By this stage the Surveyors of the Navy were sufficiently impressed with teak ships and the advantages of building new, useable tonnage in such short time that they recommended procuring as many teak ships as could be obtained. It took time for the officials of both the Navy and the Company in London and Bombay to prepare a more considered post-war policy. At this period an exchange of correspondence between London and Bombay required at least a year. On hearing of the first abdication of Napoleon, Commissioner Johnstone suggested mooring some new ships at Bombay, as a reserve. He also argued that more materials should be sent out, notably the masts, as local supplies were inadequate, and expensive. He sustained the attack on the Company, which he accused of taking no steps to ascertain the actual resources of the forests or to secure the supply. Plank was still plentiful, but curved timber was hard to come by. In addition charges for dock hire (2000 rupees a month), labour and timber were all excessive. Dock hire raised the cost per ton of the Indian-built battleships from £ 31-10s per ton to £34, not including the cost of sending them home.[24]

Building the *Trincomalee*

The durability and value of the teak warship was already established by the time of the final defeat of Bonaparte, and the Surveyors of the Navy recommended obtaining 'as many ships built of teak as possible, particularly Ships of the line and Frigates, but whether they should be constructed here or in India is for the consideration of the Board'.[25] These ships could be built quickly, without long periods of seasoning, and used in

Above: The original drawing for the figurehead of the *Trincomalee*, which was only carved when the ship was prepared for service in 1845. The design shows a native of Ceylon, as Sri Lanka was then known. The name was first used after the British captured Ceylon, and the great harbour at Trincomali from the Dutch in 1795. The subject of this book was the third and last ship to carry the name, the first two being locally captured prizes. (Public Record Office, Adm 87/15)

Right: The restored figurehead.

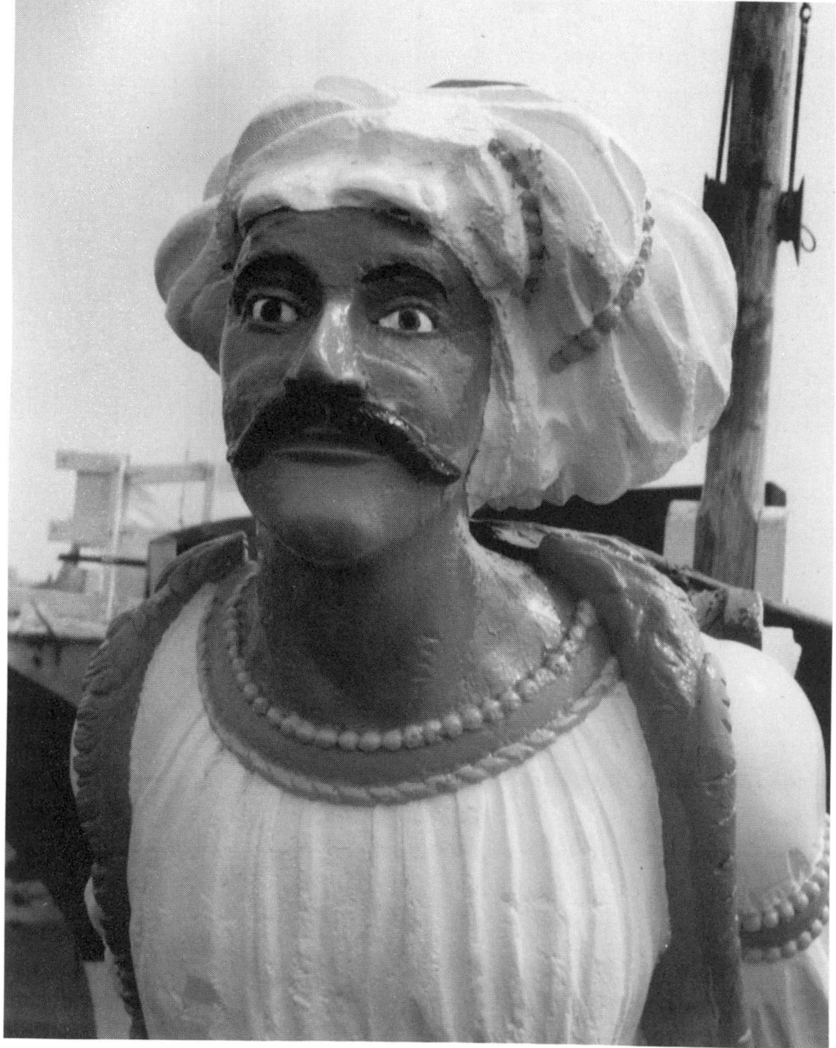

hot climates, especially in eastern waters. Among the ships already planned to be built at Bombay were a pair of frigates ordered in October 1812, as repeat versions of the successful *Leda*, but as yet not laid down.[26] The second, the *Trincomalee* was only to be built 'if there are adequate means'.[27] Their plans had been sent on board HMS *Java*. It would seem that the new ships were intended to reinforce the East Indies Station, where a threat from American cruisers was anticipated following the outbreak of the War of 1812. However, the construction of the new frigates did not proceed smoothly. The contrasting requirements of the Company and the Admiralty produced a series of misunderstandings, to say nothing more, that began to undermine the whole project of building at Bombay.

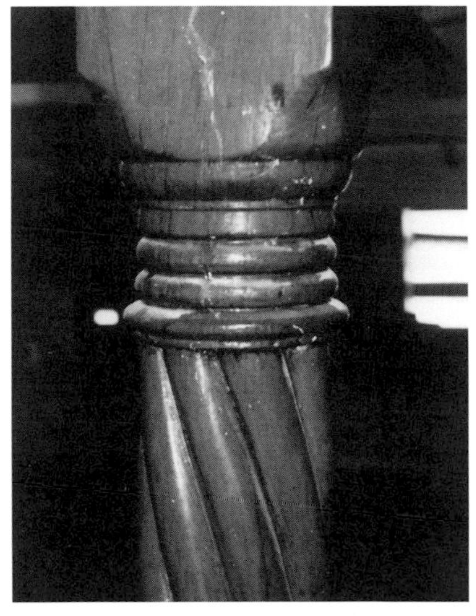

A Wadia 'trademark' was the use of a spiral 'barley sugar' moulding on stanchions; *Trincomalee* retains a number of these below decks.

The first problem arose when the first Bombay warship, the frigate HMS *Salsette* was measured at Portsmouth, and it was discovered that 'the lines of the *Inconstant*, by which she was ordered to have been constructed, have been completely departed from.' In addition, her upperworks were clumsily fitted, and irregular. The Commissioner at Bombay was ordered to ensure this did not happen again, and the following year an experienced Master Shipwright was sent out to inspect the work.[28] Fortunately the arrival of the first 74, HMS *Minden*, established the credentials of the yard.[29]

The Admiralty had expected the two new frigates to be laid down at once, but Bombay could not oblige because the necessary plans had been destroyed when HMS *Java* had been captured and burnt by the USS *Constitution* off Brazil on 29 December 1812. As the Admiralty had clearly specified a 38-gun frigate, Bombay could not, as they did with the 74-gun ship also ordered at the same time, simply re-use the one frigate design they had, which was for a 36-gun ship. However, the Company did not let the opportunity to rack up some profit pass, laying down a 'keel' for the *Amphitrite* in the Upper Old Dock, which it would later assert was the date from which dock hire was due. In fact fresh plans did not arrive until 1816, so the ship could not be have been laid down before that date.

Although Bombay had planned to build the second frigate, *Trincomalee*, in the Middle Old Dock, instructions arrived from the Court of Directors to build a 1300-ton merchant ship, the *Buckinghamshire* (named for the new President of the Board of Control), and the putative 'keel' of the *Trincomalee* was taken up. The Navy Board Commissioner Joseph Seaton protested to the Governor, and advised the Navy Board that this 'will supersede for some time the arrangement which had been made for the construction of the *Trincomalee* frigate for HM Service.'[30] He was also annoyed by the fact that the *Amphitrite* would be

25 Committee of Surveyors – Navy Board 4 July 1815: Adm 106/3205

26 The only other British frigate of this era, HMS *Unicorn* of 1826, was also built to this design, although with the post-war Seppings modifications to bow and stern and constructed on his 'small timber' diagonal trussed system

27 Admiralty – Navy Board 30 October 1812: Adm 106/3123, p20

28 Navy Board – Commissioner 31 December 1812; 20 March 1813: Adm 106/3123, p21. Gardiner, *Frigates of the Napoleonic Wars*, p12
Navy Board – Admiralty 15 December 1813: Adm 106/3123, p23

29 Surveyors of the Navy – Navy Board 4 June 1812: Adm 106/3205, no 4

30 Commissioner Seaton – Navy Board 12 December 1814: Adm 106/3205, no 39

detained in the Upper Old Dock until the new ship was ready.[31] In truth the former was a minor issue, and the latter was not significant, as she would have been delayed by her sister in any case. When reproached the Court of Directors did not apologise for their actions, pointing out

> it does not appear to them reasonable that they should restrain themselves from occasionally giving orders to build such ships as may be required for the Company's service in Docks which have been constructed solely at their expense.[32]

In addition the Admiralty had only ever asked the Company to build one 74 and one frigate a year. However, the Board of Control did tell Bombay that no charges should be levied for the period of delay arising from the inability to launch the frigate.[33] In the event *Trincomalee* could only be laid down when *Amphitrite* and *Buckinghamshire* were floated out in April 1816. The new keel was laid down in the Upper Old Dock on 25 April. One month later the ceremony of driving a Silver Nail into the keel was carried out, in accordance with Bombay tradition. *Trincomalee* was constructed quickly, and floated out on 12 October 1817. She was immediately followed by another frigate. Her construction had proceeded smoothly, although the acute shortage of curved timber made it impossible to complete a duplicate frame that year. To do so would delay the next ship of the class, and the Presidency did not want to cripple their own profitable construction and dock hire business in order to fulfil a minor stipulation.[34]

The East India Company charged £23,642 to build *Trincomalee*, and with the addition of stores valued at £6681 from the Royal Navy her total cost was £30,323. On top of this were to costs of the delivery voyage.[35] When finally delivered, on 30 May 1818 it was intended that *Trincomalee* should to be commissioned, but she was subsequently ordered to be laid up in ordinary, being turned over to the Master Shipwright and moved to the port from which she took her name. The Commander-in-Chief, Admiral Sir Richard King, had suggested laying up the new Bombay ships at Trincomalee, as the Company owned Bombay harbour and would not consent to do so there.[36] However, the cost and trouble was not deemed acceptable, while the projected dockyard was still far from complete, so the new ship was commissioned in mid-October by turning over the crew of HMS *Challenger*[37] under Commander Philip Bridges, recently Senior Officer in the Persian Gulf.[38] She was commissioned with a sloop complement of 100, comprising 77 officers and men, 7 boys and 14 marines. Her crew was almost entirely British, although there were four West Indians, a Portuguese, a Palermitan and an American.[39] She was only fitted out for a passage home, carrying condemned stores, invalids and some timber. In October 1818 Admiral King decided it

31 Commissioner Seaton–Navy Board 14 July 1817, rec 28 November 1817: Adm 49/14

32 East India House–Admiralty 29 February 1816: Adm 1/3918

33 Board of Control–Bombay 8 April 1816: E4/1033, f743

34 Bombay–Board of Control 27 March 1817: F/4/13761

35 Admiralty Progress Book: Adm 180/12, p356

36 Navy Board–Master Shipwright 5 July 1817: Adm 106/3123 p39

37 A *Cruizer* class 18-gun brig-sloop, then hulked at Trincomalee as a rice depot, broken up in 1824

38 The first of *Trincomalee*'s three captains, Philip Henry Bridges entered the Royal Navy in 1796, and was promoted Lieutenant for gallantry 1803. From 1811 to 1819 he served in several frigates, including *Leda*, on the East Indies Station, being promoted Commander, into *Challenge*, by Admiral Burlton in 1815. He served briefly in the 1820s, was promoted Captain and died in 1848

39 Ship's Muster Book: Adm 37/6135

40 Admiral King–Admiralty 25 October 1818, rec 31 March 1819: Adm 1/190, no 65

41 Lieutenant's Log 27 March 1819: Adm 52/3933
See also the Master's Log Adm 52/3960 and Captain's Log Adm 51/2916

would be safer to send the ship home in company with another vessel, the sloop HMS *Towey*, Captain Hill.[40] *Challenger*'s crew moved to their new ship on 15 October, and quickly shifted the guns and stores from the brig, set up the masts and repaired the sails.

The two ships left Trincomalee on 27 October, with Captain Hill in overall command, stopping at Point des Galles and then Port Louis in Mauritius to deliver stores and collect invalids, where two men deserted. Four men were flogged for being drunk. The ships then left for Simon's Bay at the Cape, and arrived there on 27 December. On 9 January they moved into Table Bay to load bullocks and other supplies for St Helena, where a squadron was still based to ensure Napoleon did not escape. During a boisterous twenty-day passage to the island most of the livestock, which was already in poor condition, died even faster than the invalids. After a week at the anchorage the ships passed on to Ascension Island, and when they left it took a fortnight to get through a zone of calms and baffling winds at the equator, before making passage for the Azores, arriving at Fayal on 19 March, in need of fresh water and provisions. A week later 'John Robinson (seaman) fell from the main yard, rounded too but found it impossible to save him'.[41] Having picked up further invalids at every stop the ship had become something of a floating hospital. Twenty of the sick died, but Bridges noted the rest were 'on whole, much recovered'. The similarly decayed stores–old cables, anchors, butts, barrels and such like–also collected along the way, were less troublesome. There is even a diary of the passage, compiled by the

In 1812 the United States declared war on Britain and invaded Canada. Anticipating an American threat to shipping in the region the Admiralty ordered two new frigates to be built at Bombay for service in the Indian Ocean. The plans for *Trincomalee* and her sister the *Amphitrite* were sent out to India on board HMS *Java*. On the way she engaged the USS *Constitution* off the coast of Brazil. After a brave fight the far smaller *Java* surrendered. However, she was so badly damaged that her captors decided to burn her, and the original plans were lost when the burning wreck blew up. New copies of the plans had to be sent and the two frigates were not completed until long after the War of 1812 had ended.

A contemporary drawing of a frigate sailing from Bombay. *Trincomalee* was actually sailed home with a reduced rig (which required a far smaller crew). From a manuscript in the British Library, WD303 17.

widow of a shipwright who had died at Trincomali.[42] As the two ships entered the Channel they parted company in foggy, blowing weather, before *Trincomalee* arrived at Spithead on 29 March 1819.[43]

Once at Spithead Bridges compiled a sailing report, which stressed that she had made the passage under jury masts, and was light. Even so she ran well, steered easily and made up to 12 knots before the wind, despite rolling heavily due to her light condition (and doubtless far from perfect stowage). She was ballasted with 114 tons of iron, in various forms, and 70 tons of shingle. The report is similar in most respect to those of her sisters, especially the delivery voyage of *Amphitrite*, which brought home 55 loads of timber.[44] After her crew had unloaded the invalids, the condemned stores, and the fittings used to bring her home, *Trincomalee* was stripped out, warped alongside the sheer hulk, to have her bowsprit and masts removed and then paid off at sunset on 27 April 1819. Thirty-five of her men had gone ashore without leave two days earlier, and four of those who had to come back for their pay received a flogging for their pleasure. Placed in dockyard hands the ship was prepared for long years of duty in the reserve fleet. Curiously, the next Bombay frigate, HMS *Seringapatam*, was the lead ship of a new class, and as such was commissioned throughout the 1820s to enable the Navy to assess the qualities of the new design.[45]

Once in dockyard hands *Trincomalee* was housed over from the main mast forward, to keep out the rainwater, and placed in the reserve, at the back end of the harbour. She was docked in June/July 1829, when her copper was shifted, but otherwise needed only basic maintenance for the next twenty-five years.[46]

42 Monnery, M H (ed), *From Trincomalee to Portsea: The diary of Eliza Bunt, 1818-1822* (Worthing 2001). Contains a journal of this voyage by the widow of an officer of the Trincomali dockyard

43 Bridges – Admiralty 29 March 1819: Adm 1/1566, B42

44 Sailing Report 4 April 1819: Adm 95/45, p152

45 see Gardiner, *Frigates of the Napoleonic Wars*, pp63-4, 144

46 Admiralty Progress Book: Adm 180/12, p356

Imperial Security – the First Commission

Chapter Three

The rebuild

AFTER SPENDING twenty-five years in the reserve *Trincomalee* was no longer a modern front-line warship by 1845. Not only were increasing numbers of smaller ships now steam-powered, but the standard frigate of the French and American navies had become a very large 50-gun ship, armed with a full battery of 32-pounders. *Trincomalee* was now a small frigate, no longer capable of carrying enough modern guns to remain a Fifth Rate, let alone match a Fourth Rate.

However, her well-preserved teak hull remained sound and strong, still ready for years of service. In the interests of economy she was ordered to be cut down from a 42-gun frigate to a 26-gun 'gun-deck corvette' in January 1845 by the Conservative Admiralty Board of Lord Haddington and Admiral Sir George Cockburn.[1] Three months later her sister the *Amphitrite* was detailed for a slightly more extensive conversion, in which her bow would be rebuilt along new lines provided by the Isle of White shipbuilder J Samuel White.[2] The logic of the project was to convert obsolescent frigates that were too small for front-line service with the main fleet into powerful and durable heavy corvettes for service on distant stations. The two teak ships were selected as among the best preserved, and better suited to the harsh conditions to be found on distant stations, especially extremes of heat and humidity, which their teak hulls were known to be more capable of resisting. Another frigate of the same age, the *Penelope*, was converted into a paddle-wheel frigate by cutting the ship in half, adding a new section 65 feet long with powerful engines and paddle wheels, at a cost of close on £60,000. While this was less than half the cost of a new ship, the *Penelope* experiment was not repeated. Four more frigates were to have been reconstructed as screw steamships, but only the *Horatio* was completed, in 1850, and she was not a success. Indeed the most effective conversion was that applied to *Trincomalee* and *Amphitrite*.

The process of cutting down older ships to a lower class, often termed *razeeing* (from the French *rasée*), had long been employed to improve overloaded ships, or in the French Revolutionary War and War of 1812, to produce very powerful frigates from small battleships. The post-1815 policy of building large numbers of ships to standard designs had left the

1 Admiralty to Surveyor 17 January 1845: Adm 83/34

2 Admiralty to Surveyor 4 April 1845: Adm 83/3768

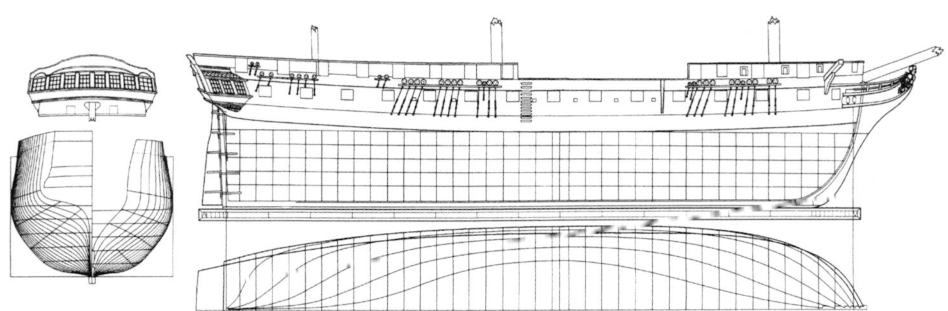

HMS Trincomalee 46 guns 1817

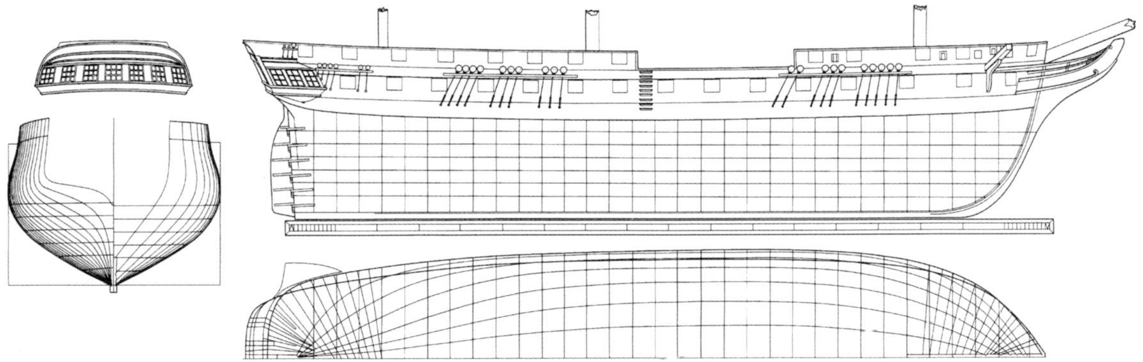

HMS Vernon 50 guns 1832

When she was ordered, in 1812, the *Trincomalee* had been a standard sized frigate. However, the events of 1812, when larger American frigates secured embarrassing victories over standard class British ships led to a steady rise in the size of this warship type. By the mid-1840s the Royal Navy was building 50-gun ships, based on HMS *Vernon*, designed by Sir William Symonds in 1832. With a full gundeck battery of long 32-pounders, and short guns of the same calibre on the upper deck, these ships were three times more powerful than the *Trincomalee* and, more significantly, could engage effectively at much longer range. (Drawing by Norman Swales)

Royal Navy with a problem of block obsolescence; a problem exacerbated by the superior durability of the new ships. By the early 1840s *Trincomalee*'s original main battery of 18-pounder guns and 32-pounder carronades was completely out of date. The critical 'point blank' range (the range at which the guns would hit the target without elevation) of new ships with heavier guns was at least double that of her intended battery, and offered far greater real firepower, not least from the introduction of shell-firing guns. In the United States a trend toward building ship-rigged sloops with a small number of very heavy guns had been taken up in the early 1840s, with ships such as the USS *Germantown.*

Length	151 feet 10 inches
Breadth	37 feet 3 inches
Depth in Hold	16 feet 3 inches
Burthen	960 tons
Armament	22 guns: eighteen medium 32-pounders, four 8-inch shell guns
Complement	210 men.

A relatively small complement made these ships more efficient for distant stations.[3] The American sloops were ordered at a time of heightened Anglo-American tension in the early 1840s, probably for commerce destroying.[4] They were fast, well armed and offered an interesting alternative to the small frigate. However, they carried their armament on the exposed upper deck, and would have suffered severely in combat with a gun-deck vessel (*ie* one with a covered battery). The British decision not to follow this model reflected a conscious rejection of such large ships armed only on the upper deck, the availability of numerous sound 18-pounder frigates, and the fact that no other major navy followed the American lead.

The new ships the Americans were building would have made short work of an old frigate armed with 18-pounder guns. However, the British response was to convert older ships to carry a modern armament. This would both reduce their crew needs, which were based on a full gun crew for one half of the guns carried, and significantly improve their effective firepower. The conversion was proposed by the ambitious Master Shipwright at Portsmouth, John Fincham, who hoped to secure the post of Surveyor of the Navy. His plan was to retain the upper deck, but greatly reduce the number of guns mounted on it. This left the upper deck and gangways as overhead protection for the main-deck gun crews, who would not be injured or inconvenienced by any rigging that fell during an action. This was considered to be a cardinal point by all contemporary

3 Chapelle, H I, *History of the American Sailing Navy* (New York 1959), p440

4 Tucker, S, *Arming the Fleet* (Annapolis MD 1989), pp142-3

Drawings prepared for the restoration of the ship showing forecastle and quarterdeck configurations in 1817 and as converted in 1847 to a 'gundeck corvette'. In this type of warship the main battery was covered by a flush upper deck, which unlike a frigate, carried only a few guns.

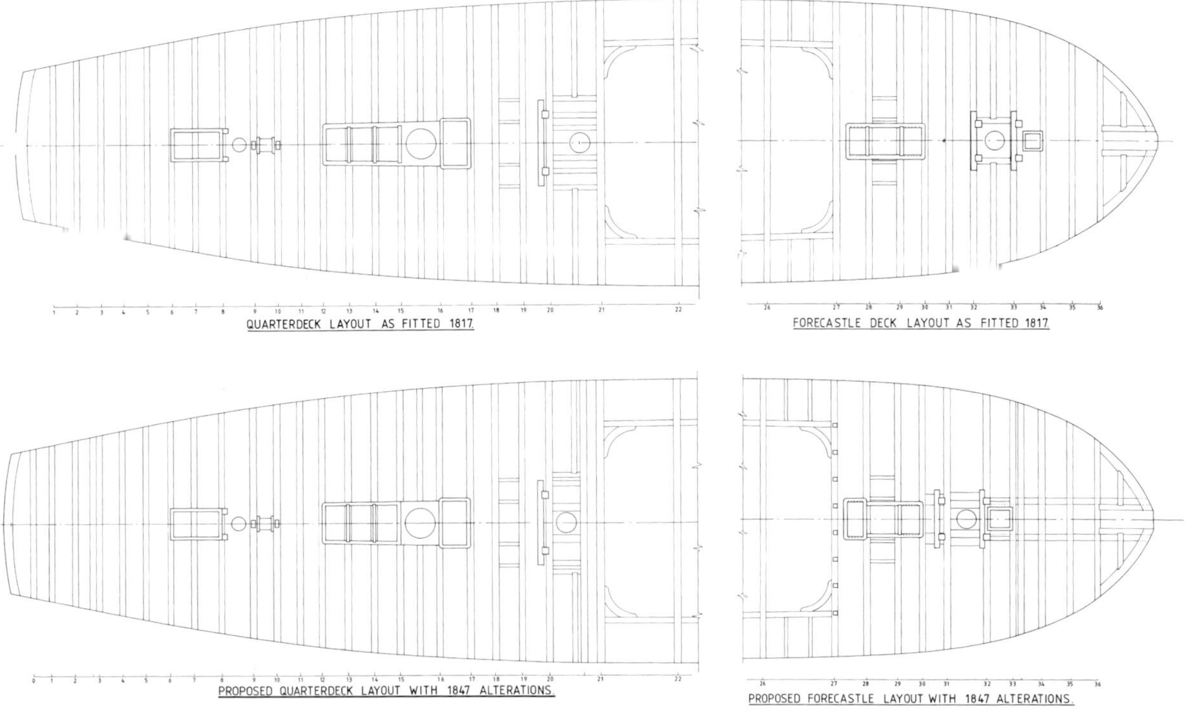

naval officers, many of whom could still remember the details of close-range action. The exposed main battery had been the major criticism of HMS *Amazon*, the only frigate *razeed* into a true 26-gun corvette by the removal of the forecastle, gangways and quarterdeck.

Trincomalee was docked at Portsmouth in mid-March 1845, and finally undocked at the end of November, having had her copper completely replaced, the upper deck altered for the new reduced armament, and been fitted for sea.[5] In July the new armament for the rebuilt ships was settled as:

Quarterdeck	two 85cwt 56-pounder guns; six 25cwt 32-pounders
Main Deck	six 8-inch 65cwt shell guns; twelve 50cwt 32-pounders
Total	26 guns

In addition, the after magazine was converted into a shell room.[6] The stern was also remodelled as a modern elliptical structure, and the masts moved.

The conversion cost £10,539 of which only £5760 was for materials.[7] The transformation produced an effective, powerful ship without using up much scarce timber. On coming into office the new Surveyor, Captain Sir Baldwin Walker, considered the work on the two teak frigates 'a very judicious alteration'.[8] His department calculated that *Trincomalee* had cost £11,721, of which £6209 was for materials. A new ship of the same

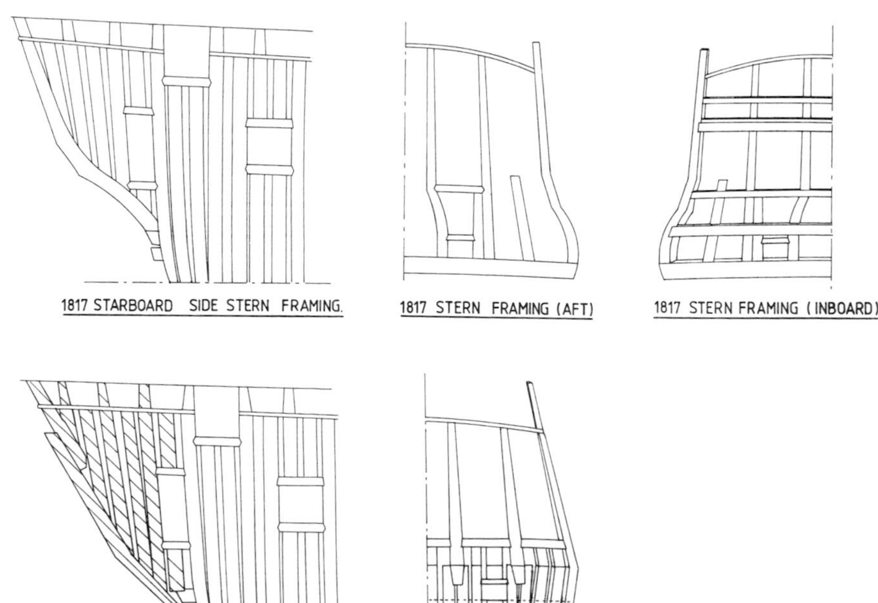

General arrangement of stern timbers as built 1817, and as converted 1847.

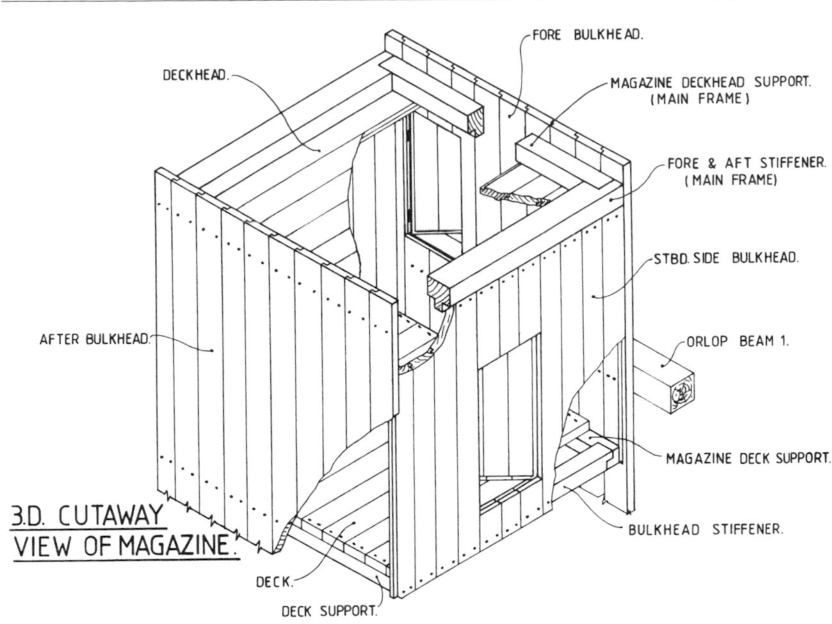

The after magazine. It was converted to a shell room in 1847.

rate would have cost £27,000, of which £21,000 would have been for materials.[9] However, Walker and his Liberal colleagues were less pleased with the larger and more costly *razee* of the 120-gun First Rate *Prince Regent* into a 92-gun Second Rate. There would be few more such conversions; the fall of the Conservative ministry in 1846 marked the end of the process, and the next major group of ship conversions, in the 1850s, transformed sailing ships of the line into screw steam battleships.

As rebuilt *Trincomalee* was a modern fighting ship, but her size and lack of steam power ensured that she did not join the great battlefleets in the Mediterranean and the Channel on which the security of the Empire rested, but served out her active career on more distant stations, where the life of an imperial cruiser was less glamorous, if no less active. It could have been worse: other frigates of similar vintage were already doing duty as harbour service hulks and depots in obscure parts of the world.

Imperial defence in the mid-nineteenth century

After 1815 the British Empire returned to the fundamental business of expanding commercial activity over oceans secured by the Royal Navy. Unlike continental empires the British did not seek territory; if possible they avoided the costs of local administration, and local security forces. Instead, they sought trading opportunities, based on global sea control, which amounted to an 'informal empire', where the economic life of whole continents was controlled from London, without British occupation. Where large territories were under effective British control, as in India and much of Canada, the authority and administration was left to

5 Progress Book: Adm 180/12

6 Admiralty to Surveyor July 1845 and 13 September 1845: Adm 83/35 & 36

7 Adm 83/40

8 Parliamentary Papers 1847-8, p161

9 These figures do not agree with those later entered into the Progress Book: Deputy Surveyor Edye, Parliamentary Papers 1847-8, pp189, 897

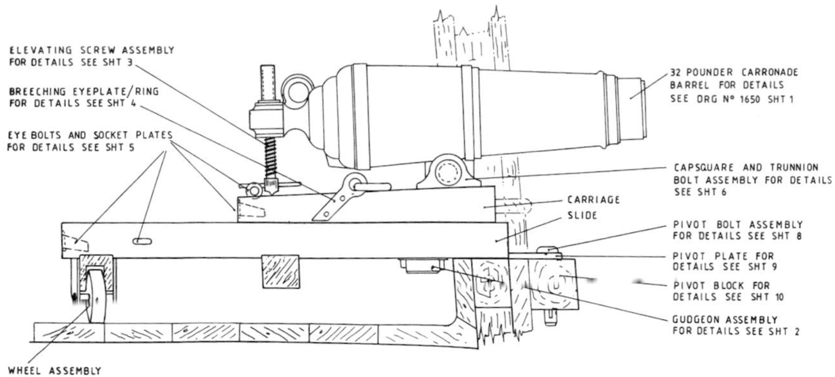

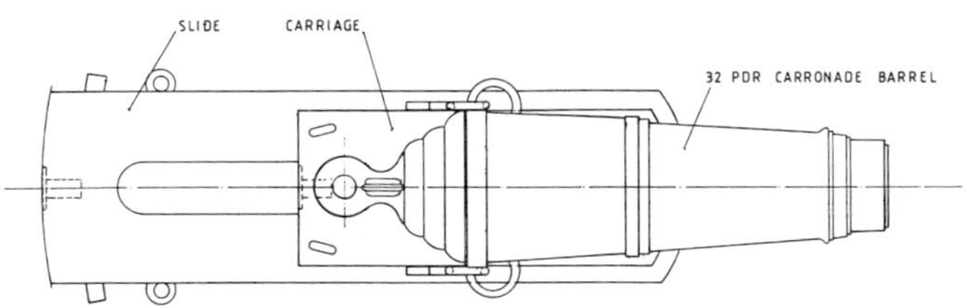

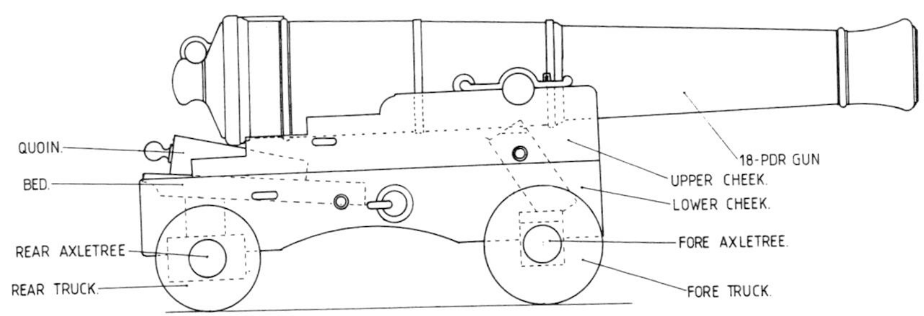

The original designed armament was chosen for the reconstruction of the ship, these drawings being used to make replica 18-pounder long guns and 32-pounder carronades. This weapon fit was obsolete by 1847, and during her first commission the ship carried only 26 guns, but of larger calibres, including 32-pounders and 8-inch shell guns.

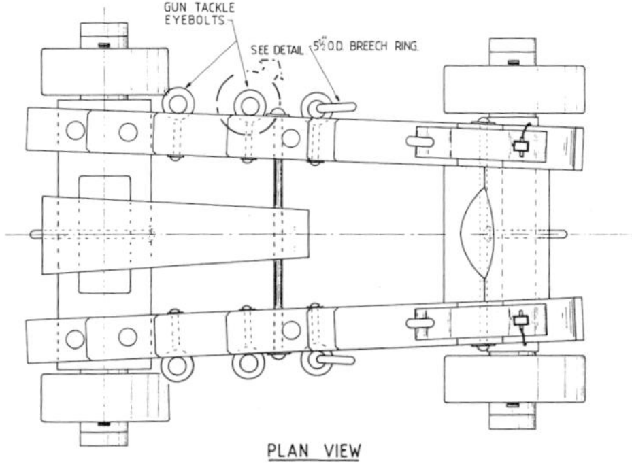

imperial agencies, the East India and Hudson's Bay Companies, who carried out imperial tasks in return for commercial privileges. The key overseas possessions of the British Crown were almost invariably small, easily defensible naval bases, either insular, or peninsula, with little or no commercial value, but strategically vital. Gibraltar, Malta, Bermuda, Halifax (Nova Scotia), Singapore, Hong Kong, Aden, and even the isolated, windswept Falkland Islands, were links in the imperial position. They were held together by sea communications, and secure as long as Britain ruled the waves. From these positions Britain could project power into any theatre around the world, should that be necessary. In truth it was rarely necessary, for the other major powers lacked the naval power to challenge the Royal Navy, and consequently were easily deterred from attacking British interests, while local difficulties over trade or frontiers rarely required additional naval forces to be sent.

While the European mainland was stable and no one power or bloc threatened to dominate it, as Napoleon had, Britain was content to stand aside and focus her energies on the opportunities opening up elsewhere. As Lord Palmerston, by turns Foreign Secretary or Prime Minister for much of the period between 1830 and 1865 once famously declared: 'We have no eternal allies and no eternal enemies, only eternal interests, and those interests it is the duty of the Government to uphold.' Palmerston was a particularly aggressive exponent of opening new commercial opportunities, as his treaties with Turkey in 1837, and war with China between 1839 and 1842 demonstrated. Indeed, much of the work of the Royal Navy in this era involved putting pressure on other regimes to open up their markets, from Burma and the Gulf states to West Africa and Latin America.

The various squadrons operating around the world were accorded differing degrees of independence. The Channel and Mediterranean Fleets, the key indicators of British power, were closely directed; the West Indies Squadron was less closely watched, but still within range for effective direction, but the Pacific Squadron was necessarily allowed a good deal of latitude. The increased degree of local responsibility also flowed down to captains, for the bigger the station the more likely it was that the admiral would have to delegate important decisions to trusted subordinates.

The first commission, 1847-1850

On 23 July 1847 *Trincomalee* finally commissioned for active service, on the North America and West Indies Station, some thirty years after she had been built. Her captain was Richard Laird Warren. Warren, the son of an admiral, had entered the Navy in 1822, and been commissioned in 1829. His family and political connections, on the Liberal side, ensured his

Captain Richard Laird Warren commanded the *Trincomalee* on her first commission. He proved to be a sound officer of the old school, maintaining discipline with a firm hand, and not a little flogging. Although seen here in a later photograph, as an admiral, he was in his mid-30s when the commission began.

career prospered, and within ten years he had become a Captain. Sent afloat in 1841, just as his political friends left office, he had not had to wait long for fresh employment after they returned in late 1846.[10]

Complement

1	captain
172	officers and men
33	boys
35	Royal Marines
240	in total

The crew was largely composed of experienced men-of-war sailors, and boys. Of the 284 seamen who would serve on board the ship on this commission only 84 were first entrants into the service, and some of them would have been experienced seamen or boys fresh from a training ship.[11]

Warren came aboard, and read his commission to a largely empty ship. Over the next few weeks a crew was assembled, beginning with the Royal Marine detachment, who usually ended up doing all the hard work associated with getting up the masts and rigging. A month later the Admiralty Board visited the ship, and then she was docked for an inspection. On 20 August the ship was visited by a piece of living history. Captain John Pascoe of the flagship HMS *Victory* mustered the ship's company and read new regulations authorising the use of imprisonment in place of corporal punishment. Pascoe had been Nelson's signal lieutenant at Trafalgar, and played a part in composing the immortal signal 'England expects . . .'. Once out of dock *Trincomalee* used her main yard to hoist in her guns. While fitting out, Warren noted that her sister, the *Amphitrite*, had left harbour. A week later *Trincomalee* followed her out to Spithead, where she was inspected by the commander-in-chief, Admiral Sir Charles Ogle, and the crew paid 21 months' wages. She also embarked 40 supernumerary boys for the squadron she would be joining.[12] The two ships then anchored in St Helen's Roads, before proceeding to sea together, and heading for Lisbon. On 2 October they stood up the Tagus, saluted the flag of Rear-Admiral Sir Charles Napier, and joined the Western Squadron anchored off Black Horse Square.

The two ships had been sent to Napier to 'have a fair trial' before they

10 O'Byrne, W, *Naval Biographical Dictionary* (London 1849), p1253. Another officer, William Warren, is listed as captain of *Trincomalee*, but this is an error

11 Ship's Muster Book: Adm 38/9204

12 Admiralty – Austen 9 September 1847: Adm 2/1605, f425

13 Admiralty – Napier 6 August 1847: Adm 2/1605, f371-9. Admiral Dundas (First Sea Lord) – Napier 10 September 1847: BL Add 40,022, f104

14 Auckland – Napier 20 September 1847: NAP/1 NMM

15 Promoted Rear-Admiral in 1849 Moresby (1786-1877) would meet *Trincomalee* on her next commission, as C-in-C Pacific station, in 1850-53, his last sea service.
Moresby, J, *Two Admirals* (London 1911)

proceeded to distant stations, where they would have little opportunity to sail in company and carry out comparative exercises, as the Admiralty was anxious to ascertain the value of the lengthened bow fitted to *Amphitrite*.[13] Although only recently promoted to flag rank, Napier (1786-1860) was the most dynamic, popular and effective senior officer in the service. Lord Auckland, the First Lord of the Admiralty, sent a series of ships, from sailing corvettes to the first screw warships, to him for exercises. His reports influenced the development of new ship designs. Auckland declared: 'Pray try *Amphitrite* and *Trincomalee* well, but do not keep them long.'[14]

On 7 October the squadron put to sea, and the following day began with gunnery practice against targets, but unfortunately Able Seaman William Roberts was lost overboard. Despite heaving a life buoy and launching the cutter, no trace was found of the man; the life buoy was recovered, and the ship rejoined the squadron astern of the battleship *Canopus*, which had been taken by Nelson at the Nile. Between the 10th and the 14th the two sister ships were tested under sail, with the 84-guns ships *Canopus* and *Vengeance*, under the command of Captain Fairfax Moresby (1786-1877) of *Canopus*.[15] On the 10th the four ships spent two hours beating to windward, with *Canopus* making between 1000 and 1500 yards on the other ships; *Trincomalee* ended up 400 yards astern of the rest. On the 11th the ships ran free before the wind for six hours, covering up to 35 miles. This time the frigates made 9000 yards on the *Canopus* which beat *Vengeance* by another 1200 yards. On the morning of the 12th

A large squadron under sail was an impressive sight, although it was one that the *Trincomalee* experienced but briefly at the beginning of her first commission. In this view Sir Charles Napier is leading the Baltic Fleet out from Spithead, going to war, in March 1854. In August 1847 Napier commanded the Western Squadron, as it beat out of the Tagus, with *Trincomalee* in company, for sailing and gunnery exercises.

the ships exercised fore-reaching and weathering, with the frigates once again well ahead of the battleships. In the afternoon they returned to working to windward, with similar results. Finally on the 14th the squadron worked to windward for a third time, with *Trincomalee* beating the battleships by over one mile an hour, and *Amphitrite* by a more modest 120 yards an hour.[16] Not only did *Trincomalee* get the better of *Amphitrite*, but she did so with less canvas spread.

On the 15th the two ships left the squadron, heading into the Atlantic together. When they parted company, *Amphitrite* for the west coast of Africa, while *Trincomalee* arrived at Bermuda on 6 November. Here she was towed into harbour, and saluted the flag of Vice-Admiral Sir Francis Austen (1774-1865), the older of Jane Austen's two naval brothers.[17] After many years on shore the widowed admiral had brought his family with him. His two daughters lived on board, one of his sons was the flag lieutenant, another the chaplain, and he would have employed his eldest son as flag captain had the Admiralty not refused to sanction the move.[18] Such 'family' ships were a dying breed by 1848, but Austen still managed to reduce his expenses, and promote his son and his nephew who relieved his son as flag lieutenant. In addition his eldest son was serving on the station.[19]

The North America and West Indies Station stretched from the Arctic in the north to the Brazilian border in the south, and from Mexico out to the mid-Atlantic (Latitude 55° to the coast of Brazil, and from Longitude 36°to the coast of the Americas). Within these extensive boundaries were the British territories of Canada and Newfoundland, along with their important, contentious, fisheries. These, together with the West Indian islands, from Bermuda to Trinidad, and the continental outpost of Belize, all required external security, and more frequently, a degree of support to the civil power, either for disaster relief or the suppression of local tensions.

This was not a happy time for the British West Indies: the final abolition of slavery in 1832, and the falling value of local produce were rapidly transforming it from an economic motor into a backwater. Sugar prices had been kept high for two centuries by slave labour and a protected home market, but the former had gone in the early 1830s, while the latter was ended after a period of very high prices in the early 1840s, which caused political problems in Britain. These resulted in the Sugar Duties Act of 1846, as revised in 1848, which ended the customs discrimination between free and slave-grown sugar. This was followed by the 1847 commercial crisis. When the Bank of England tightened credit restrictions, this exposed the speculative trading patterns of several leading West Indian merchants, who were immediately bankrupted. The knock-on effects included the failure of the two major West Indian banks, while sugar estates were abandoned, and wages cut by 25-50 per cent, leading to strikes, riots and economic distress for the newly emancipated population. Wrapped in the flag of Free Trade the British Government would do little to help, simply waiting for better times. In the interval local forces would have to support the civil power.[20]

British territories on the mainland, Belize and Honduras, were threatened by Nicaraguan attempts to claim the mouth of the San Juan River, and the ethnic strife between Mexico and the native American population on the Honduran border. Nor were the problems of the region confined to the British domains; instability was endemic, from Venezuela to Cuba, especially in Haiti and the breakaway Dominican Republic. Even if the British military force in the region – some 10,000 men – had been adequate, it was largely immobile, and could not be deployed into foreign countries. Consequently, much of the work of supporting British interests necessarily fell to the small force of warships. Typically, *Trincomalee*'s captain soon received his warrants from the various maritime nations who did not permit slave ships to operate under their flag, authorising him to stop and search their national merchant ships on the high seas in pursuit of slavers. Only two nations refused this right, Portugal and the United States, and they did so from economic weakness or political division.[21] The uncertain policy of the latter was a particular problem.

The expansionist policies of the United States, which had invaded Canada and attacked British merchant shipping in 1812, provided the main challenge to British interests in the western hemisphere. Another Anglo-American war was the most serious threat that the local forces could face, and there were many crises between 1815 and 1861.[22] These necessarily focused attention on the fleet, and the bases from which it operated. While no longer at the heart of the Empire, the West Indies still warranted a vice-admiral, with his flag in a 50-gun frigate, like Austen's *Vindictive*, or a small battleship, supported by frigates, corvettes and steamers totalling no more than a dozen ships.

The only fortified bases on the station were Bermuda and Halifax. After the War of 1812 both had been developed to fulfil the key role of securing the western hemisphere. By the late 1840s they were tolerably secure against a fleet of sailing ships, although the Admiralty was anxious that the Americans should not gain any detailed knowledge of the seaward approaches to Bermuda.[23] They possessed enough firepower to protect an inferior fleet, if only temporarily. The navigation and fixed defences of Bermuda were being upgraded in the late 1840s, a process that would be almost constant until the end of the century.[24]

Port Royal in Jamaica, English Harbour at Antigua and Castries Bay, Barbados provided local support. The dockyard at English Harbour in Antigua had been devastated by an earthquake in 1843, and was only

16 Reports by Captain Moresby 10-14 October 1847: Napier MSS BL Add 40,022, f147-56

17 Hubback, J H & E C, *Jane Austen's Sailor Brothers* (London 1906), pp 283-6

18 Hayward, K, *Cruise of HMS Vindictive on the North America & West Indies Station 1845-1848* (Bermuda 2000), pp7-8

19 Wilkinson, H C, *Bermuda: From Sail to Steam* (London 1973), Vol II, p569

20 Burns, A, *History of the British West Indies* (2nd edn London 1965), p659. Holland Rose, J, Newton, A P, & Benians, E A, *The Cambridge History of the British Empire* Vol II 1782-1870 (Cambridge 1940), pp707-12

21 Admiralty – Austen 22 November 1847: Adm 2/1606, f14

22 Bourne, K, *Britain and the Balance of Power in North America 1815-1900* (London 1967) provides a detailed survey

23 Admiralty – Austen 25 November 1847: Adm 2/1606, f20-1

24 Willock, P, *Bulwark of Empire: Bermuda's Fortifications 1860-1920* (Princeton NJ 1962), esp pp41-3

slowly recovering.[25] Bermuda had a garrison of 1300 British troops, from a total of 7000 in the West Indies. The three local West India Regiments added another 3400 men to the available force, and being locally raised were considered better suited to the hostile climate.[26] These forces were already being reduced. The Secretary of State for War and the Colonies, the third Earl Grey, sought economy and efficiency through the concentration of troops in larger, but less numerous garrison, with a home army being built up for a more 'expeditionary' strategy. Given the large number of British possessions in the region, few were garrisoned on a scale commensurate with external defence, and most garrisons would be reduced or removed. Grey argued that there was no longer any external danger, while the abolition of slavery had ended the internal threat.[27] In the former case he was correct, but internal security would remain a problem. Reducing troop numbers merely increased the demand for naval forces to provide internal security and disaster relief. Little wonder the admiral was always short of ships.

From Bermuda *Trincomalee* cruised to Barbados, where Warren took command of the local division of the squadron.[28] On moving to Antigua, John Gillingham, a Royal Marine, was drowned while bathing at the dockyard on 16 December; a week later AB George Stone fell overboard at sea, and was not found. Other ports of call included Jamaica, St Vincent, St Lucia and Demerera. The routine of sailing between ports was interspersed with target practice, until the problems of Venezuela called

The restored captain's cabin of HMS *Trincomalee*, compete with a captain from the era in which she was built. The squared floor pattern, on painted cloth, greatly enhances the sense of space in the largest single occupancy area of the ship (although during the Napoleonic Wars the captain shared his living space with a couple of 18-pounders a side). Here the captain planned his passages, wrote his reports, occasionally entertained local dignitaries and foreign officers. He also had his cot behind a partition, and two sets of toilet facilities, to be used according to the direction of the wind, the lee side being preferred.

the British squadron. British trade with Venezuela was worth well over one million pounds a year,[29] and Austen received instructions from Foreign Secretary Lord Palmerston to support the British diplomatic agent Mr Wilson in person, or 'send an officer in whose judgement and discretion he can place confidence', to support a variety of claims against the Venezuelan government, and ensure local political disturbances did not threaten the lives and property of British subjects.[30] Austen immediately dispatched Warren from the anchorage at St Vincent to liase with Wilson at Caracas. The flagship, HMS *Vindictive* and the steamer HMS *Vesuvius* joined *Trincomalee* at La Guaira, the port for Caracas, in late February 1848.

The turbulent politics of independent Venezuela reflected the growing political power of the commercial elite in Caracas, which was replacing the provincial military leaders of the Independence Wars, the agriculturalist *caudillos.* The shift from a cacao staple crop to coffee in the early 1830s, in response to external demand, led to a boom, and brought in large amounts of external capital. When coffee prices fell in the early 1840s the country, which had little cash and no major banks, witnessed numerous bankruptcies. The election of the liberal General Monagas as President in 1848 prompted a conservative rebellion by the most powerful of the *caudillos*, General Paez. This brought warships representing the major foreign investors in Venezuela scurrying to la Guiara, but Monagas quickly defeated the old war hero, who went into exile.[31]

Relative calm had been restored by the time Austen arrived. He noted that with only eight vessels in his command any unusual activity would cause severe problems.[32] Auckland concurred, and advised the Foreign Office that the continued presence of a warship would be 'most inconvenient'.[33] Austen arrived on the 22nd to discover that *chargé d'affairs* Wilson wanted his support to secure compensation of £500 from the Venezuelan authorities for William Massey, who had been illegally imprisoned. In addition, he was trying to get the suspected murderer of a British seamen put on trial. The British demands were quickly conceded, although the *chargé* advised that they should be treated as if they had been voluntarily made. Austen met the President, noted the disturbed state of the country, and advised regular visits, before departing, leaving *Trincomalee* to protect British interests.[34] Warren carried the court officers to Angostura for the murder trial, but Massey died, and his claim lapsed. Warren continued to cruise along the coast until the trial was over. The French presence, the corvette *la Boussole* ('Compass') missed her bearings off the coast, and ran aground on the island of Little Curaçao. Already bilged with a broken back, the French ship was beyond help, and her officers refused Warren's offer of assistance.[35] Her situation was complicated by the revolution in Paris, which had just brought down

25 Blackburne, K, *The Romance of English Harbour* (6th edn Antigua 1994), pp17-8

26 Burns, *British West Indies*, p665

27 *Cambridge History of the British Empire*, Vol II, pp812-3

28 Admiralty–Warren 4 December 1848: Adm 2/1607, f177

29 Williams, J B, *British Commercial Policy and Trade Expansion 1750-1850* (Oxford 1972), pp280-2

30 Admiralty–Austen 25 January 1848: Adm 2/1606, f169

31 Lombardi, J V, *Venezuela* (New York 1982), pp170-183

32 Austen–Admiralty 17 February 1848, rec 27 March 1848: Adm 1/5587

33 Auckland marginalia ibid

34 Austen–Admiralty 1 March 1848, rec 6 April 1848: Adm 1/5587

35 Warren–Austen 18 March 1848 encl in Austen–Admiralty 19 April 1848, rec 23 May 1848: Adm 1/5587

the Orleans dynasty in favour of a republic. The Foreign Office advised officers to adopt the utmost discretion in any dealing with the French, who might be looking for an excuse to fight. Warren's tact on this occasion was commended.[36] In April, when the local situation had cooled, Warren followed Austen's orders and took *Trincomalee* to refit at Antigua, before returning via Trinidad to cruise between St Thomas and Porto Rico. In future only occasional visits would be required.[37]

By this time *Trincomalee* was serving under a new commander-in-chief, Vice-Admiral the Earl of Dundonald (1775-1860), who arrived on board HMS *Wellesley*, one of the Bombay-built 74s. After thirty years in disgrace and unemployment Dundonald (better known as Lord Cochrane) had been given a command by Lord Auckland, a lifelong friend who believed that Dundonald would command one of the principal fleets in the event of major war, and therefore would need some practice. Auckland had also checked that Dundonald's plans for the use of poison gas, first developed in 1812, remained secret, and would work.[38] Like Austen Dundonald relied on sons and cousins for his staff.[39] His command, which began well, became a tedious exercise in routine after Auckland's sudden death in late December 1848. The new First Lord, Sir Francis Baring, was not a personal friend, and as a former Chancellor of the Exchequer did not share Auckland's enthusiasm for radical admirals or his enlarged view of the needs of the service.[40] Typically, Dundonald filled his days with a far more vigorous regime of inspection and report writing than Austen had considered necessary. Where Auckland had commended his activity, Baring was pointedly less enthusiastic.[41] At Trinidad in early 1849 Dundonald observed the tar lake at La Brea, and with his usual insight developed the first bituminous road system, which he patented. Unfortunately, the horses slipped on the new surface, and as was ever the case with the impecunious earl, he lost money. The main impact of the new commander-in-chief was to increase the amount of time *Trincomalee* spent at sea.

The demands on the squadron increased when the internal affairs of Haiti dissolved into turmoil. When the British consul wanted protection for British merchants and their property, Dundonald, then at Halifax, sent the corvette *Daring* to assist. Back in London Lord Auckland thought a more powerful ship ought to have been sent: 'It does not appear why the *Trincomalee* has not been called up to Haiti. She must have been more wanted there than in the neighbourhood of Barbadoes.'[42] In fact there would be work to do where she was: on 21 August *Trincomalee* experienced her first severe weather, a Caribbean hurricane, while lying off English Harbour, Antigua. The approaches to the harbour were difficult, so ships not using the yard tended to anchor outside. That night the barometer began to fall rapidly, and three guns were fired to signal to the shore as the wind picked up to full force. At 1am on the 22nd the wind veered round to the north-west, with a succession of tremendous squalls that began to abate an hour later. At sunrise, 4am, the scene on shore was one of devastation; the rigging house had been blow down, along with part of the dockyard officers' quarters and many other buildings both public and private. At 8am Warren sent a party to the dockyard to help clear away the wrecked storehouses; part of the crew would be ashore almost every day until the end of September. Only in mid-October was it possible to return to the Venezuelan coast, before calling at Port of Spain, Trinidad. Christmas was spent at Carlisle Bay, Barbados, although a fire on shore on 28 December required assistance from the ship.

In February Dundonald arrived at Carlisle Bay, for his first meeting with Warren, who then took the *Trincomalee* along the Venezuelan coast, reporting the situation quiet.[43] After calling at Haiti to supply the endangered British consul with six muskets, ammunition and accoutrements, *Trincomalee* sailed north for the fishing grounds off Newfoundland at the end of April. She stopped at Halifax, Nova Scotia in mid-May, to be joined by Dundonald, who inspected the ship on 3 June. By the 8th *Trincomalee* had arrived off the tiny French island of St Pierre on the coast of Newfoundland. This island, along with Miquelon, were used by the French as fishing stations, and they provided ample opportunity for complaint and counter claim over fishing grounds, treaty rights and French smuggling. The French government treated the Newfoundland fishery as a major source of seafaring labour for their fleet, paying a handsome bounty for the fish, which gave their ships an economic advantage. In 1848 360 French craft were active in the area, with 17,000 fisherman. By the late 1840s discussions were underway to separate the British and French sectors, but without any result.[44] The French Governor came on board, receiving the customary salute of 13 guns. Moving west to Burgeo Island, Warren placed the ship in quarantine for a week after an outbreak of smallpox. She then worked back to the east, passing Cape Race on the 27th, and anchoring in St John's harbour on the 30th. The capital of Newfoundland, which did not become part of Canada until after the Second World War, was located at the end of a long and narrow inlet, which provided ample opportunities for fortifications. The commodious harbour had a naval wharf, while the town of some 20,000 people had been burnt down in 1846, and was rising from the ashes in an improved, and rather safer brick-built form.[45]

Over the next two months *Trincomalee* did duty as a fishery protection vessel, moving along the south coast of Newfoundland, and anchoring in various isolated bays, almost all of which contained some habitation connected with fishing. She often detached the ship's cutter to work inshore. In early September she stopped at Red Bay, Labrador for a week, before

36 Admiralty Circular 1 March 1848: Adm 2/1606, f253. Admiralty – Dundonald 2 May 1848: Adm 2/1606, f365

37 Admiralty – Dundonald 3 April 1848 & 23 May 1848: Adm 2/1606, ff330, 406

38 Grimble, I, *The Sea Wolf* (London 1978). Thomas, D, *Cochrane: Britannia's Last Sea King* (London 1978), pp326-7, 330-1

39 Wilkinson, *Bermuda*, p600

40 Baring would end Napier's command in the interests of economy, causing a minor scandal

41 Admiralty – Dundonald 2 August 1848: Adm 2/1606, ff507, 534

42 Dundonald – Admiralty 4 August 1848; Auckland marginalia: Adm 1/5587 Admiralty – Dundonald 11 September 1848: Adm 2/1607, f41

43 Dundonald – Admiralty 31 March 1849, rec 25 April 1849: P92: Adm 1/5596

44 Thompson, F F, *The French Shore Problem in Newfoundland* (Toronto 1961), pp31-2

45 Moyles, R G, '*Complaints is many and various, but the old Divil likes it': Nineteenth Century views of Newfoundland* (Toronto 1975), Ch 1

passing through St John's on her way back to Halifax. Here the squadron formed up, re-provisioned and set sail for Bermuda on the 27th. Unlike some of his contemporaries on the station Warren did not develop any local expertise on the fishery patrol, spending only one summer in the north. This limited period in the north reflected both the relatively large ship he commanded, and the need for *Trincomalee*'s services in the West Indies. Just before leaving Halifax Naval Cadet Albert Hurt joined the ship from the *Wellesley*, doubtless to gain further seagoing experience in the more active frigate.[46] He would not have long to wait.

Dundonald had been ordered to patrol off Cuba, to counteract the sudden increase in slave trading, the Admiralty sending him a ship to facilitate the operation.[47] While *Trincomalee* was on passage south Commodore Bennett at Port Royal changed the ship's destination from Bermuda to Haiti and Havana, taking a course south of Cuba. Bennett had been warned of a projected American filibustering expedition from New Orleans to seize Cuba, and acted accordingly.[48] After an uneventful passage the ship, by that stage only 245 miles from Havana, was struck by a gale just after midnight on 28 October, reckoned to be between Force 10 and 11 on the Beaufort scale. This lasted for almost six hours, veering round from ENE to SW. Warren recorded: 'A sea struck the ship and stove in cabin windows and the starboard quarter gallery.' He also reported damage to the rig and the barge. Hurt's report is more graphic: he had probably not seen anything like it before.

> 12.30 am carried away weather foretopsail, sheet split from topsail to ribbons, in securing main topsail it also split to ribbons, carried away weather maintopsail brace and preventer main brace. The barge was blown into the mizzen rigging, after fall carried away . Secured d[itt]o. A sea struck the ship stove in cabin windows and stern gallery. 5.40 shipped fore and main topsails. First reef of d[itt]o. 11.30 mustered by divisions.

The company was mustered to check if anyone had been lost. Three days later *Trincomalee* put into Havana, saluted the Spanish Captain-General and Admiral, and set to work to repair the sails and the headrail. Cuba would dominate the last year of this cruise. While many ships were seen, *Trincomalee*'s main task was to maintain a strategic presence, and none were stopped.

The seaward approaches to Havana, the capital of Spanish Cuba, were dominated by a massive new lighthouse, although on closer inspection the complex of fortifications made a more profound impression. Havana was the finest harbour in the West Indies, and the most powerfully defended. Nor were these defences by any means obsolete. For the past

46 His personal log of the cruise has survived: 'Proceedings of HMS *Wellesley*' currently on loan to the *Trincomalee* Trust. Hurt served in *Trincomalee* from 27 September 1849 to 12 March 1850

47 Admiralty – Dundonald 15 July, 26 June 1848: Adm 2/1607, ff530, 550

48 Admiralty – Commodore Bennett 3 October 1848: Adm 2/1608, f132

49 Martinez-Fernandez, L, *Fighting Slavery in the Caribbean: The Life and Times of a British Family in Nineteenth Century Havana* (New York 1998), pp12-20

In this 1860 photograph the frigate HMS *Narcissus* is fitting out, and has her main and fore yards lowered to the hammock nettings while the rigging is completed. The same approach would have been required to repair any major damage to the rigging. The seeming confusion of ropes and gear is more apparent than real; an experienced crew would soon reduce the chaos to order.

thirty years the island had been the last major Spanish possession in the New World, a key contributor to her economy, and the last hope of recovering her once great American empire. The Cuban economy was dominated by the export of sugar, which accounted for 84 per cent by value, with tobacco, cigars and coffee completing the list. Sugar was grown and processed on large, newly created plantations, which depended on advanced machinery, and slave labour to harvest the crop. The recent shift to sugar production required a major increase in slave labour, so the Spanish authorities had persistently violated their treaty agreements with Britain to suppress the trade. Between 1800 and 1860 over half a million African slaves were bought to Cuba, more than 300,000 of them after the trade became illegal. By 1850 41 per cent of the population were black, almost all slaves: some 49 per cent were white, and, with smaller mixed race groups, were all free.[49] Ironically, the dramatic growth in Cuban sugar production was largely inspired by the British decision in 1845 to end the tariff barrier against sugar produced in countries that still permitted slavery. This measure had been used to protect the British West Indian islands' market-share after their labour costs rose as a consequence of abolition. This clash of economic ideology and humanitarian concern would create bitter cross-currents in British politics, forcing the government to fight for its survival in the House of Commons while *Trincomalee* cruised off Cuba.

At the same time Cuba was coveted by the expansionist, aggressive United States, which had already seized the last element of Spain's North American empire, Florida. More recently the Americans had despoiled Mexico of California and Texas, and their ambition seemed to recognise no limits. In 1848 the United States Government offered to buy Cuba, and when this approach was rejected a series of filibustering expeditions were mounted from New Orleans, hoping to exploit local rebellions, overthrow the Spanish regime and invite American annexation. This approach, already successful in Texas, was driven by southern politicians seeking to expand the slave-owning element in the state, and find a outlet for their own surplus servile population. The threat of filibustering and local creole independence movements led the Spanish authorities to station large forces in Cuba, under a military governor, the Captain-General.[50]

British interests in Cuba were complex. Foreign Secretary Lord Palmerston considered the abolition of slavery, and the suppression of the trade to be the proudest boast that Britain could make. His astonishing action in the late 1840s in using the Royal Navy to destroy the Brazilian slave trade, acting inside Brazilian territorial waters, demonstrated his determination.[51] However, he could not follow the same principle in Cuba. Weak and divided as she was, Spain was vital to the success of his liberal policies in Europe, and Palmerston could not simply bully her over slavery, which the Spanish ministers knew was the key to the Cuban economy, and through that to the loyalty of the Cuban elite. To act against slavery would prompt a rebellion, American intervention, or the terrifying prospect of slave revolt and race war, leading to political and economic disaster of the scale first witnessed on San Domingue in the 1790s. Palmerston accepted that the West Indies was not the best place to stop slave ships, stepping up activity on both sides of Africa instead.

The leading members of Lord John Russell's government (1846-1852) recognised the dilemma. British attempts to end the slave trade could drive Cuba into American hands, a development that would threaten the strategic basis of British power in the New World. The crisis arrived in September 1849, when the acting British Consul-General in Havana, alarmed by reports of an impending filibustering expedition wrote to Commodore Bennett[52] at Port Royal, Jamaica: 'the period is very near at hand of this island being annexed to the United States.' Bennett diverted *Trincomalee* to Havana. The next spring the Governor of the Bahamas stressed the danger of allowing Havana to fall into American hands: 'she would, in time of war obtain the complete control over the navigation of this vast gulf . . . they could shut us from the Gulf of Mexico.'[53]

Trincomalee was one of many Royal Navy ships to call at Havana over the next decade, concerned to protect British lives and property, and warn off American invasions, official or unofficial. Britain was highly unpopular with the leading elements in Cuban society, where American propaganda that London controlled Madrid and wanted to destroy the Cuban economy was widely believed. Consequently visits to Havana were neither friendly nor relaxing. In addition the city was pervaded by an air of lassitude and decay, reflecting the enervating climate, endemic fevers and maladministration. It was not a place to remain if the ship's health and happiness were to be considered. Even so, the stern Warren kept his men up to the mark, securing a highly favourable battle readiness report from Dundonald, a high authority on anything connected with fighting at sea.[54]

Back in London, government policy came under sustained attack in Parliament, from economists who wanted to end the attack on the slave trade and West Indies landowners who wanted protection for their interests. Palmerston and Russell made the question an issue of confidence, and won a clear majority in the House of Commons on 19 March 1850. This allowed them to push on with their programme of defending Cuba against American intervention, and it was this, rather than the suppression of the slave trade, that determined the deployment of British warships in Cuban waters.

Even so, the slave trade persisted. There had been a fall in demand in the mid-1840s, as old coffee estates were converted to sugar production, and slaves moved within Cuba, but by the late 1840s the trade was growing, partly through increased demand, and partly from increased supply after the closure of the larger Brazilian market. The 5-1 imbalance between male and female slaves, and the loss of 5 per cent of the slave population every year, ensured a steady demand, even without overall expansion.

Sugar, Slaves and the Cuban Trade 1845-51

	British Cuban Sugar Imports (cwt)	*Slaving Voyages*	*Slaves imported into Cuba (Actual)*	*(British Estimates)*
1845	197,000	6	950	1300
1846	411,000	4	0	1500
1847	875,000	4	0	1000
1848	694,000	5	1500	1500
1849	664,000	20	6525	8700
1850	489,000	7	2325	3100
1851	811,000	7	3689	5000[55]

50 Murray, D R, *Odious Commerce: Britain, Spain and the abolition of the Cuban Slave Trade* (Cambridge 1980), pp ix-x, 223.
Martinez-Fernandez, *Fighting Slavery*, p15.
Schroeder, J H, *Shaping a Maritime Empire: The Commercial and Diplomatic Role of the American Navy, 1829-1861* (Westport CT 1985), pp92-5

51 Southgate, D, '*The Most English Minister*' (London 1966), pp147-51

52 Captain Thomas Bennett, a captain of 1828 with considerable experience on the station, commanding the Leeward Islands station

53 Murray, *Odious Commerce*, pp223-4

54 Admiralty–Dundonald 23 April 1850: Adm2/1608, f185

55 Drawn from Murray, *Odious Commerce*, pp243-4

Although she would stop many suspicious vessels off the Cuban coast, mostly the American style schooners that were the standard slaving ship of the era, *Trincomalee* was too large, unhandy and costly for this service.[56] Her presence had more to do with Cuban security than the campaign against slavery. Warren left Havana after nine days, taking another ten to reach Port Royal, where the Commodore of the Leeward Islands section of the station, Thomas Bennett, flew his broad pendant in the hulked ex-74 *Imaum*, yet another product of the Bombay dockyard. The deck was recaulked, and then *Trincomalee* returned to Cuba, stopping at St Jago to correspond with the British consul; after a brief return to Port Royal Warren was detailed back to St Jago. Moving along the Cuban coast to Cumberland harbour he landed part of his crew on 30 and 31 January, conducted firing drill with his field gun and muskets, and cut local timber 'for boat knees'.[57] The landing and firing of artillery, without permission, on the soil of a foreign state, was insensitive at the best of times, but with the constant threat of filibuster invasions it was irresponsible and more than the proud Spanish authorities could tolerate. British protection was one thing, but to be insulted was quite another. Four months later Dundonald responded to a Spanish complaint that

The war against the slave trade went on right up to the American Civil war: here the 500-ton brig-sloop HMS *Arab* chases a slave ship off Cuba in 1856. These smaller ships were better suited to the preventive role of chasing the slightly built schooners used in this loathsome trade. (Royal Naval Museum, Portsmouth)

Trincomalee had infringed their territorial rights: 'I consider that Captain Warren acted with great want of caution, but as the Consul General is satisfied that no insult was intended, I trust no further notice will be taken of the affair.'[58] Despite an official complaint from the Foreign Office this seems to have been the case, for Warren's career certainly did not suffer.[59] Having passed on the Spanish complaint the Foreign Office did not pursue the matter–Palmerston doubtless thought it would do no harm to remind the Spaniards that their security against American threats was based on British power. As Sir Francis Baring, the First Lord of the Admiralty, remarked the following year, 'the interests of England are strongly concerned in America not having Cuba–whether Spain retain the island or not.'[60] *Trincomalee* had played her part in that process. As with so much of her work on the first commission it lacked drama, bloodshed or controversy, but it was highly effective in maintaining British interests in the region, opening new markets for commerce, and resisting foreign encroachment.

Unaware of the problems he had caused, Warren continued in 1850 much as he had ended 1849. *Trincomalee* returned to Cuba twice more, between visits to Port Royal, arriving at Havana on 13 April with HMS *Helena* in company. Returning via Grand Cayman Henry Pidworth fell overboard on 7 May, but was recovered, along with the life buoy. The ship's next task was to cruise along the coast of Belize, Nicaragua and Mexico to uphold British interests,[61] including the Mosquito Coast protectorate, and ended with *Trincomalee* back at Port Royal on 18 June. Here she began preparations for her return home, which had been ordered in April,[62] loading condemned stores, mainly from the old frigate *Galatea*, which had been broken up in the harbour after thirteen years service as a coal hulk, and taking on a party of invalids. She left harbour on the 26th, and headed out into the Atlantic, past Bermuda. The Isles of Scilly were passed on 27 July, and *Trincomalee*, cast anchor at Spithead on 5 August to discharge the invalids, before beating back down the Channel, and entering Plymouth Sound on the 9th. After an inspection by Admiral Sir William Gage, the Port Admiral, she discharged her powder and was towed into the Hamoaze. The guns were hoisted out, the rigging dismantled for storage ashore, the *Galatea* stores were landed, and on the 15th *Trincomalee* was moved alongside the sheer hulk to have her masts hoisted out. She was paid off the following day by Commodore Lord John Hay, the Dockyard Superintendent.

Warren went on to command the steam battleship *Cressy* in the Baltic campaigns of 1854 and 1855, and to fly his flag afloat and over a dockyard. As we shall see, he was very much a product of the old navy, and his attitude toward the lower deck was at the brutal end of what was tolerable in 1847-50.

56 See Hurt Journal & Log Book

57 Hurt confirms the details

58 Dundonald–Admiralty 3 May 1850, rec 27 May 1850: Adm 1/5602

59 Admiralty–Dundonald 7 May 1850: Adm 2/1608, f505

60 Bartlett, C J, *Great Britain and Sea Power, 1815-1853* (Oxford 1963), p275

61 Bourne, *North America*, p177.
Admiralty–Bennett 1 May 1850: Adm 2/1608, f498

62 Admiralty–Bennett 15 April 1850: Adm 2/1608, f461

Chapter Four

The Changing World of the Royal Navy, 1815–1860

IN THE years that separated *Trincomalee*'s construction and voyage home from her active service, the social structure of the Royal Navy had begun a process of fundamental change. The old navy was an eighteenth-century world of short-term employment, taking little responsibility for the men, creating no reserve of seamen in peacetime to mobilise for war, and relying on impressment from the general pool of seafaring labour to put the fleet to sea. The discipline of the service, from conduct in combat through social structures and subordination, was upheld with theatrically contrived displays of controlled violence. The food and drink were liberal in scale, but less than appetising to modern sensitivities. Officers were practical men, in the main, with few of the scientific attainments of their French contemporaries. Before anyone forms the opinion that there was anything wrong with the old navy it should be stressed that it had a well nigh unbroken record of success in war, based on all-round excellence and large-scale funding.[1] This navy, despite a few problems over pay and food, fought and won the greatest maritime conflict yet seen between 1793 and 1815, defeating every other navy of any significance in the process.

The two commissions of HMS *Trincomalee* spanned the origins of the modern Royal Navy, and of all professional naval services. The process whereby the eighteenth-century Navy, relying on casually raised men, impressment and flogging, gave way to the twentieth-century Navy of long service specialist ratings quite distinct from other seafarers, has often been represented as one in which simple conservative resistance to change on the part of the elite, resistance based on nothing more than prejudice, held up the inevitable. In truth the Royal Navy met the challenge of modernisation head on, and did so rather earlier, and more effectively than any of its rivals. The inspiration for change came from two distinctively modern developments: guns and steam.

The world of a nineteenth-century British warship was based on discipline, the order and structure of the ship that ensured every man knew his task, and his place, both physically and socially. The crew were located within the ship according to their station at sea, or in action. Two-thirds of the crew were divided into two watches, since the mid-1840s termed starboard and port. These included all the seamen, relevant petty officers and deck labour required for heavy hauling. Each watch had enough

1 Rodger, N A M, *The Wooden World: An Anatomy of the Georgian Navy* (London 1986) for a sustained analysis of this complex organisation in an earlier era

2 Melville, H, *White Jacket, or the world in a man of war* (Boston 1850) for the most compelling statement of this perception.
Higgins, B & Parker, H (eds), *Herman Melville: The Contemporary Reviews* (Cambridge 1995), pp293-349 for contemporary British and American reviews of *White Jacket*

Bible reading on the gundeck of a frigate about 1830; an oil painting by Augustus Earle (fl 1806-38). Formal divine service was conducted at the main mast, the centre of shipboard life, but educational and self-improving activities like this one became more common as a new, more religiously motivated generation of naval officers entered the service. The presence of women is noteworthy, as is the sick man in his cot. (National Maritime Museum, London)

manpower for all but the most demanding ship-handling requirements. The rest of the company – officers, marines, servants, tradesmen working below deck, cooks and such like – were not watched. In an emergency the whole company could be summoned, but normally the ship was worked through the night by a single watch. Men were assigned to stations within each watch according to their ability, and the needs of the ship. The elite seamen, the topmen, who worked above the tops, comprised between 100 and 150 men, depending on the ship. They took enormous pride in their own ability, and viewed the ship from a superior position aloft.[2] The crew were also divided into messes, of 4 to 8 men, and often men from the same stations would prefer to live and eat together. The First Lieutenant would station the men at the guns, basing his decision on the skill and experience of each man, rather than their rank, taking care to build effective combat teams under good leaders. This was the basic fighting unit of any wooden man-of-war, providing both firepower and combat cohesion. Some topmen would be stationed at the upper-deck guns, so that they would move more quickly to guns and back aloft again, to deal with the inevitable damage to the ship's motive power. The men were also mustered into four Divisions, each under a lieutenant. This officer was directly responsible for the health, cleanliness and welfare and pay of his men. In this way the cohesion of the unit was reinforced, authority tempered by a duty of care. Everything had to function smoothly to ensure success, and any friction, human or material, that hampered this smooth, well-oiled effort had to be removed.

Nor were women excluded from this world. Nineteenth-century accounts perpetuated the official fiction that they were not on board, but the reality is different. There is no certain evidence of women on either of *Trincomalee*'s cruises, but it is highly probable that the wives of at least some petty officers lived on board.

In 1815 post-war planning was based on the expectation that 100,000 men could be raised for service in the first year of a major war. These figures were based on the slightly higher numbers of men that were in service at the height of the Napoleonic conflict, but the time-scale of twelve months reflected the absence of any method of recruitment beyond offering a financial inducement, or impressing men by force. In the age of sail the time-scale was acceptable, no other power would be able to do much better, and Britain's superior reserves of ships and men would soon establish effective command of the sea. In peacetime crews were recruited on a commission basis, men entering of their own free will, as and when they chose, and being paid off at the end of the commission three to four years later.

If any single image can be said to define life in the sailing navy it is that of corporal punishment, the use of a nine-stranded whip, the 'cat o'nine tails' to beat men on their bare backs, creating a bloody spectacle as revolting to twentieth-century sensibilities, when it was so graphically described by the poet John Masefield in 1905,[3] as it is today. In fact flog-

Gunnery was the driving force behind the creation of a professional career structure for naval ratings. Between 1830 and 1853 HMS *Excellent* trained gun captains for long service, while the rest of the lower deck were still raised on a commission-only basis. After 1853 all ratings were raised for long service, which allowed time to master the wide range of seamanship skills required in the increasingly technical steam and sail navy, and to handle very heavy guns, like the Armstrong 110-pounder breech loading rifle and the 68-pounder muzzle loading smooth bore, seen here on the gundeck of the restored ironclad HMS *Warrior* of 1861.

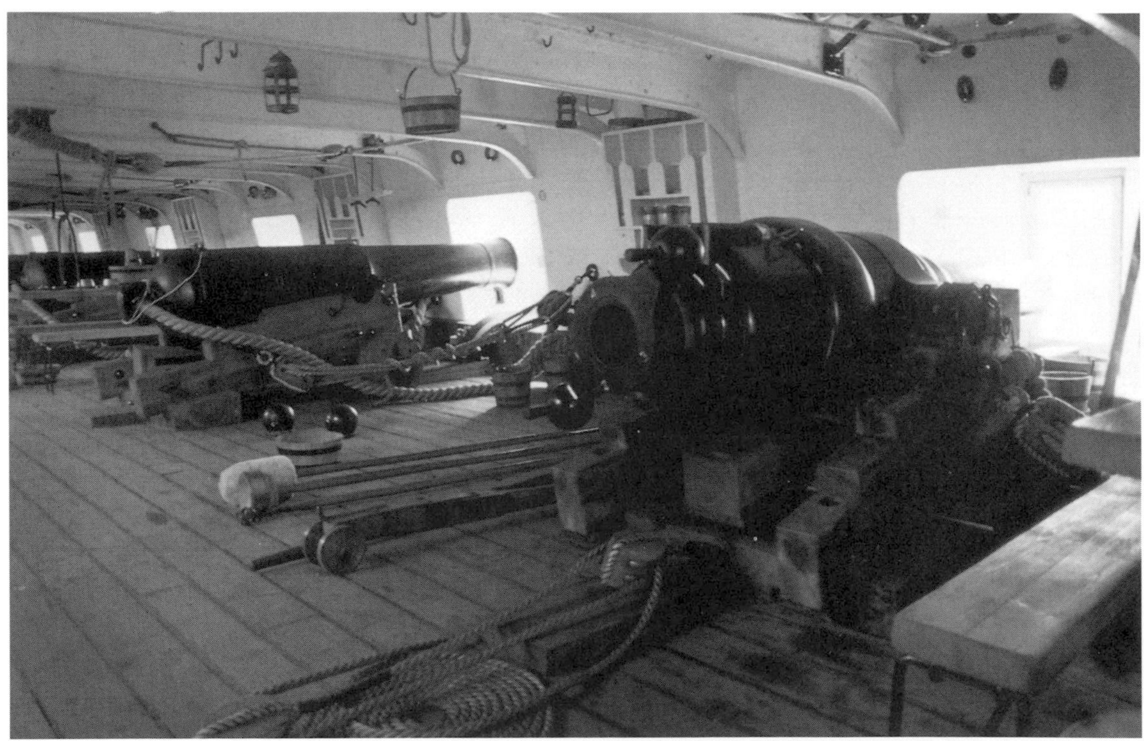

ging and other forms of corporal punishment were the accepted form of correction in society on shore. The Navy only began to change its approach when society changed, and the prison was a nineteenth-century development, one that took a little time to work its way into the naval world. It should be stressed that all formal naval punishments were enacted in a contrived, theatrical manner, to act as a deterrent to the assembled ship's company, who were forced to watch and profit from the example. Far from beating men to a bloody pulp, or hanging them, the naval officer, ever short of skilled hands, was more likely to pardon offenders than the equivalent shore-based magistrate. In the absence of any alternative flogging was the standard naval punishment used by captains to maintain order and discipline on board ship. There were no prisons on warships until the 1850s, and many critics of corporal punishment believed it was wrong to take men off work as a punishment for disciplinary offences. Only in the late 1850s were prisons built into new ships; HMS *Warrior* with a crew of 650, had only three cells, which is indicative of the usage envisaged. In truth changing punishment regimes were only one facet of the far wider changes that were to transform the Royal Navy, adopted to facilitate greater efficiency and professionalism.

Post-1815 reforms

The first great change was inspired by the awesome spectacle of the shattered gundeck of USS *Chesapeake* (Chapter One). Everyone could see the difference that fully trained gun crews made to the combat effectiveness of the *Shannon.* For most of the war success had come because the old-style British tar was both a better seaman, and far quicker with the great guns than his French opponent, but Philip Broke's men looked to the future. They were a thoroughly professional team: they fired fast, they hit the target, and they fought in silence. Seventeen years later Broke, who never returned to active service after his terrible injuries, stood as godfather to the first establishment specifically set up to train seamen, HMS *Excellent*, initially housed on board the ship Collingwood had commanded at the battle of Cape St Vincent (1797). *Excellent* combined the roles of training ship for seamen gunners, and their officers, with that of artillery trials platform. In campaigning for the gunnery training Broke's followers had relied on his name, and those eternal eleven minutes off Cape Ann to secure the project.

Having trained the seamen gunners, and prepared them for higher ranks, the Royal Navy wisely secured their services beyond a single commission. In return for higher pay and, once promoted, immunity from the lash, seamen signed on for a term of years, initially five. Here was the basis for a professional rating career, but it would not be applied to all

3 Masefield, J, *Sea Life in Nelson's Time* (London 1905), pp157-69

seamen for another two decades. When Broke died in early 1841 the value of his system had just been demonstrated in the Syrian campaign of 1840. After the Bombardment of Acre one *Excellent*-trained officer observed:

> The very first broadsides were murderous. . . . It is also an historical fact that for guns of that period, in wooden ships, something like perfection had been attained. Officers and men had been thoroughly trained under the newest system; and all matters connected with gunnery worked with the regularity of clocks.[4]

These trained gunners hit the target. It was vital that they did, for attempts at rapid, voluntary recruitment during the emergency had failed, leaving the Navy to fight short-handed. Only the high professional standards of the peacetime-manned ships carried them through. On *Trincomalee*'s second commission eight men and four boys from *Excellent* provided a nucleus of gunnery expertise, including two gunner's mates.

The second impetus for a modern system of lower deck careers followed the humiliation of the French in that crisis. Too weak to support their Egyptian protege Mehemet Ali against the British, the French shifted the focus of their naval effort from battleships to the paddle steam warship, and with the completion of the new base at Cherbourg reopened the threat of invasion. Although France had a far smaller maritime population than Britain, her system of classifying and controlling the enrolment of seafarers into the navy, the *Inscription Maritime*, promised to mobilise more men in a short space of time. By 1844 the French claimed to have 45,000 registered, and another 10,000 trained. The British continued to rely on the age-old system of voluntary enlistment in peacetime, supplemented by impressment, the forced recruitment of seafarers, in wartime. These traditional measures had been adequate in the age of sail, but steam markedly increased the tempo of operations, and made it imperative to get the fleet to sea in a matter of days, not months. This would require more men at sea in peacetime, and the creation of a naval reserve.

There had been several attempts to create a reserve from the 1820s, but these were half-hearted, piecemeal and quite ineffective. Sailors did not stay in the Royal Navy, the merchant service often paid better, and the Navy had a bad reputation for excessive corporal punishment. It should be recalled that the major objects behind Captain Frederick Marryat's pioneering naval fiction were the ending of impressment and corporal punishment. He had campaigned against both measures from the early 1820s, arguing that they were inefficient and expensive, while impressed men could only be kept in order by the use of the lash. Ending impress-

4 Burrows, M, *Autobiography* (London 1908), p128

5 Marryat, F, *Suggestions for the Abolition of the Present System of Impressment in the Naval Service* (London 1822)

6 Warner, O, *Captain Marryat, a Rediscovery* (London 1953), pp61-2

7 Van der Voort, P J, *Pen and Quarter Deck: A Study of the Life and Works of Captain Frederick Chamier RN* (Leiden 1972), pp20, 141

8 Between 1815 and 1865 HM ships *Solebay* (ex-*Iris*), *Iphigenia* and *Venus*: Lyon, D J, *The Sailing Navy List* (London 1993), p347

9 Marine Society Annual Reports, 1833-1856: Marine Society Library

10 Lloyd C, *The British Seaman* (London 1968), p269

ment would remove the need to flog. However, his alternative was a form of conscription, which was unlikely to have been any more popular.[5] By the end of the decade Marryat had turned to fiction to secure a wider audience for his ideas. His first two novels, *Frank Mildmay* (1829) and *The King's Own*, (1830) were savage pictures of brutality squarely aimed at a public no longer tolerant of eighteenth-century ideas of punishment.[6] Like his friend and fellow naval novelist, Captain Frederick Chamier, Marryat was only prepared to tolerate flogging because he could see no alternative on board ship; ashore he considered it inexcusable.[7] It should be noted that impressment was never employed after 1814, although it remained an option into the 1860s. The events of the era simply did not warrant such an extreme measure.

Instead the post-1815 Navy was increasingly manned by seamen who had entered warships as boys, and grown up in the service. They came to form a distinctive type, the 'man-of-war's man' who re-entered the service commission after commission. These boys were largely drawn from southern England, often through the Marine Society and the Royal Hospital School. The management of both institutions was dominated by senior naval officers and statesmen with experience of naval administration, while the Admiralty provided an old frigate as a stationary training ship,[8] an officer and petty officers to the Marine Society free of charge.[9] In effect the Society was acting as a recruiting agency for the Navy, with any surplus of trainees going to the Indian Navy and the merchant marine. The Admiralty, recognising the long-term importance of the boys, ensured that they were not paid off at the end of a commission, but turned over to the harbour flagship, to be re-assigned to the next ship to commission.[10] On both commissions *Trincomalee* was partly manned with these boys, and over the years transformed them into able seamen. In the process the Navy developed a unique character.

These boy entrant naval ratings manned the peacetime fleet, and by the 1850s had created a new popular image, one that would be reinforced by their heroics in the Crimean War. By 1852 four-fifths of men entering HMS *Excellent* were such boy entrants. However, the need to raise men for war service, in short time and from

The officer cadet training ship *Worcester*, previously the steam battleship HMS *Frederick William*, with the yards fully manned. There were also boys training ships preparing young seamen, a response to the social problem of urban poverty and manpower needs which was employed for a hundred years.

useful sources, had still to be addressed. After 1815 the Navy had largely ignored the merchant service, from which it drew few men, and as the man-of-war's man became more specialised, other seafarers became less useful. The need was for a system that would generate time-served naval ratings, retained by a pension, to be recalled in an emergency.[11]

The new type of rating recruited as boys, and often trained on board the *Excellent*, was too discriminating to tolerate the old system, and too valuable to be allowed to leave. The combination of public pressure and seamen's preferences led to change. The process was hastened by officers of a new generation, more sensitive, better educated, and often deeply imbued with an evangelical Christianity. These officers considered it both inefficient and morally wrong to resort to physical chastisement to impose discipline. In 1842 a newly entered naval cadet observed the spectacle:

> The other day there was a man flogged for being drunk, He had 4 dozen lashes, it was very dreadful to hear them, I could not look. We were all obliged to be on deck. The Capt. [Henry Bruce] was so much affected that he could hardly read the articles of war.[12]

We will meet Captain Henry Bruce again (Chapter Five).

The situation in the other major navies was far less satisfactory. Captain Henry Martin recorded an incident at Tahiti in 1846, and made a general point.

> This morning a sailor underwent the punishment of la Cale from the main yard arm of *L'Ariane*. His crime was having struck a petty officer. This punishment is not uncommon in the French navy. The culprit having a shot attached to his feet, is trussed up by the shoulders to the yard arm, & from thence dropped into the sea, and then hauled on board. Sometimes for very grave offences 3 dips are given–which generally prove fatal. There is more flogging in French ships than in English ships & a vast deal of vexatious minor punishment.[13]

Such medieval punishments had not been used in the Royal Navy for over a century. The United States Navy of the 1840s had made far greater use of the lash, at least in part to reflect the cosmopolitan nature of American warship crews, and other minor corporal punishments, like starting.[14] On his brief cruise Melville would have witnessed over 150 such punishments, and these made him a passionate advocate of abolition.[15]

By the mid-1840s the strategic need to man the fleet more rapidly on the outbreak of war, and the social pressures from without to abolish both impressment and flogging, made change inevitable. While the latter issue attracted all the public attention, both then and now, the thoughts

11 For a full length discussion of this problem, and the solution see Taylor, R, 'Manning the Royal Navy: the Reform of the Recruiting System, 1847-1861' (University of London unpublished MA thesis 1954). Rasor, E L, *Reform in the Royal Navy: A Social History of the Lower Deck, 1850 to 1880* (Hamden CT 1976) provides a wider context

12 Harrod, D (ed), *War, Ice and Piracy: The Journals and Letter of Samuel Gurney Cresswell* (London 2000), p26

13 Martin, H, *Polynesian Journal 1846-1847* (Salem, MA 1981), p85

14 Melville's *White Jacket* contains a long discourse on the inefficiency, illegality and demoralising impact of flogging. 'Starting' comprised random blows from a short end of rope or stick, and was intended to 'start' the men working

15 Parker, H, *Herman Melville: A Biography Vol 1, 1819-1851* (Baltimore MD 1996), pp262, 655, 716-22

16 Admiralty Circular 26 May 1848: ADM 2/1606, f417

17 Bridge, Sir C, *Some Recollections* (London 1918), pp158-9 relating to HMS *Brisk* (Pacific) 1855-57

of naval policymakers were dominated by the former. In 1845 Joseph Hume, MP moved for the punishment returns of the Navy to be published every year. This was conceded, making the level of punishment common knowledge. Hume had already drawn attention to military flogging. Sensing the shift in public mores the Queen's Regulations of 1844 had cautioned officers to use 'great discretion and all due forbearance' in the administration of corporal punishment. Some officers responded to the new regulation by adopting new forms of punishment, 'severe in nature and contrary to the usages of the service' to avoid flogging. These were condemned and replaced by the introduction of a 'Defaulter's Book' in which all infractions were to be recorded, along with the punishment awarded. Captains were to be accountable for the 'justice and necessity' of any punishment.[16] This general warning was replaced by strict guidelines in 1853, just as *Trincomalee* was starting her second commission. Even so some captains still adopted novel and annoying methods of discipline.[17] Public attention led to a marked reduction in punishment, and while the ability to use the lash was retained, the actual employment of the instrument was abandoned once a new navy had been created by recruiting the sailors on a system of continuous and general service, a measure introduced in mid-1853.

The improved character of the men was one reason for the reduction in corporal punishment. The major cause of disciplinary problems on board

An image of the mid-century sailor is conveyed in this lively sketch from the army camp before Sevastopol. Here a mess from the battleship HMS *Bellerophon*, ashore to serve the heavy guns bombarding the Russian city, disport themselves in piratical rig. Their carefree attitude is not to the taste of the Army officers in the distance. The skill, courage and initiative of the Naval Brigade was noted by all those who served in the trenches, and such brigades became a standard feature of all subsequent military campaigns. (Royal Naval Museum, Portsmouth)

ship had always been drunkenness, with men carefully monitoring their daily input of 'grog' (a rum and water mix) to ensure they had the opportunity to become oblivious to all cares every once in a while. Drunkenness was the norm, among officers as well as men. This too had changed by the 1840s. The standard half pint of grog, mixed from four parts water to one part rum, had been reduced to a quarter pint in 1825, and then the mix cut to eight to one in 1850, with the offer of alternative beverages, tea, cocoa and coffee, and money in lieu. The effect was immediate: as drinking was reduced, discipline problems declined in parallel. However, the men still tended to drink themselves into a temporary oblivion once they reached the shore, something that would be a feature of both commissions.

A marked increase in pay helped to win over the sailors, with additional provisions clearly aimed at encouraging long service and good conduct.

	1844	1852
Ordinary Seaman	26 shillings (£1.30p)	34 shillings (£1.70p) per month
Able Seaman	33 shillings 7 pence (£1.63)	41 shillings 4 pence (£2.07p)

Seamen gunners received an additional 3 pence (1p) per day.

In 1849 Good Conduct badges were introduced, following their success in the Army. Sailors who received a good character from their officers for five years received one badge, which was worth 1 penny per day, up to a maximum of three badges. In this way a seaman gunner with three badges would earn another 18 shillings a month, adding fifty per cent to his pay. The new system also provided a disciplinary incentive, as the badges could be removed if the sailor disgraced himself.

Such systems worked well in the enclosed, restricted world of the wooden warship, where a good captain knew all of his men by name, and could recall their merits and faults from memory. Throughout his private journal Henry Martin noted the men by name and rate, but was particularly moved by one loss:

> This morning died Lindo Sheaf, a remarkably fine young man, a good seaman and as honest a fellow as is often seen. He bore the highest character, and there are few in the ship whom I should have regretted more.[18]

By the late 1840s the dress of the warship sailor had taken a recognisable form, with a broad-brimmed black straw hat, blue jacket and white or blue bell-bottomed trousers, designed to be easily rolled up when washing the deck. Any sailor worth his salt carried a clasp knife, for work. This outfit was finally standardised and issued to all the men in January 1856, too late for the *Trincomalee*'s crew, although they would have been similarly dressed, as these clothes were the standard types carried by the ship's purser for sale to the crew, or made by them from standard materials stocked on board. However, as long as there was no official standard, officers were free to indulge their own inclinations, and on the second commission Captain Houstoun had the entire crew turned out in red shirts and fancy caps. Nor was he alone in this: *Harlequin*'s gig crew were dressed to match their ship's name, while *Caledonia*'s had 'Scotch Bonnets'.[19]

The institution of a uniform was the outward sign of a far deeper process that had affected every aspect of life afloat for the naval rating, emphasising the professional nature of the new warship sailor and creating standardisation. It would help to identify the naval rating seaman, who by the High Victorian age had been transformed from a colourful rogue into a model of working class rectitude. The fact that these men now served longer raised the average age of naval seamen, while the superior pay, promotion opportunities and the acquisition of transferable skills made the naval career, which had hitherto been a short-term choice, more attractive to settled and ambitious men.

By the late 1840s the literate public was well aware that changes were occurring, and almost entirely in favour of improved conditions. In 1847 Commander Cospatrick Baillie Hamilton paid off HMS *Frolic* after four and a half years in which he had only resorted to the lash on one occasion, and lost only two men through desertion. The vessel ended her commission in outstanding order, and Hamilton was praised in both *The Times* and *The Morning Herald*.[20] Finer yet, and more important, was the feat of Commander Bartholomew James Sulivan, commanding HMS *Philomel* in South American waters between 1842 and 1846, including arduous active service on the River Plate and River Parana. Sulivan was an ornament to the service, being at the same time an outstanding seaman, a brilliant navigator and surveyor, an inspirational combat commander and a tactician of genius. If his courage, humanity and professionalism marked him out above his contemporaries, his humility saved him from arrogance. Sulivan treated his men kindly, but firmly. The men received extra liberty, and more considerate treatment, but Sulivan made them understand that if they let him down, he would punish them. He then trusted them to go ashore without supervision. No-one reported back drunk, no-one deserted, and no punishment was required.[21] Sulivan understood that if the sailors were treated as grown men, rather than foolish children, they responded. The *Philomel* was a happy ship, and her record in war was outstanding. Her captain went on to play a major role in the Crimean War, and to develop the first effective naval reserve system in 1859.

By contrast Vice-Admiral Sir Fleetwood Pellew, son of Lord Exmouth, was recalled in disgrace from the command of the East Indies Station in

18 Martin, *Polynesian Journal*, p135 (26 April 1847)

19 Clowes, Sir W L, *The Royal Navy: A History*, Vol VI (London 1901), p212

20 Bartlett, *Great Britain and Sea Power*, p315

21 Sulivan, M N, *Memoirs of Admiral Sir B J Sulivan* (London 1896) p56-8

January 1854 after he had flogged men on his flagship without proper warrants.[22] Pellew's old-fashioned ideas about discipline and punishment, especially his refusal of shore leave, had already sparked a mutiny. The importance of the issue was demonstrated when the entire Board of Admiralty signed the letter of recall.

The level of physical punishment in the service declined markedly in the 1840s. The decade opened with 2028 men flogged in a year, but by 1844 this had fallen to 1441, by 1846 to 1077 and by 1847 to 860. By 1852 the number had fallen to 500, but it rose rapidly back to nearly 1500 at the end of the 1850s, as the size of the active fleet increased steadily from 1854 to 1862. However, in percentage terms expressed as the number of floggings per seamen enlisted, the trend was clearly downward throughout. Officers who were thought to have resorted to excessive punishment had to account for their actions, and those who erred were disciplined. By 1860 the regime of Captain Warren while he commanded *Trincomalee* in 1847-50 would have earned him a public censure. In 1871 corporal punishment was 'suspended', but the change had begun far earlier. In 1848 new regulations were issued, just as *Trincomalee* commissioned, that allowed captains to substitute terms of imprisonment for corporal punishment. However, as no warships had any purpose-built prison accommodation until 1861 the new order could only be used by ships in harbour.

The need to raise large numbers of seamen at the outbreak of war was one of the related issues that dominated the strategic thinking of the Board of Admiralty between 1846 and 1853. The increased tempo of French steamship construction, the break-down of Anglo-French relations in 1845, and the appearance of alarming pamphlets written by the French king's naval son, all contributed to a deep sense of unease among the wider public, which was blown up into a regular invasion scare in 1847, and again in 1850-51, by soldiers, political opponents and naval officers outside the Admiralty. It was claimed that 'steam had bridged the Channel', that the French would decoy the Royal Navy away so they could land an army, and that all the old certainties of war at sea under sail were gone. In this period the Admiralty put in place a number of measures–new harbours and bases on the South Coast and in the Channel Islands to counter the French base at Cherbourg, while improved charts and tidal information enabled the British to predict and intercept any French moves in the Channel with some of the newly constructed steam warships. Plans to arm merchant steamers on the outbreak of war, and incremental additions to the small group of seamen who could be used as a reserve–those working in the dockyards for land defence, the Coastguard and the Customs for service afloat–all improved readiness and reserves. To man the vast fleet required for a war with France the

Navy had to accept a new relationship with the seamen. They would have to be treated as scarce and valuable resource, to be nurtured and rewarded for their loyalty, and paid a retainer for future service.

By 1852 the Admiralty was ready to act, and a Committee on Manning was set up under Vice-Admiral Sir William Parker, one of Nelson's favourite frigate captains, and Earl St. Vincent's nephew.[23] The real work of the committee was carried out by a civil servant, Charles Pennell, who had been working on the subject for the past decade and had already produced a scheme.[24] When Parker and his colleagues reported in early 1853, they recommended that seamen should enter the Royal Navy for a term of years, with twenty years of this 'Continuous and General Service' qualifying for a pension. The pension was a retainer so that the sailor could be recalled in the event of war. Building on the reality of the post-war Navy these new ratings would be naval specialists, distinct from merchant seaman. Half of *Trincomalee*'s men signed on when Continuous Service became law in April 1853, although they were among the last to hear of the measure. By one of those ironies that mark history, the Royal Navy went to war the very next year, before the new measure had taken effect. As the Russians did not pose much threat at sea impressment was not used, no bounty was offered, and consequently few men came forward for service.[25] Nor were the earlier reserve measures much help, providing only a few aged seamen.

However, the new system would generate a reserve over time, and to reinforce the effect other seafaring men were drawn into the reserve, direct from the merchant service. In 1857 a regulation uniform for all sailors was introduced, emphasising the professional nature of the new warship sailor and creating standardisation. It also helped to build the unique identity of the seaman. In 1859 Captain Sulivan's naval reserve plan, put forward in 1857, was largely adopted, building the Royal Naval Reserve into the Continuous Service System, thereby creating the modern naval career structure for ratings. Prompted by an Anglo-American war scare in 1861 the reserve quickly developed into an effective resource. The reservists were regularly drilled on board a ship, and a number of old sailing warships were turned over to this task. Among them was the obsolescent, but still strong and durable *Trincomalee*. In 1914 the Royal Navy could mobilise the largest fleet the world had ever seen, entirely from its own resources in a matter of days.

Six months after Continuous Service was introduced it was followed by a marked improvement in the regulation of minor punishments, whereby men with certificates of good conduct were not to be flogged for a first offence. The use of physical punishment continued to decline, until 1866, when it was effectively suspended, although the right to use it was retained.

22 Admiralty - Pellew 9 January 1854: ADM 1/1611, ff414-23

23 Phillimore, A, *Life of Sir William Parker* (London 1880), Vol III

24 Duke of Northumberland to Parker 24 July 1852: Northumberland MSS E/374, Alnick Castle (by courtesy of his Grace the Duke of Northumberland). Bromley, J, *Manning Pamphlets*; 1694-187, Navy Records Society (London 1974), pp xiv-xv

25 Lambert, A D, *The Crimean War: British Grand Strategy against Russia 1853-1856* (Manchester 1990), pp74-6

Trincomalee's experience

Sadly, the *Trincomalee* on her first commission could not be described as a happy ship. Although she did not have a particularly severe record, being below the statistical average, the officers and crew never achieved that level of common community that made Sulivan's *Philomel* such a success. During the years of that commission the Navy as a whole flogged less than one thousand men a year, from a total in service of between 44,000 and 39,000. On average 38 men in every 1000 were flogged, with an average of 30 lashes. (As punishments were given in dozens this suggests that two and three dozen were the standard.) Warren flogged 23 men and boys, two of them were punished twice, six men were imprisoned on shore; he also disrated 16 men from positions of trust, and placed the Marine Lieutenant under arrest for overstaying his leave. The total of 51 offences noted as receiving punishment were spread across the entire commission of 33 months. This provides a yearly average of less than 20 punishments.

Drunkenness was the main problem, being the sole cause of punishment in 23 cases, and a contributory factor in several more, such as Henry Perriton, the Armourer, who was disrated to Able Seaman for being drunk, 'and pissing on the main deck'. This was a serious offence in a service that rated cleanliness next to, and only just below, godliness. Many of the punishments were drink related. They included insolence while drunk, smuggling drink onto the ship, 'abusive and disgusting language', leave-breaking, theft, sleeping on duty, false accusation of the Ship's Corporal, and being incorrigibly dirty. The beatings ranged from 4 to 48

By the middle of the nineteenth century naval uniforms had settled on a style that would remain largely unaltered for decades. These were the established patterns when HMS *Trincomalee* left Plymouth for her second commission, although they would only have been worn for formal occasions. (Royal Naval Museum, Portsmouth)

lashes, with the two repeat offenders having 84 in total. In the middle of the cruise the Ship's Corporal, Whittaker, was disrated to Able Seaman at his own request, only a month after one of the boys had received 48 lashes for falsely accusing him. Clearly this was not a happy ship, with the men seeking solace in drink, to the extent that several were unable to do their duty, or control their conduct in the presence of their officers. Nor were the offences restricted to the seamen. The elite to whom the other seamen looked for leadership, the captains of all three tops, and those with responsibilities around the ship, all fell prey to drink.

The second commission would be similar, if less brutal. There were fifteen floggings, one man being beaten twice. The occasion for the punishment was either aggravated drunkenness or desertion, although the former probably played a major part in encouraging the latter. A large number of men were disrated, lost their good conduct badges, and even more were fined various sums, ranging from £6.10 shillings to a few shillings, for straggling, often with the costs of their imprisonment, any damages they caused, and the cost of recovering them added. The worst offenders managed to run through almost every system of discipline, taking every opportunity to disgrace themselves ashore. The most persistent offender was the Blacksmith, Mr Beer, who was mulcted pay on eight occasions for straggling and related offences, and ended the commission being disrated, first to Armourer, and then Ordinary Seaman, before being promoted back to Armourer, at which rate he was paid off, to his considerable pecuniary disadvantage. He still did duty at the forge. The other grievous offender, Robert Gullet, AB paid a heavier price: he died early on 21 February 1854, after his seventh over-long run ashore.

Even senior petty officers were not immune to the temptations of drink: the Mate, Mr Young, reported for duty drunk, and was arrested. When faced with the prospect of formal punishment he elected to be discharged with disgrace at Honolulu. At the end of the commission an acting lieutenant would be found insensible from drink while on duty, while the final act of the commission, paying off, was marred by the drowning of Alex McDonald. This may well have been drink related. A frequent straggler, McDonald had received 30 lashes for drunkenness, and several fines. Perhaps the most revealing disciplinary episode, at least as far as Captain Houstoun is concerned, came late in the commission, when one of the worst of the drunks, recently flogged Thomas Wright, AB, accused two other men of 'taking indecent liberties with each other'. Born just across the Tamar at Cawsand, Wright, by now 32, was a small, fair skinned man with an anchor tattooed on his right arm. Although a veteran he had a fairly ordinary character on joining, and was one of only three men to leave the ship officially rated as a bad character. Under examination Wright retracted his claim, and this was read to the assembled ship's company. Houstoun understood that such claims, even if well founded, were a threat to the cohesion and order of the ship, and this was something he had managed to instil and then sustain throughout five years crossing and re-crossing the trackless wastes of the Pacific. His hardened crew of experienced hands did their duty, but were still in thrall to the vices of the old Navy. Houstoun was a very good officer and, if not the equal of Bartholomew Sulivan, he earned the trust of three admirals, and kept his ship efficient.

Trincomalee remained a ship of the old Navy, full of men who sought solace in drink, and were struggling to come to terms with good conduct badges, disrating and prisons. In their turn the officers were trying to work with alternative systems to discipline based on beating. The most modern element was the regular practice with guns great and small, afloat and ashore. Back in 1813 Broke and the *Shannon* had probably been unique in this respect, but since 1830 it had been compulsory. Had it come to a fight, the *Trincomalee* would have acquitted herself well. Her new, more powerful armament, served by trained crews under *Excellent*-prepared seamen gunners, and qualified gunnery officers, could have engaged the enemy more effectively at 500 yards than the navy of 1805 had at 100, while the use of shells made each hit far more telling. The big 56-pounder or 10-inch shells could inflict serious structural damage to a wooden frigate, and gave the ship the offensive power to take on forts and larger ships.

Elsewhere life afloat remained much as it had been for centuries and, unlike lean-manned merchant vessels, the work of the ship was relatively easy, given the very large crew required to fight the guns. Even so, a disproportionate burden fell on the topmen, the elite group of ratings who worked aloft, furling, loosing and shifting sails, as well as shifting the topmasts and yards as necessary. This work demanded strength, dexterity, confidence and a cool head. It was also physically demanding, with the men bent almost double out over the yards, hauling up the wet canvas being prone to ruptures and back injuries, and always in danger of a fall, relying on footropes and the occasional handhold for their safety. In the main fleet competitive evolutions aloft led to fatal falls. These could have a demoralising effect on the rest of the crew, and it had been the deaths of three topmen that sparked the *Hermione* mutiny back in 1797. Given the importance of the elite sailors, a wise captain would treat them well.

On deck a larger body of men served the ropes, providing the power to work the ship. These 'waisters', men who did not go aloft, were a lower element in the ship's society, although they also included some of the petty officers. Some of them were now too old to work aloft, others too inexperienced. This was also the station of the Royal Marines, who would join in the work of the ship, when not required to fulfil their military and police function. A Marine, or 'bootneck', a term of derision derived from the leather stock collar that was part of their army-style uniform, was a lower life form, and the younger and more intelligent among them were encouraged to better themselves by becoming seamen. Men who worked below deck were even lower in the eye of the seamen, for they required no true seafaring skills.

The men slept in hammocks, closely packed on the berth deck, and ate in their self-selected 'messes' of four to eight men, with their own table and benches, and shared the cooking duties of preparing and collecting their food from the galley, where the ship's cook ran the cooking range. After years of experience arrangements on board a Royal Navy warship were simple and effective. Other services missed key points: the Americans left their men to eat sitting cross-legged on the gun deck, the French and especially the Russians did not pay the same quasi-religious attention to cleanliness, and other fleets lacked the strict subordination and observance of orders that made the Royal Navy so effective.

In the Crimean War the peacetime raised seamen of the old Navy demonstrated skill, daring, flexibility and commitment of the highest order. They fought afloat and ashore, with skill and earned a number of

The confined messing arrangements of 1817 as replicated in the restored ship would not have been very different during the first commission, although of course the established complement of 1847 was smaller.

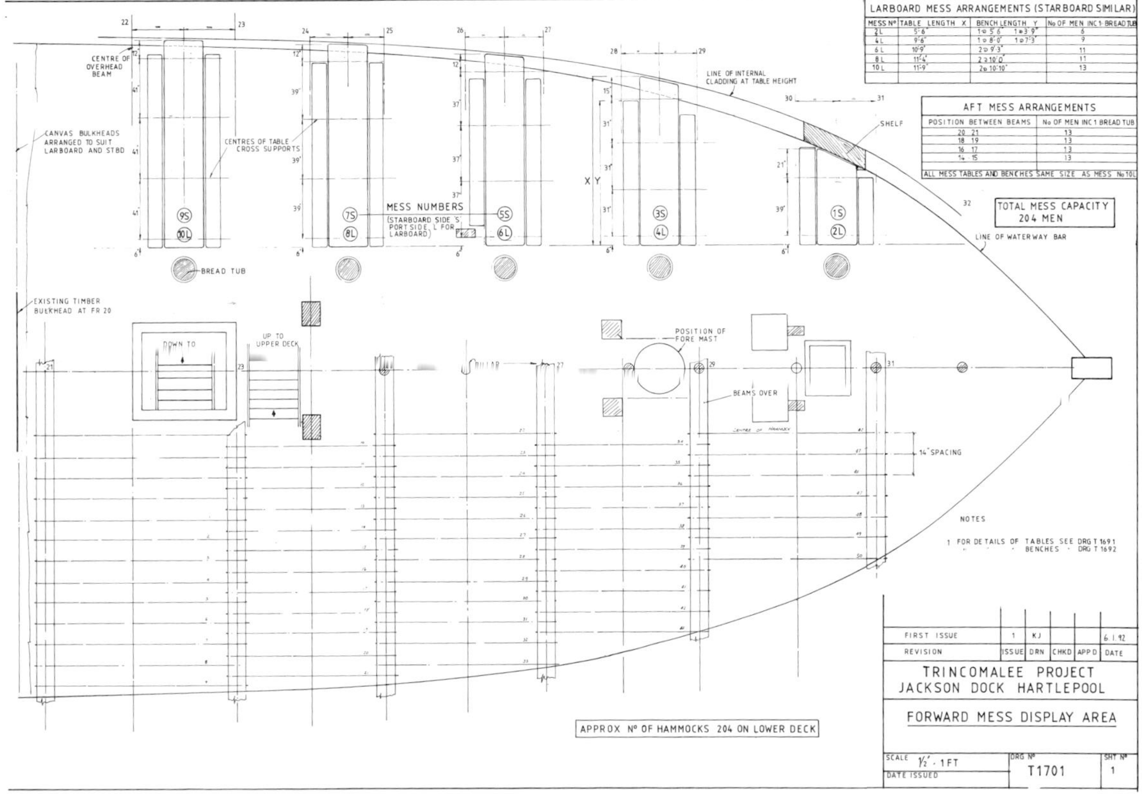

the newly created Victoria Crosses for their efforts. Along with the junior officers who led them, they were the real heroes of the war. From this basis a new fleet could be built.

Health and diet

Food on board was still based around the salt meat, beef and pork, hard biscuits, dried fruit and peas, cheese and lime juice of Nelson's day, although the story that some of the meat eaten in the 1840s was of his vintage is almost certainly apocryphal.

This diet offered about 3500 calories, and although rather dull was adequate for a working seaman. Training for ship's cooks was only introduced in 1873. Improved standards of preparation, cooperage and handling had been established immediately after the Napoleonic wars, when two integrated victualling depots had been built, at Portsmouth and Plymouth, while the Deptford yard was overhauled. These facilities enabled the Navy to bring in raw materials–livestock, grain, limes, timber and iron–to be slaughtered, milled, salted, baked, cut into staves, welded into hoops, and sent out again as packed provision–meat, biscuit and beer–all ready for the fleet. The introduction of canning offered greater variety, although early problems with lead solder may well have poisoned the men of Franklin's Arctic expedition, and contributed to their deaths. From 1847 ships in regular commission were also occasionally issued with canned food, especially beef, which was quickly termed 'bully', from the French term *boulli*. Baking on board British warships was not begun until the 1860s.

Although lime juice was effective, it only possessed half the anti-scorbutic value of lemon juice, but was used for cheapness. Perhaps the well-

The 1844 Food Allowances for Seamen:

	Biscuit	*Spirits*	*Beef*	*Pork*	*Flour*	*Peas*	*Sugar*	*Chocolate or Cocoa*	*Tea*	*Oatmeal & Vinegar*
	pound	pint	pound	pound	pound	pint	ounces	ounces	ounces	pint
Sunday	1	¼	¾	-	¾	-	1½	1	¼	
Monday	1	¼	-	¾	-	½	1½	1	¼	½ pint
Tuesday	1	¼	¾	-	¾	-	1½	1	¼	per
Wednesday	1	¼	-	¾	-	½	1½	1	¼	week
Thursday	1	¼	¾	-	¾	-	1½	1	¼	
Friday	1	¼	-	¾	-	½	1½	1	¼	
Saturday	1	¼	¾	-	¾	-	1½	1	¼	

This was the preserved ration: where possible fresh provisions were substituted especially meat, vegetables and fruit.[26]

known American slang 'limey' has the same connotations as 'cheapskate'. Even with inferior remedies the terrible scourge of scurvy, caused by the lack of vitamin C on long sea voyages, had been conquered by 1800. However, even in the mid-1850s a long passage could still end with the crew showing signs of the disease, as happened to *Trincomalee* at least once while in the Pacific. When a warship entered port fresh provisions would be obtained and used, and as leave opportunities increased the men had more opportunity to supplement their diet, even if drink was the priority. This supplementary supply was easier and more frequent among the well-established and closely linked West Indian islands than on the long passages across the Pacific. Experienced officers knew that the British sailor was more inclined to think about his food than anything else, a fact that Pepys had noted two centuries before. With the improved conditions of service, and the greater value placed on the men, their overall conditions improved markedly in the 1850s and 1860s. Without those improvements the service could not have recruited the long service professional ratings who, then as now formed the backbone of the fleet.

The other necessity of life, fresh water, was more easily supplied from 1815 with the introduction of iron water tanks, which increased the quantity that could be stowed, and the length of time it would remain drinkable. Even so the supply could deteriorate quickly into a vile concoction, covered in green slime and reeking of rotten eggs.[27] Little wonder the rum ration remained popular; it made the water bearable, if not palatable.

Medical services also improved. Although the understanding of disease made little advance, the increasing acceptance of cleanliness and adequate sanitation as important elements in prevention halved the death rate of the war years. The figures were still markedly higher than comparable civilian populations, but less than half those of the army. Improved ventilation, clean clothes and higher standards of personal hygiene were all factors in the change, while the old scourges of yellow fever and malaria were avoided, where possible. Even these advances were not, however, without side effects. The mania for washing the decks made some ships permanently damp, promoting an increase in tuberculosis. Doctors were better trained, and increasingly involved in other aspects of the work of the service.[28]

A scientific officer corps

Nor were the officers of the Navy immune to change. They entered the Navy aged 12 or 13, and served six years as cadets and midshipmen before qualifying for the examination in seamanship and service knowledge that qualified them to be commissioned as lieutenants. After 1836, when the

26 Lloyd, C & Coulter, J L S, *Medicine and the Navy: Vol IV 1815 -1900* (Edinburgh 1963), p93

27 Lloyd & Coulter, *Medicine and the Navy: Vol IV*, pp105-6. Gardiner, *Frigates of the Napoleonic Wars,* pp104-7

28 Lloyd & Coulter, *Medicine and the Navy: Vol IV*, pp 69-90

optional entry level Royal Naval College was closed, those serving on larger ships, battleships and flagships, had the benefit of a Naval Instructor who might also be the Chaplain. These university-educated men taught maths, science, and languages. In addition the ship's officers and warrant officers taught the cadets about an officer's duty, and the professional skills they required to carry it out. Most of the learning was by example, and was tested through small scale opportunities to act the part, such as keeping watch under supervision, or commanding one of the ship's boats. While this system lacked the formal intellectual rigour of more modern systems, and often led to clashes between the First Lieutenant, who wanted the cadets to help run the ship, and the Instructor, who wanted to educate them, it produced fine sea officers. They benefited from the long apprenticeship at sea, learning how to handle the complex and dangerous square rigged ship while still young, and to exploit the fickle power provided by the wind. Only long years and hard lessons could teach a man to anticipate danger, to read the weather and get the best from his ship. This early experience gave British officers a head start over those of all other services, in practical seamanship, gunnery and man-management that no amount of book learning could replicate.

The limitations of the system became obvious only later, when the best of these young men became captains and admirals, men who had to assimilate and assess large amounts of written material, and work in the fields of policy, politics and technology. While French officers were better grounded in science and theory, they were hampered by limited sea

The officers of HMS *Reindeer*, 1871-3, with warrant officers and a solitary rating. This type of steam sloop replaced the old sailing corvettes on distant stations in the 1860s, notably the Pacific, where she followed in the track of the *Trincomalee*. The uniforms are now formalised. Captain William Kennedy was delighted with the qualities of his ship; she carried six guns on the upper deck, and had a crew of 175.

experience and short-service conscript crews, a combination that did not make for confident ship-handling. Fortunately for the Royal Navy there were normally enough individuals who could rise above the system and equip themselves for higher posts through self education, hard work or innate capacity.

In practice the greatest limitation on the Royal Navy's officer corps between 1815 and 1860 was the slow promotion caused by the swollen list of officers left over from the French Wars. With a limited number of appointments to flag rank, and these only by seniority, Charles Napier, a young captain of 1809, had to wait until 1846, almost forty years to become a rear-admiral. The admirals of this book, Napier, Moresby, Adam, Dundonald, Price and Bruce, the fleet commanders under whom *Trincomalee* served, were all past 60, and Dundonald past 70, when they came to fly their flags. All were veterans of the French wars. By the time *Trincomalee* paid off the blockage had been eased by the passing of time; the Napoleonic veterans were rapidly dying off so younger men like Warren and Houstoun only had to wait nineteen and seventeen years to go from captain to rear-admiral. Attempts to introduce a system of retirement for officers too old, infirm or incompetent to serve again, to speed up the promotion of younger men, all foundered on the pride of the service, and the political weight of the senior officers.

Despite the blocked list of officers the mid-nineteenth-century Royal Navy produced a crop of outstanding captains, men who made their mark in all areas of naval service. The skill and professionalism of Bartholomew Sulivan, the cool heroism of William Peel, VC, the policy input of Baldwin Walker, the seamanship of William Mends, the administrative capacity of Alexander Milne and the strategic input of John Washington, were merely highlights from an excellent performance by Royal Navy captains in the Crimean War. Sadly, Peel died during the Indian Mutiny, and Washington of over-work in 1863, while Mends and Sulivan moved into administrative posts, but Walker and especially Milne went on to lead the service into the 1870s. While Mends, Milne, Sulivan and Washington were educated at the Royal Naval College, Walker was not, and Peel entered the service after it closed.

Education had become more important to the Navy and the nation by the middle of the nineteenth century. However, much of the initiative was left to the individual. Officers on half pay had always been at liberty to improve their education, with the consent of the Admiralty. In Nelson's day this was would have been either service in a merchant ship, or residence in France to learn the language. By the 1830s it was more likely to be a period of study at one of the major marine steam engine factories of London or Glasgow. After 1836 the College was linked to the Gunnery Training Ship HMS *Excellent* and offered specialist education in gunnery, steam and the relevant sciences to half-pay officers, and preparatory courses for those undertaking advanced level gunnery training. From the 1850s these *Excellent* officers provided the Navy with well equipped technical minds, able to meet the challenge of new technology: men like Astley Cooper Key, John Fisher and Arthur Wilson. Not that the educational value of the study was limited to service matters, for Montagu Burrows went from the *Excellent* to be Chichele Professor of History at Oxford;[29] while Francis Blackwood went to Cambridge to study astronomy, to aid his surveying work.[30] In truth the Royal Navy was becoming a scientific organisation, at much the same rate as the rest of the country, just in time to meet the new challenges of iron, steam and shell guns.[31] It is worth noting that Houstoun was rated as 'conversant with steam' in April 1852, and suitable for a frigate command, just before being appointed to *Trincomalee*, which indicates a course of private study.[32] Although not noted for any knowledge of steam, Richard Warren was already slated to command a battleship in the event of war, and was the youngest on the battlefleet list.[33] Evidently his solid seamanship and gunnery skills were highly regarded while his record on discipline was not a problem.

From the end of the French wars the role of science had steadily expanded, first with advanced mathematics as the basis for serious gunnery training, then for steam engineering, and increasingly as the basis for a more accurate understanding of the environment within which the Navy had to operate. The precise recording of relevant information had long been a feature of naval life, but the nineteenth century would transform the position. The creation of the Hydrographer's Office in 1795 reflected the growing potential of surveying, and the value of this knowledge for operations.[34] After 1805 much of the Navy's work had been close inshore, projecting power against an increasingly land-bound enemy, and this only reinforced the need for accurate charts. While the main run of Admiralty charts were released for use by the merchant navy, and other commercial users of the sea, the Admiralty was careful to keep secure information concerning key foreign naval bases, and similarly strategic intelligence. Until the 1880s such information formed the basis of war planning, with the Hydrographer of the Navy as the key planner. In 1848 triplicate copies of charts for foreign coasts and harbours were issued to all ships, to permit young officers 'to become acquainted with them'.[35]

With the return of peace in 1815 the thoughts of British empire-builders, traders and shippers had returned to the little known fringes of the world. Sir Joseph Banks, by now a venerable, if declining institution, was still pressing the cause. His naval connections still prospered with men like the Hydrographer, Captain Thomas Hurd, and the Second Secretary at the Admiralty, John Barrow. These men quickly resumed the

29 Burrows, M, *Autobiography* (London 1908); see Ch IV & V for this transformation

30 Ellison, D, *Quarterdeck Cambridge: The Quest of Francis Price Blackwood Captain RN* (Cambridge 1991), pp27-8, 36; Blackwood's protege Charles Shadwell inspired John Fisher to follow a technical path, and played a major role in developing naval education in the 1870s

31 Clowes, *Royal Navy*, Vol VI, pp189-221 for an overview, and Hamilton, C I, *Anglo-French Naval Rivalry 1840-1870* (Oxford 1993), pp144-199 for a thorough comparison of the British and French officers and men

32 Confidential Memorandum by the Duke of Northumberland (First Lord of the Admiralty) April 1852: Northumberland MSS E/4/514

33 ibid E/4/528

34 Ritchie, G S, *The Admiralty Chart* (London 1967)

35 Admiralty Circular 8 March 1848: ADM 2/1606, f277

36 Lloyd, C, *Mr Barrow of the Admiralty* (London 1970), Ch 6-9. Fleming, F, *Barrow's Boys* (London 1998)

37 King (1791-1856) was the first Australian-born admiral. His later career and residence in Australia brought him into contact with such key figures as Sulivan and Darwin. See below

38 Hordern, M C, *King of the Australian Coast: The work of Philip Parker King in the Mermaid and Bathurst, 1817-1822* (Melbourne 1998), pp13-15, & Colonial Office memo February 1817 p406

39 Edited by Sir John Herschel (London 1849)

The upper deck of HMS *Minotaur*, a large ironclad battleship completed in the late 1860s. The crew are being drilled on a 7-inch muzzle loading rifled gun, by a Royal Marine Artillery gun crew. These weapons required skilled handling, and two were fitted to HMS *Trincomalee* in 1872, to train the reservists. The training arcs can still be seen at the amidships gunports on either broadside.

strand of scientific, acquisitive and economically expansive exploring that had been the *leitmotif* of Bank's career. Barrow's vision led on to the North West passage, the source of the Niger, the Congo basin and Timbuktu.[36] The more practically-minded Hurd wanted to fill in the gaps in the charts, many of which were in the Pacific basin. From Kamchatka to Van Diemen's land, including much of the Australian coast, ignorance of the navigation hampered commercial shipping.

This work called for officers of scientific merit and they were recruited by Hurd into the Royal Naval Surveying Service formed in 1817, with a generous additional allowance of 15 shillings a day for a lieutenant while on duty. This was a fine career opening for a poor but able man at a time of mass unemployment among younger officers. However, it did not normally lead to high rank. One of the first officers sent out was Lieutenant Philip King,[37] who spent the period 1817 to 1822 filling in much of the unknown coast of Australia, and seeking a safe passage through the Torres Straits for commercial shipping to India. Nor were charts his only concern: he had to take physical possession of important sites, especially the mouths of major rivers, even if his only tools were a marker post and a handful of seeds. He was also to note the climate, terrain, population, prospects for trade, minerals, flora and fauna, especially any species that might be economically useful, and 'such woods as may appear to be useful in ship-building; hard woods for tree nails, block-sheaves, &c, of all which it would be desirable to procure small specimens labelled and numbered, . . . to ascertain the quantities in which they are found; the facility or otherwise of floating them down to a convenient place for shipment &c.'[38] Banks helped to write these instructions, and provided a botanist to join the ship at Sydney, continuing the scientific role in naval expeditions that he and Cook had pioneered sixty years before.

The ambition of the Admiralty and the Colonial Office in framing these instructions was limitless, and yet they had few problems finding men with enthusiasm and physical endurance, not to mention cartographic, drawing and scientific skills, to carry out such missions. That many of the same skills were critical to serious war planning was soon recognised, and by the 1850s the Hydrographer was the leading source of strategic advice and a key player in many aspects of naval policy and planning. In addition to the more obvious information, such as charts of naval bases and strategic narrows, the Royal Navy also developed an understanding of oceanic phenomena that would influence operations, notably tides, currents and wind patterns. The first fully reliable set of tidal data, prepared for the English Channel in the 1840s, was the key element in planning to deal with a possible French invasion.

Down to the mid-1840s the collection of such information was usually undertaken by specially detailed surveying and exploring expeditions, led by trained officers. In addition all offices were requested to report any information they considered useful, and their journals were scrutinised by the Hydrographer for useful information. While specific missions would continue, especially for hydrographic work, it was recognised that the improved educational standards of the officer corps meant that they could be given more detailed instructions on marine science, and expected to conduct enquiries. In 1849 the Admiralty issued their instructions, *A Manual of Scientific Enquiry prepared for the use of Her Majesty's Navy: and adapted for Travellers in General.*[39] Edited by Sir John Herschel, it covered astronomy, magnetism, hydrography, tides, geography, geology, earthquakes, mineralogy, meteorology, atmospheric waves, zoology, botany, ethnology, medicine and medical statistics, and statistics. The authors were all Fellows of the Royal Society, the scientific elite, including Airy, the Astronomer Royal, Darwin, the botanist, and Director of Kew Gardens Sir William Hooker, palaeontologist Richard Owen, and other luminaries. The initiative had been launched by Lord Auckland's Admiralty Board in December 1847, with an appeal to the public spirit of the selected contributors.[40] The object was to guide observation and recording for all branches of science, and written for men of 'good intelligence and fair acquirement'. A hint of pecuniary reward was held out to encourage application. In addition to the exact sciences, social and ethnographic evidence should be acquired. The potential of the volume was immense, for 'They have cruisers in every sea; and where the ships of the navy are not present, it sometimes happens that the vessels of the merchant are conducted with much intelligence and enterprise.'[41] It did not need to be said that such information had a direct naval utility.

The mixture of high science and practical naval intelligence-gathering enshrined in the *Manual* demonstrated the wider ambitions of the Admiralty. Foreign ports were to be assessed, their docks, repair facilities, engineering works, coal stocks, tides and other key aspects recorded.

40 Admiralty William Hooker 29 December 1847: RBG Kew Archives Admiralty Volume no 4

41 *Admiralty Manual* preface piv

42 ibid; for specific examples see: pp62, 95-7, 105-7, 129, 139-41, 153-4, 156 & 421-2

43 Desmond, A & Moore, J, *Darwin* (London 1991), pp101-193.
Desmond, A, *Huxley: The Devil's Disciple* (London 1994), pp 53-129.
Lloyd, & Coulter, *Medicine and the Navy: Vol IV*, pp 69-80 for a survey of these men

44 Deacon, M, *Scientists and the Sea 1650-1900: a study of Marine Science* (London 1971), pp290-2

45 ibid, p291

46 Williams, F L, *Matthew Fontaine Maury, Scientist of the Sea* (New Jersey 1963)

Charts were to be made, and the example supplied included a fort, in case the strategic purpose should escape the less gifted officer. Unknown coasts and seas were to be analysed, and the north Pacific was a major area of ignorance, a fact the Russians exploited to escape the allies in 1855. Man's impact on the coast was to be observed, along with local trade, political issues, history, geology, and of course any timber resources suitable for shipbuilding must be reported.[42]

Many ships on exploring and surveying missions carried scientists. Some were passengers, notably Darwin in HMS *Beagle* (1831-1836) where he met Lieutenant Bartholomew Sulivan, who became a lifelong friend. Others were junior naval surgeons like Thomas Huxley in HMS *Rattlesnake* (1846-1850) off New Guinea.[43] For both men the opportunity to work in unknown regions and focus on their subject proved critical.

The 1840s were a key point in the development of marine science, with a number of individuals and organisations across the world assembling data and attempting to develop theories of more universal application.[44] Significantly, Beechey's chart of oceanic currents in the *Manual* was intended as a guide for further experiment,[45] with much of the evidence being supplied by the position bottles thrown at frequent intervals to help determine the tides and currents. The American naval officer Matthew Fontaine Maury developed a theory of oceanic circulation based on such data which, although flawed, was a marked improvement on the previous haphazard approach.[46] In 1853 an International Conference on Meteorological Observation at Brussels resolved that participating governments should issue their ships with adequate instruments, and standardised logbooks so that useful data could be gathered. In the age of steam navies sought certainty. Captain Houstoun would be one of the men who contributed, in his small way, to the process by his use of position bottles, astronomical observations and detailed logbook full of information on winds, currents, and meteorology. In addition, both Houstoun and the ship's Master, Horatio Norway, produced more

Harbour service. This collection of old ships made up the torpedo training school HMS *Vernon* at Portsmouth between 1904 and 1923. All three ships were completed between 1856 and 1861. The central unit is HMS *Warrior*, now restored to her 1861 glory; her funnel reveals that she is serving as the power house and workshop for the school. The other two ships are used for accommodation. The left-hand unit is HMS *Marlborough*, one of the last wooden steam three-decker battleships, and the other is HMS *Donegal*, a contemporary steam two-decker. Such collections of old hulks were a common sight at all naval bases.

detailed Remarks Books, which were also sent to the Hydrographer, who extracted any useful information from them. By contrast to her first commission HMS *Trincomalee*'s second period of sea duty took on a more 'scientific' character. The commission included a period in the Bering Straits, supporting the North West passage operations of HMS *Enterprise* and *Investigator*, where Houstoun made charts. He also charted on the coast of British Columbia, and compiled detailed reports on foreign harbours, their resources, trade and prospects exactly as set out in the *Manual.*

In essence, the Royal Navy changed alongside the society that it served and which supported it. It moved away from eighteenth-century ideas and practices because they no longer met the needs of the day, and in the process created the basis of all modern professional navies, the long-service volunteer rating entered for general and continuous service, backed up by paid reserves who could be mobilised for war. To secure this key step, it had been necessary to reform almost every aspect of the service for officers and men, from pay and conditions, through discipline and retirement. While HMS *Trincomalee* did not cause any of these changes, her career spanned the great divide of 1853, as an active cruiser and a reserve drill ship. Indeed, without the Naval Reserve system she may well have been sold in the early 1860s.

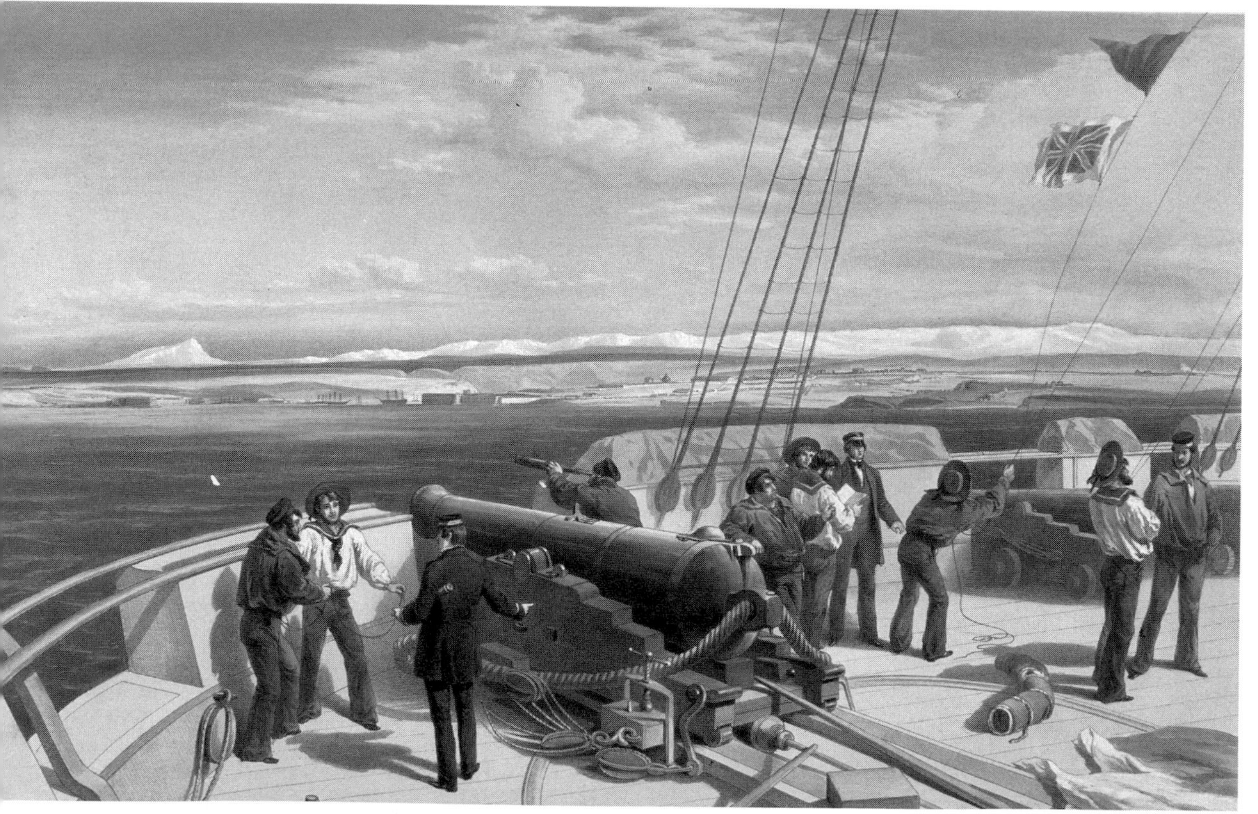

The quarterdeck of a steam frigate, seen here off Sevastopol during the Crimean War. The sailors are wearing the new uniform, with the low cut blouse-like frock, with the sleeves gathered at wrist bands, and a large square collar. The broad brimmed straw hats must have been a trial in blowing weather. The officers are wearing their undress or working uniform. The gun is a 68-pounder on a pivoting upper deck carriage, and is fitted with sights. (Royal Naval Museum, Portsmouth)

Imperial Security – the Second Commission

Chapter Five

TRINCOMALEE did not have long to wait for another tour of duty: she was brought forward to commission at Plymouth for the Pacific station in 1852. The Pacific Squadron, responsible for the largest ocean area of any British naval station, had only been established in 1837, in recognition of the growing importance of regional trade both on the West coast of the Americas and in the oceanic islands of the central Pacific. It stretched from the Arctic Circle to the Antarctic, bounded to the east by Cape Horn and to the west by the 170th meridian, the longitude of Samoa. Unlike other major stations there was no Royal Navy base within the station limits.[1] Depot ships in the Chilean harbour of Valparaiso and the Peruvian base at Callao, the shore-side support of the Hudson's Bay Company at Esquimalt, San Francisco and Honolulu,[2] together with purchases from local peoples in the islands and lesser ports, had to suffice. The sheer scale of the station placed a premium on good sailing capabilities, adequate stowage and relatively small crews. Between 1850 and 1860 there were normally twelve British warships on station, with a total manpower of approximately 3000.[3] *Trincomalee* would be an average unit of this squadron, in size and complement, one of four razee frigates to serve there during the decade. Her voyaging would reach astonishing proportions, as the track charts reveal. In 1853 alone she sailed over 20,000 miles, on an extended round trip from Valparaiso, calling at Esquimalt, Sitka, San Francisco and then back to Valparaiso.

Armament

Main Deck	8 x 32-pounder of 56cwt (standard heavy solid shot gun) 10 x 8-inch shell guns of 65cwt (standard broadside shell gun)
Upper deck	1 x 10-inch 85cwt shell gun 2 x 32-pounders of 39cwt (light solid shot gun for the upper deck)
Complement:	240, comprising: 24 officers 39 petty officers 115 seamen 33 boys 29 Royal Marines

1 For contemporary accounts of the station in the 1850s see: Bridge, Admiral Sir C, *Some Recollections* (London 1910), pp111-160; Bridge was a midshipman in HMS *Brisk*, 1855-57. John Moresby served in *Amphitrite* 1850-55; Moresby, J, *Two Admirals* (London 1911). Akrigg, G P V & Akrigg, Helen B, *HMS Virago in the Pacific 1851-1855* (Victoria, British Columbia 1992)

2 Barrett, G, *Russian Shadows on the British Northwest Coast of North America, 1810-1890* (Vancouver 1983), pp43-4

3 Gough, B, *The Royal Navy and the Northwest Coast of North America, 1810-1914* (Vancouver 1971), pp245-7

Stowage: 140 tons of salt provisions
70 tons of bread
95 tons of water in iron tanks
10 tons in wooden casks

80 tons of ballast were required.

The main change since 1847 was the improved armament. The new main-deck guns were the standard heavy pattern 32-pounders and 8-inch shell guns issued to battleships, while the 10-inch was the largest shell gun used by the Royal Navy.

Trincomalee's third, and last sea-going captain was Wallace Houstoun. The son of a Scottish general, Houstoun, like his ship, began life in India, in 1811. He entered the Navy in 1824, passed his commissioning examination in 1830 and became a lieutenant in 1832, serving in several ships on the South American station, including the flagship. Between 1836 and 1839 he was a lieutenant in the Bombay-built frigate *Madagascar* on the North America and West Indies station, under Captain Provo William Wallis, senior surviving lieutenant of the *Shannon.* After serving in Admiral Sir Graham Moore's flagship at Devonport, he went back to the West Indies in 1841 as Flag Lieutenant to Admiral Sir Charles Adam, earning automatic promotion to commander, and a transfer to command a brig, and then the Bombay-built Port Royal depot ship *Imaum* in 1843. He paid off in 1844. Promotion to post captain in July 1847 only reinforces the impression that Houstoun's politics, and his naval friends, were liberal. Houstoun's appointment by the tory Admiralty Board of the fourth Duke of Northumberland was based on merit, and would prove to be among the better of the Duke's sometimes controversial decisions.

The muster opened on 23 June 1852, Houstoun came on board and read his commission on the 24th, and a month later the guns were hoisted in. The ship was quickly manned, the Pacific being a popular station.[4] Only 30 of the 240 sailors who would serve in the ship during this commission were new entrants to the service. The original crew comprised 157 names on the Muster List, excluding marines, boys and officers. Many of the men came from other warships that had just paid off at Devonport; the great 110-gun three-decker HMS *Queen*, lately Admiral Sir William Parker's flagship in the Mediterranean and a 'crack ship' in every respect, paid off on 2 July; she provided forty-two men. When the 80-gun two-decker battleship HMS *Superb* paid off on 19 June, seventeen of her men joined, along with thirteen from the razee frigate HMS *Amazon*, paid off on 11 May, and eleven from the paddle sloop HMS *Gladiator*, paid off on 15 June. Together with eight top rated men and four promising boys from HMS *Excellent*, these sources provided Houstoun with over half his crew. The vast majority of the men were local, with places of birth and residence on either side of the Tamar,

4 Moresby, *Two Admirals*, p100, refers to *Amphitrite* commissioning in 1850 for the same station.

5 Muster Book: Adm 38/9205

6 Houstoun–Admiral Sir J Ommaney (C-in-C Plymouth) 7 July 1852: Houstoun Letter Book, British Columbia Archives, Victoria (hereafter LB)

although Devon men were the more numerous. Other seamen came from Ireland, many from *Superb* which had called at Cork while serving in the Western Squadron, some from Portsmouth, Chatham and London.[5] The marines were predominantly from Somerset. The petty officers were all veteran naval seamen, some with over thirty years service, and an appropriate number of good conduct badges. They promised to be steady men, but by contrast one able seaman deserted while the ship was still in port. Nor was this the worst problem, as Houstoun may have realised when he mustered the crew. The Purser's Clerk, George Twiggs was too drunk to read his own writing, and this was not the first time he had been drunk on duty. Houstoun persuaded him to apply for a discharge.[6] This was an early taste of the major disciplinary problem of the cruise.

The final element of the crew was a draft of twenty supernumerary boys for the Pacific Squadron. The boys would all develop into seamen. The twenty-six first class boys mustered when the ship commissioned were all rated as seamen by late 1854, while many of the second class boys were promoted to first class, and also rated before mid-1857, being replaced by fresh drafts brought out by other ships. The last of the eighty first class boys to be entered on *Trincomalee*'s books was George Prince. Born in Plymouth in May 1841 he entered the service at Devonport in July 1855, and went out to the Pacific with one such draft. He joined *Trincomalee* as a second class boy in October, was rated as a first class boy in July 1857, and transferred back to the Devonport flagship HMS *Impregnable* at the end of the commission. The boys, like the men, were predominantly from the south-west, thirty-eight from Devon and eleven from Cornwall out eighty. Not only was the ship, like every other unit of the sea-going Navy, a machine for creating naval ratings, these ratings were largely boy entrants and local to the ship's home port.

Trincomalee sailed out of Plymouth Sound on 21 August. Only nine days later Bennett, one of the first class boys sent from HMS *Excellent,* fell from the mizzen topsail yard, hit the chains and was picked out of the sea dead. He was returned to the sea, with all due ceremony the following day. After stopping for provisions and water at St Vincent in the Cape Verde Islands the ship found some light relief at the Equator, when members of the ship's company dressed up as King Neptune and his host, 'boarded' the ship from the bow and conducted the customary 'Crossing the line' ceremonies, involving soap, tar and comical razors. The next port of call was Rio de Janeiro, where

Captain Wallace Houstoun, seen here in old age, was 41 when he took command of the *Trincomalee* in 1852. He proved to be an outstanding officer, demonstrating excellent seamanship, impressive scientific and surveying skills, considerable tact and a firm, if benevolent control over his occasionally unruly crew.

in rather fraught circumstances Rear-Admiral W W Henderson, with his flag in the paddle frigate *Centaur*, was policing the ending of the Brazilian slave trade.[7] He was accompanied by the steamers *Plumper* and *Torch* and the exploration vessel *Herald*.[8] Also in the harbour was the USS *Congress.* Here four men were invalided, and Houstoun checked his compasses at the Brazilian navigational depot ashore. Finally the 10-inch pivot gun was struck into the hold for the next leg of the voyage, which would take the ship round Cape Horn. Houstoun was reminded of the drink problem when Nathaniel Tucker, his coxswain, drank himself into a stupor and failed to turn up when expected. Having embarrassed his captain, Tucker was promptly disrated, the first of many.

Admiral Henderson ordered Houstoun to stop over at Port Stanley in the Falkland Islands, following a request from the Colonial Office.[9] Houstoun provided a thorough report on local resources, noting the marked increase in shipping calling at the harbour, but the visit was spoiled when *Trincomalee* was run into by the merchant ship *Helena* of Liverpool while working out of harbour, suffering some damage to the starboard main mast rigging and yards. The merchant skipper accepted the blame, complaining that his unruly crew had ignored orders. Leaving aside the question of blame, it still took the carpenter's crew four days to repair the two ships. *Trincomalee* then headed for Cape Horn, one of the most dangerous places on any ocean. A combination of mountainous seas, high winds and deceptive fogs allied to the severe cold and a horrific coast, made passing the Cape a unique experience. This time, despite Force 10 to 11 winds, the passage was quick, and trouble-free. On 21 November the ship finally entered the waters of her station, once again coming under the command of Fairfax Moresby, now rear-admiral and Commander-in-Chief Pacific Station.

Moresby was at Valparaiso when *Trincomalee* arrived on 12 December. Valparaiso, which could supply large quantities of food and water at low cost, was the headquarters of the station It was also a popular run ashore for officers and men, although it could be a dangerous place.[10] Within days her crew were savouring the delights of the town, and paid heavily for the pleasure in lost rates, good conduct badges, mulcted pay and fines. Two boys were flogged. Bosun's mate Thomas Knowles was disrated to able seaman and lost his good conduct badge for 'drunkenness and riotous conduct'. Although Knowles regained both his post and his badge, he lost the badge again before the commission was over. Three men deserted. Even so the ship passed an inspection by the Admiral the next month, and when Moresby exercised her at general quarters, the crew demonstrated the benefits of constant drills while at sea, passing the inspection, even with the 10-inch gun still in the hold.[11] Later *Trincomalee* sent her boats out to tow *Amphitrite* into the harbour. Her

7 Bethell, L, *The Abolition of the Brazilian Slave Trade* (Cambridge 1970)

8 *Centaur*, 1200-ton paddle frigate of 1845; *Herald*, Cochin-built 500-ton Sixth Rate, doing duty as a survey vessel; *Plumper*, wooden screw sloop, 490 tons, built 1848; *Torch*, iron paddle gunvessel, 340 tons, built 1846. The steam force had just finished suppressing the Brazilian slave trade.

9 Houstoun – Henderson 8 November 1852: LB, pp11-12

10 Bridge, *Recollections*, pp111-2

11 Admiralty – Moresby 26 March 1853: Adm 2/1611, f68

12 Log: Adm 53/5838

13 Houstoun – Admiralty 29 March 1853: LB, p22

14 Admiralty – Moresby 23 April 1852; 11 May & 26 June 1852, 13 August 1852: Adm 2/1611, ff271, 305, 364, & 408

15 Longstaff, F V, *Esquimalt Naval Base* (Victoria, British Columbia 1941). Bridge, *Recollections*, pp121-3

sister ship had been on station for nearly three years. In April the two ships, with Moresby's flagship HMS *Portland*, a 50-gun frigate of 1822, put to sea and conducted the usual gun drill and exercises. By this time Houstoun had got a feel for his ship, and reported that she sailed well, comparatively speaking, and 'That she is easy both at sea and at her anchors, and that she is generally speaking a strong and well built ship.'[12] He had also decided to shift the shell room, to increase stowage in the bread room, as had been done in *Amphitrite*. The work was carried out at Esquimalt, although the Admiralty later disapproved.[13]

The Pacific North West

After a passage of over two months *Trincomalee* arrived at Esquimalt on the coast of modern-day British Columbia to watch over a gold rush and possible American filibustering.[14] The area around Fort Victoria and Esquimalt was then a small settlement, with a few British families.[15] The

The 1852–1857 commission took the *Trincomalee* to the Pacific, where she spent much of her time making a grand tour of the region, following the winds and currents in a largely cyclical pattern of movements from Chile to Hawaii and Vancouver, with occasional diversion to the Bering Straits, Petropavlovsk and Tahiti, returning through San Francisco. This modern chart is based on the surviving track charts of the first half of the commission. (Roma Beaumont)

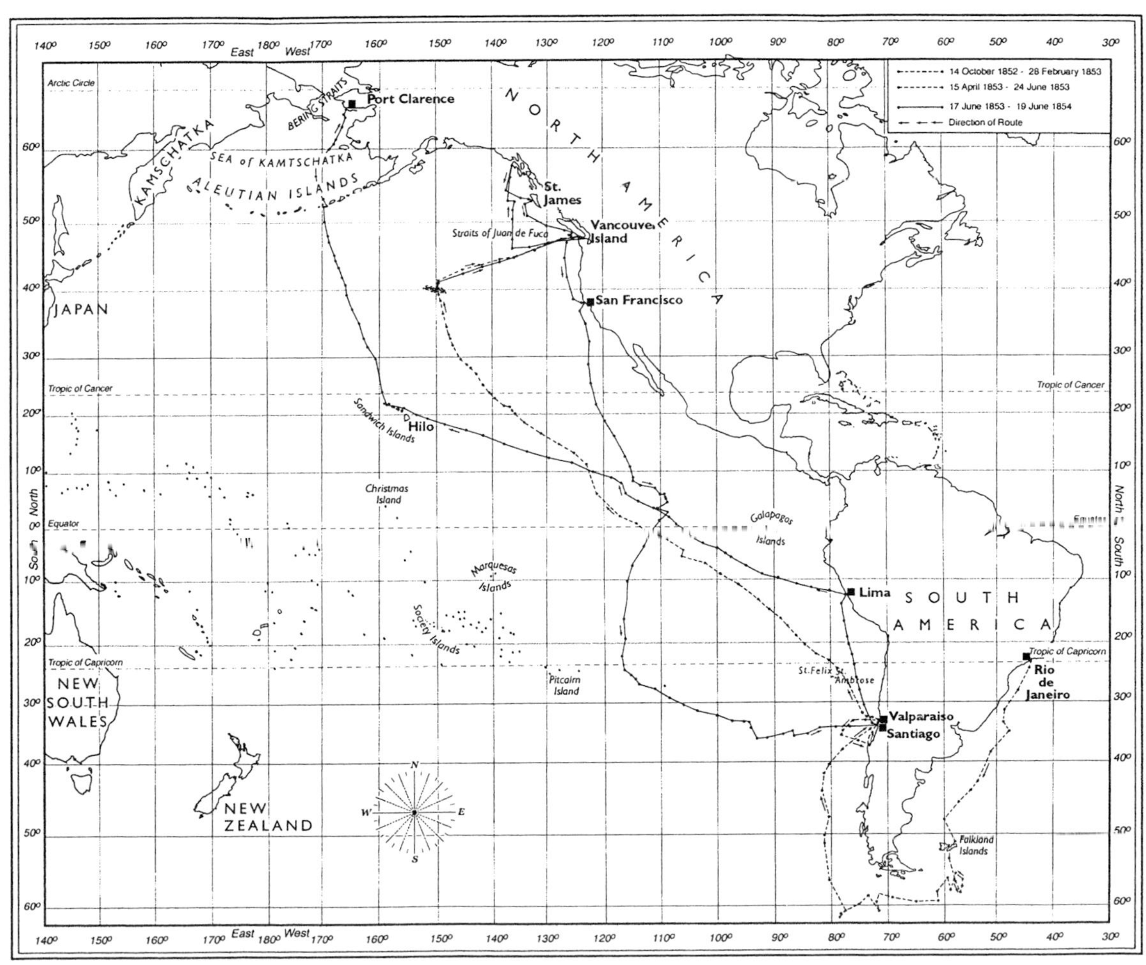

British Government made it a Colony in 1849, essentially to put a limit on American encroachment in the area. Even so, the Colonial Office was content to leave the fur trading Hudson's Bay Company, which had no interest in settlement, to run the territory.[16] While Houstoun was quick to use his seine net to supplement meagre local stores of beef and vegetables, the crew once again took the opportunity to overstay their leave on shore, get drunk and straggle back. Two more were flogged for drink-related offences. The naval run ashore, a time-honoured tradition, took on an altogether less savoury aspect in frontier settlements like Fort Victoria, where the interaction between native and colonising peoples was worked out. Cultural arrogance, assumed superiority and the impact of European goods like whisky, together with such medical disasters as smallpox and venereal diseases, added to conflict over land, provided ample occasion for inter-racial violence. Despite the best efforts of missionaries and high-minded administrators, the native Americans came off second-best in almost every encounter. When a watch of bored and thirsty seamen came into this heady environment, the potential for trouble was high. They piled into the bars, brothels and gambling dens and, when drunk, often wandered into the outlying native village in search of girls. The consequences of this activity invariably ended up being considered by the Captain, with punishments being awarded.[17] Nor were the men of the lower deck the only ones to be tempted by the opportunities of the colonial frontier.

Trincomalee had entered the world of the Hudson's Bay Company, the seventeenth-century chartered fur trading concern that ruled this distant outpost of empire. While increasingly coming under government control, both imperial and Canadian, the Company jealously preserved its independence while looking to London for security against its American and Russian neighbours and the local native population.[18] This curious relationship led the Company to prefer a Royal Navy presence, which was

Sitka, the capital of Russian Alaska. *Trincomalee* visited the post in August and September 1853, less than a year before going to war with Russia. Captain Houstoun conducted his mission with skill, but two of his midshipmen could not resist the temptations of the shore.

necessarily confined to the coast, to a military garrison. Fort Victoria was a stockaded trading post, not equipped for defence against warships.[19] However, the need for armed force to support authority ensured a steady stream of requests from the Governor of Vancouver Island, Sir James Douglas, who was also the local Company chief officer and founder of Fort Victoria.

The Colonial Office recognised the problem, and considered it 'highly desirable that a ship of war should frequently visit Vancouver's Island'.[20] This was at variance with the Admiralty view that warships should not be tied to police functions in peacetime. Unfortunately, the complex and extensive coastline made the use of large sailing ships problematic. The coastal waters were largely uncharted, and could only be safely navigated under tow from one of the Company steamers, the appropriately named *Beaver* and *Otter.* These were able to operate relatively easily because coal was mined locally, and they could also burn wood, of the which there was an abundance close to the shore. While *Trincomalee* might appear powerful, her local role was restricted to landing marines and sailors, in pursuit of a variety of disreputable characters: murderers, pirates, slavers and liquor smugglers.[21]

In August a Hudson's Bay Company officer came on board as a pilot and the ship was towed out of harbour and set sail for New Archangel (Sitka), the capital of Russian America (Alaska), a commercial colony with a similar relationship to the Russian Government as that of Hudson's Bay Company.[22] While the business of the visit led Houstoun to seek information about the British Arctic expeditions, one of which had gone north through the Bering Straits, he also compiled a detailed report on the population, climate, coast, water supplies, coal, furs, fish and trade of the settlement. Much of the fish was exported to San Francisco and Hawaii, along with ice at $35 a ton.[23] Around these discussions the two chartered companies were agreeing that they would remain neutral should their home nations go to war. The ship's company had leave, and salutes were fired to mark Prince Albert's birthday, and on 2 September the anniversary of Tsar Nicholas's coronation. However, Captain Houstoun had more serious things on his mind, noting in the ship's log:

> Mr W E O Massey midshipman, was disrated to Naval Cadet and suspended from duty to await the Order of the Commander in Chief for grossly obscene conduct when officer of the Watch on the afternoon of Thursday 1st September.[24]

In a letter to Admiral Moresby Houstoun was more explicit: Massey had been discovered 'having connection with an Indian female on the Accommodation Ladder'.[25] Massey had been a problem throughout the

16 Morrell, W P, *British Colonial Policy in the Age of Peel and Russell* (London 1930), pp444-6

17 Gough, B M, *Gunboat Frontier: British Maritime Authority and Northwest Coast Indians, 1846-1890* (Vancouver 1984), p76

18 Galbraith, J S, *The Hudson's Bay Company as an Imperial Factor 1821-1869* (Berkeley CA 1959)

19 Barrett, *Russian Shadows*, p43

20 Admiralty–Moresby 2 March 1853: Adm 2/1611, f47

21 Gough, *Gunboat Frontier*

22 The Russians sold Alaska to the United States in 1867

23 Houstoun–Moresby 2 January 1854 (Report of Proceedings): LB, pp34-46

24 Log 3 September 1853: Adm 53/5838

25 Houstoun–Moresby 3 September 1853: LB, p31

commission, being disrated in January for not having a quadrant or a telescope, and receiving a poor report from Houstoun, which led the Admiralty to censure him and expect a better report in future.[26] After the ship had returned to Esquimalt Massey was in trouble again, going ashore in a canoe while suspended from duty, with the assistance of Midshipman William Pearson, who was also disrated. Pearson was another bad character, disrated with Massey for having no navigational instruments, aiding and abetting Massey and then for 'insolent and offensive behaviour to his superior officer' at Sitka. His conduct was, Houstoun pointedly observed, 'not that of a gentleman'.[27]

On the return voyage Houstoun called at Virago Sound in the Queen Charlotte Islands, one of the many local features named for British warships, to check on the local gold rush, and make a visible display of force to impress the Haida tribe, who were generally reckoned to be pirates. Just in case they missed the point, he conducted a demonstration of shot, shell and rocket fire against distant targets. This had a suitable impact, although Houstoun reported that settlers should avoid trading with the Haida.[28] Sailing Master Norway charted part of the sound, which Houstoun then named Trincomalee Harbour.

In November *Trincomalee* joined *Amphitrite* in San Francisco Bay, before heading south for Valparaiso. Here a court of enquiry was assembled on 4 January, the Captains of HMS *Dido* and HMS *Virago* finding against the two errant midshipmen. They were discharged from the ship on 7 January 1854, to await a passage home. Their naval careers were over. A younger officer, Naval Cadet Sir Lambton Loraine had been doing duty as a midshipman since joining the ship at Valparaiso in early 1853 and proved to be altogether more acceptable: 'Sir Lambton Loraine Bart. Has very good talents, and promises to make a good draughtsman and surveyor'.[29] His character, and his talents, would play a major part in his long career.[30] The Russian Company, and the Hudson's Bay Company agreement to remain neutral in the event of war was confirmed by the Admiralty, but the news only reached the Pacific in November 1854.[31] Critically, the arrangement only applied to settlements ashore, ships at sea remaining fair game.

Moresby reached Valparaiso just before his relief, Rear-Admiral Sir David Price, appeared in HMS *President*, another 50-gun frigate. *Portland* turned over her surplus provisions, ammunition and other gear, before *Trincomalee* headed north for Callao, a small port some eight miles from the Peruvian capital of Lima. Here Robert Gullett, the most persistent straggler and drunk finally reached the end of his earthly span, dying on board the day after a final run ashore. Plymouth-born Gullett, then 30 years old, was a career naval rating, and entered for Continuous Service. He was buried ashore. Three days later the burial detail was back with

26 Admiralty – Moresby 16 March 1853: Adm 2/1281, f288

27 Houstoun – Moresby 10 October 1853: LB, p33

28 Gough, *Gunboat Frontier*, pp102-3

29 Captain's Remark Book 1852: Hydrographic Office Archives, Taunton

30 Loraine was a baronet. In 1873 Commander Loraine demonstrated his confidence, and his character, when he took HMS *Niobe* into Santiago harbour, cleared for action and demanded that the Spanish Governor-General of Cuba stop the execution of American citizens taken on board the insurgent ship *Virginius*. This was the third time he had overawed or overpowered local authorities in the West Indies into releasing British or American citizens held illegally

31 Captain Frederick of *Amphitrite* – Admiralty 13 November 1854: Adm 1/5655, Y75

32 Barrett, *Russian Shadows*, p44; Gough, *Royal Navy*, pp112-3

33 Gough, *Royal Navy*, p113

34 Barrett, *Russian Shadows*, p46

35 Martin, Captain Henry RN, *Polynesian Journal, 1846-1847* (Salem MA 1981), p14. Martin's private observations provide a useful addition to Houstoun's public correspondence, not least because he was a man of rare talent and considerable penetration

mate James Saumarez, while the contagious hospital cot in which he had died of yellow fever was hove overboard. In April Admiral Price arrived, to provision *Trincomalee* for a voyage to support the Arctic mission of HM Ships *Enterprise* and *Investigator* that had gone north through the Bering Straits to search for Sir John Franklin. The Russian frigate *Aurora* arrived at Callao on 15 April. Although war had broken out between Britain, France and Russia three weeks earlier, the news would not reach Price, still at Callao, until 7 May; Esquimalt only heard in mid-July.[32] Price's main concern was to deal with the two Russian frigates and rumoured privateers operating against British trade.[33] *Amphitrite* was dispatched to look for privateers at San Francisco, but found none and Captain Frederick dismissed the rumour.[34]

Hawaii

Meanwhile *Trincomalee*, still unaware of the war, sailed to Hawaii, where she met another Russian frigate, the *Diana.* Anchored at Honolulu, her men encountered 'a large straggling village, whose streets are lanes', while the most prominent buildings were chapels, temperance houses, rival grog shops, a few consular and merchant dwellings and the king's palace, all standing amidst native huts.[35] After loading coal, lime juice and fresh provisions for the Arctic ships, *Trincomalee* left harbour at the end of May, and after a brief stay on a mud bank, kedged off and headed north. A month later she rendezvoused with HMS *Rattlesnake*, one of a class of sloops frequently used for exploration and surveying, at Port Clarence, where salt provisions for the Arctic ships were discharged to the shore. *Rattlesnake* required help with repairs and caulking, and after she left the exploration ship HMS *Plover* arrived, needing even more work. Invalids from both ships were sent on board *Trincomalee*, and replaced by twen-

Seen here drying her sails, *Trincomalee* spent a significant part of her second commission at Honolulu, supporting British policy and Hawaiian independence. This view reveals that she carried her nine broadside guns in the aftermost ports, a choice determined by her sailing qualities. (H L Chase Bishop Museum, Honolulu, Hawaii)

ty-two volunteers from her crew, along with spare clothes. On quiet days Houstoun surveyed a local river, as instructed by the *Admiralty Manual*, had the ship cleared and conducted gunnery practice. After two months inside the straits *Trincomalee* headed south, arriving in San Francisco Bay after 28 days at sea. This prolonged period in northern latitudes took a toll on the crew, who were showing signs of scurvy. Not only did they receive an additional allowance of pay for Arctic service; but:

> In consequence of the representation of the Surgeon Captain gave paymaster an order to supply ship's company while in port with a double allowance of vegetables, and to procure six tons of potatoes to take to sea.[36]

With her hold full of potatoes the ship put to sea on the 23rd, working out to sea in company with *Amphitrite* and the French frigate *Artemise*; they parted company in a thick fog just outside the harbour, before heading back to Hawaii.

In Oahu and London it was feared that Hawaii, like Cuba, would be annexed by America.[37] With Russian-American relations suddenly very friendly, it was feared that San Francisco merchants, already suspected of promoting filibustering expeditions to Hawaii, might fit out privateers under the Russian flag and intercept the steamers of the British Pacific Steam Ship Company. These were attractive targets, carrying large quantities of treasure.[38] This Russo-American partnership would, if consummated, secure control of the north Pacific, to the detriment of British interests, notably those of the Hudson's Bay Company, whose local agent provided support for the Royal Navy at Oahu, and coincidentally reported these troubling rumours. Fortunately the new Anglo-French partnership could operate at Hawaii, unlike other areas of the Pacific where they claimed ownership, and the French had to accept British primacy, having alienated the Hawaiians by their heavy-handed policies in the 1840s. Building on trade and missionary contacts the Americans dominated Hawaii in the early 1850s, while their merchant ships and whalers filled the harbours. Their agent possessed great influence with King Kamehamaha III. Described by those who met him as courteous, good natured and indolent,[39] Kamehamaha allowed Americans to run his government.

The British were determined to resist American annexation, and any such thoughts had been rudely interrupted by the arrival of Price's combined allied squadron in July 1854, en route to the Russian coast, an effect reinforced by the duration of their stay.[40] This was an important mission, and delayed the move to Petropavlovsk. Once the allies had departed, the Americans hastened to settle the status of the islands, but the king went on a drunken spree, without signing away his sovereignty. Californian merchants and southern slave owners saw golden opportunities to advance their own particular interests in a new American state across the ocean. Fears that a filibustering expedition from California would open the way to annexation prompted the preparation of a treaty, but the king died suddenly on 15 December, leaving it unsigned. His successor was anti-missionary, and to an extent pro-British, while new forces among the settlers shifted the balance of power away from the Americans.[41] Throughout the critical period of change *Trincomalee* would be a frequent visitor to the islands, offering security against filibustering, and a visible presence to support British interests.

On arrival *Trincomalee* was towed into Port Diamond at Honolulu by teams of oxen, the difficult and narrow entrance being too dangerous to be attempted under sail. Houstoun found two American corvettes at anchor, firing minute guns for the recently deceased Commodore John Downes. *Trincomalee*'s pretensions as a sailing ship were confirmed when *Artemise* arrived three days later, with *Amphitrite* a further day astern of the French ship. The small harbour of Honolulu soon contained five American warships, two of which were big paddle steamers, and a pair each of British and French frigates. With so much naval power at hand it was obvious the issues at stake were important.[42] The allied ships had been sent to stop any American attempt to seize the islands.[43] While at anchor Houstoun produced a detailed report, noting a far superior anchorage that would hold the key to the islands' future.

> Ten miles to the North West of Honolulu is a magnificent harbour, spacious and deep enough to hold all the navies in the world, but its entrance through the Reef has only 12 feet water. Its adjoining district, Ewa or Pearl River, is flat and fertile for the most part.

In addition to the future prospects of Pearl Harbor, he was impressed by the location and trading prospects of the islands, and advised that Honolulu should be a free port.[44]

The funeral of one Hawaiian King, and the ceremonies for his successor, Kamehamaha IV, the following day (16 December), were attended by the British, French and American navies. Unfortunately, the attractions of the shore and the presence of large numbers of American merchant ships proved altogether too much for the crew, leading to a rash of straggling, and the far more serious offence of deserting. Those caught on board American ships were fined several months wages, and unless they were immune given 48 lashes. Houstoun spread the punishment over 27 days, to get the maximum deterrent effect from the spectacle. In addition, two British seamen who joined the ship, claiming to be free agents were still bound to American whalers and Houstoun was obliged to return them.

36 Log 18 September 1854: Adm 53/5839

37 Admiralty – Price 31 January 1854: Adm 2/1611, f463

38 Admiralty – Price 21 March & 7 April 1854: Adm 2/1612, ff10 & 80

39 Gough, *Royal Navy*, pp112-4. Martin, *Polynesian Journal*, p[illegible]1

40 Gough, *Royal Navy*, pp112-4

41 Brookes, J J, *International Rivalry in the Pacific Islands 1800-1875* (Berkeley CA 1941), pp208-18. Dudden, A P, *The American Pacific: From the Old China Trade to the Present* (Oxford 1992), pp54-61

42 Kuykendall, R S, *The Hawaiian Kingdom; 1854-1874* (Honolulu 1953), pp33-43

43 Gough, *Royal Navy*, p123

44 Houstoun Report December 1854: LB, pp81-7

The Russian War

Elsewhere the Pacific Squadron had already been to war. News that the Anglo-French Pacific squadron attack on Petropavlovsk had been repulsed with heavy losses after Admiral Price had committed suicide[45] had reached Houstoun in mid-December. *Trincomalee* sailed for Valparaiso at the end of January, with HMS *Eurydice*, and reached her destination at the end of March 1855, to be joined by a new flagship, the 84-gun HMS *Monarch*. Here *Trincomalee*'s crew helped a distressed British merchant ship:

> sent pinnace away to weigh the anchors of the British ship *Great Brittain* of Liverpool, which ship, owing to several of her crew having run away & some having struck work was unable to put to sea.[46]

After a stop at Callao *Trincomalee* and *Monarch* headed into the war zone, Russia's distant Pacific coast. They anchored in Awatska Bay off Petropavlovsk on 14 June with the rest of Rear-Admiral Henry Bruce's squadron.[47] Bruce had been sent out as soon as news of Price's death reached London, arriving at Valparaiso via the overland route through Panama in February 1855. He had arrived in time to blockade the Russian port as the ice cleared,[48] but the Russians had better local knowledge and slipped past the allies, leaving the town deserted. This was a pointed reminder that the Royal Navy could not afford to leave any part of the ocean uncharted. After Bruce and the fleet departed to seek the Russian ships at Sitka, Houstoun negotiated with the Russian Governor of Siberia for an exchange of prisoners. His selection for the role reflected the high opinion Bruce had formed of him, and a degree of linguistic competence (at least in French) above the average for Royal Navy officers of the day. In return for several days hard work he recovered two wounded sailors, one British, one French, for whom three Russians were exchanged.[49]

Trincomalee then set course to re-join the fleet at Esquimalt, hastened by an outbreak of scurvy.[50] Unable to find the Russians, Admiral Bruce was convinced that British interests required his support against American challenges over San Juan Island, and local unrest. Isolated from London by time and distance, Bruce was prepared to fight for the island.[51] The latest mail included the official register numbers of those crew members who had elected to join the Continuous Service scheme.[52] When the option was offered, 82 out of the initial muster of 157 seamen had signed.

Admiral Bruce was convinced that Esquimalt was a better location for the naval base than Victoria. The colony was making rapid progress, even in the past twelve months, with the price of supplies like meat and grain falling. He noted, with regret that government land recently sold would

45 Gough, *Royal Navy*, pp114-20. Stone, I R & Crampton, R J, 'A Disastrous Affair; the Franco-British Attack on Petropavlovsk, 1854', *The Polar Record* (1985), pp629-41

46 Ship's Log 4.00pm 1 April 1855: Adm 53/5389

47 Admiral Sir Henry William Bruce (1792-1863), Irish-born officer and protege of the brilliant Irish frigate Captain Henry Blackwood, had distinguished himself in action with Danish gunboats and American frigates before taking part in the Chesapeake Campaign of 1814 under Admiral Cockburn. In 1822 he married the daughter of Admiral Alexander Cochrane, Lord Cochrane's uncle, serving him and his son Sir Thomas Cochrane as flag captain in the 1820s and 1840s. He finally reached flag rank in 1852 after three years as Commodore of the West African Anti-Slavery patrol, where he captured Lagos.

48 Bruce – Sir Charles Wood (First Lord of the Admiralty) 10 April 1855: BL Add 49,549, f4

49 Bruce – Admiralty 17 July 1855: Adm 1/5655, Y83

50 Houstoun – Bruce 27 August 1855: LB, p109

51 Bruce – Wood 18 September 1855: BL Add 49549, f7

52 Houstoun – Admiralty 17 October 1855: LB, p114

53 Bruce – Admiralty 11 September 1855: Adm 1/5655, Y111 noted and sent to the Colonial Office

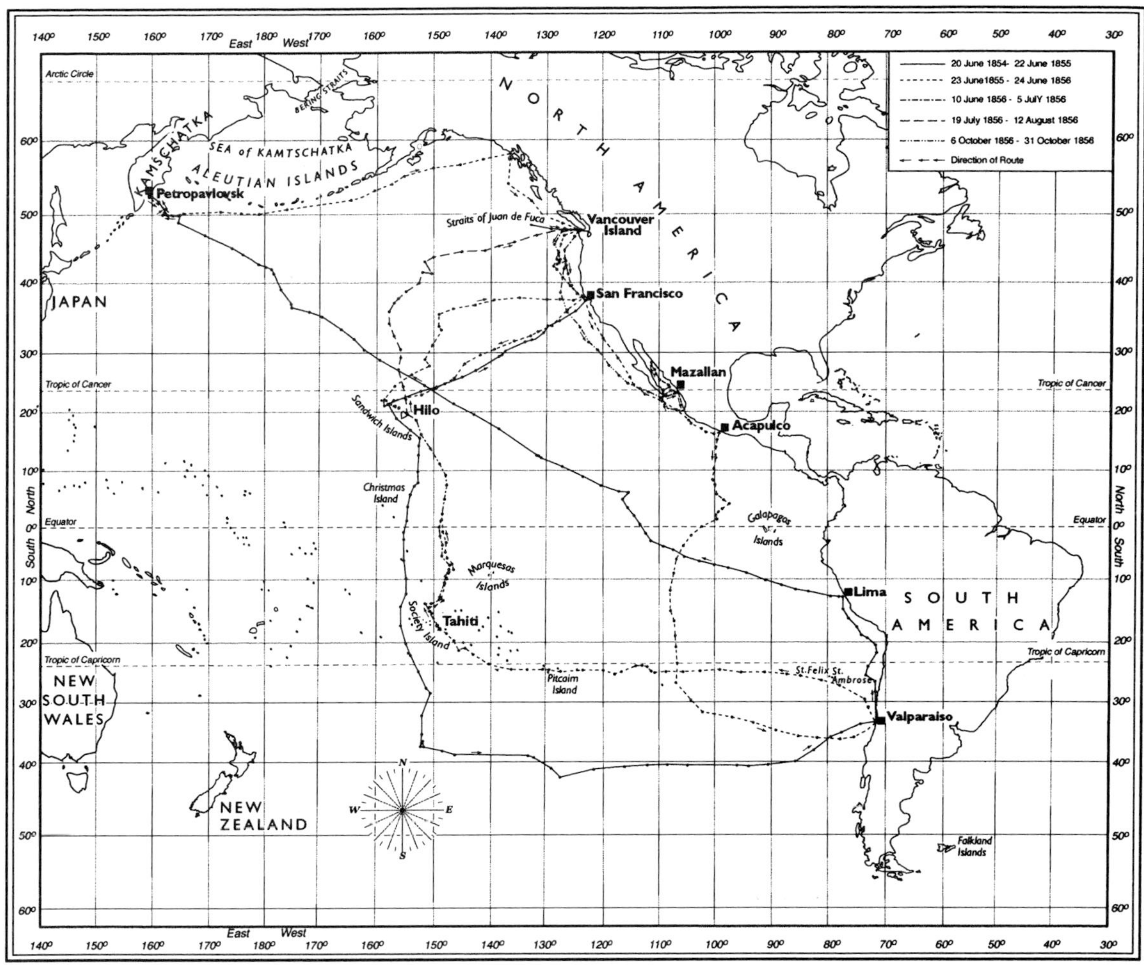

have to be re-purchased for a naval depot. Local timber would be a valuable resource,[53] as *Trincomalee* demonstrated, replacing her rotten bowsprit with a fresh stick in a week.

By 10 October *Trincomalee* was back at San Francisco. Here *Amphitrite* was anchored off Alcatraz on the tedious task of watching for any American or Russian ships trying to take supplies to Sitka or Petropavlovsk. *Trincomalee* then headed for Honolulu, where the usual team of oxen hauled her into harbour. On 16 November the French ensign was hoisted and guns fired to celebrate the capture of Sevastopol, which had occurred on 9 September. The same day the ship was heeled over to replace nineteen sheets of decayed copper. A very pointed salute to the anniversary of Hawaiian independence was fired, and two deserters had to be hunted down by a mounted party. Sailing east in December, *Trincomalee* called at Acapulco, and then went to Valparaiso where many of the squadron were assembling, *Amphitrite* to sail for home, while new ships arrived to replace her. Having heard that the Russians were now

The second part of the second commission. In total, during 1852–1857 the ship covered over 110,000 miles, with 944 days spent at sea, and 882 in harbour. The crew ate salt provisions for 978 days, and fresh for 848, and 144 of the original 240 man complement were still on board when she returned home; most of the changes were transfers, resignations or dismissals, for few men had died. (Roma Beaumont)

Wooden sailing ships have always been maintenance-intensive, with every aspect of their hulls and rig requiring constant attention, and not infrequent full services. In this view *Amphitrite* is refitting at San Francisco. The topmasts have been struck, and the main yards are lowered to the hammock netting. Despite appearances she could be ready for sea in a single day.

deep in the Amur valley, out of reach of his ships, Bruce chose to stay put, focused on denying the Russians supplies from San Francisco, and watching for American filibustering in Central America.[54] He also took the opportunity to analyse the prospects of the region, noting that it was at 'an immense distance from England, and contiguous to envious, grasping neighbours, it is difficult of access. . . . And would require the presence of a naval force to protect it from Indian as well as American aggression.' The naval force would have to be based at Esquimalt.[55]

Trincomalee's next cruise, which began in mid-April, was a search for the overdue HMS *Dido*, on a circuit heading west past Pitcairn Island, calling at Tahiti and Honolulu. Houstoun and his ship were already the Admiral's favourites, 'a pattern ship and captain'.[56] They heaved to in Bounty Bay, off Pitcairn Island, whose inhabitants had received much help from Admiral Moresby. This time there was no response from the shore. By this time the ship was showing evidence of wear and tear, her rigging frequently required running repairs, and she was in need a complete overhaul. In May *Trincomalee* arrived at Tahiti, where Houstoun was visited by Queen Pomare, who invited him to dine at the palace. The compliment was not quite what it seemed, for as Henry Martin had noted a decade earlier, the romance 'vanishes when the reality stands revealed in the form of a fat, oily woman without a particle of clothing but a cotton shirt.'[57] Houstoun took his ship north to Hawaii, where more copper was shifted. After loading a supply of bullocks she put to sea, and went through the fresh meat supply at the rate one animal every two or three days, while Houstoun heaved a position bottle overboard every five days.

A local police action

After a passage of twenty-four days the ship moored in Village Bay at Esquimalt, re-joining *Monarch*. This was a timely arrival, for the local situation required additional force. A native chief had shot and wounded a settler he suspected of seducing the woman he had intended to marry. Admiral Bruce instructed Commander Connolly of the *Monarch* to assemble a landing party of marines and seamen from the two ships, drill them, and place them all on board the *Trincomalee*. After the landing party had been exercised ashore, the ship was towed into the fairway. On

54 Bruce–Wood 25 February 1856: BL Add 49,549, f17

55 Bruce–Wood 16 April 1856: BL Add 49,549, f22

56 Bruce–Wood 16 April 1856, 25 May 1856: ibid, f22-5

57 Martin, *Polynesian Journal*, p56

30 August *Monarch*'s marines joined the ship, and the Hudson's Bay steamer *Otter* took *Trincomalee* in tow. With the Admiral and Sir James Douglas on board she moved along the coast and anchored in Cowichan Bay on the 31st.

The landing party went ashore the following morning, with Houstoun acting as Douglas's ADC. The nature of the operation can be gauged from the level of force deployed: two field guns, 159 marines, 254 seamen and 24 ambulance men. Clearly the Admiral and the Governor wanted to overawe the troublesome natives. After some deliberation, and intelligence gathering, Douglas decided to march five miles inland. The force set off on 2 September, and camped in a position inland of the village, on higher ground. A 'formidable force of armed indians' soon came out to face the landing party, with the suspect Tathlusut in their midst. They were armed, their faces painted black and they gave every appearance of being determined to resist. However, the British theatre of power proved too strong for them. When the two forces came to within arm's length Houstoun, probably on the advice of the Governor, drew his sword and grabbed the suspect; once Tathlusut had been secured the situation was defused. The British still had to endure a night in the open, exposed to torrential rain, but the following day a court of six officers and six petty officers was assembled, the prisoner was tried, found guilty of attempted murder and condemned to death. Just in case the point had not been grasped thus far, the proceedings occurred on the same spot where the crime had been committed. The execution was conducted that evening, and although it was clear the natives were far from satisfied, they were in no position to challenge the power of the Empire. The landing party left the scene the next day, and by the 5th had re-embarked, without a single casualty or accident. The officers remaining in the ship took the opportu-

A watercolour by Harold Wyllie depicting gun drill during this phase of the ship's career. (By courtesy of Captain D T Smith OBE, FNI, RN)

nity to survey the bay while waiting for the landing party to return, and they had heard gunfire on the 3rd. *Trincomalee* was towed out by *Otter* that evening, and arrived at Esquimalt the following day, when *Monarch*'s marines returned to their own ship.

Admiral Bruce was evidently well satisfied with the whole affair, commending Connolly, who had been given the command, to earn his promotion, along with Houstoun and the men. The Admiralty accepted Bruce's view, expressing their 'approbation of the judgement with which this expedition was conducted'.[58] Sir Charles Wood was pleased that everyone had done their duty 'remarkably well'.[59] Admiral Bruce was sufficiently impressed by the area, after the experience of operating ashore, that he produced a second report on the region. It would be an important colony, strategically placed between the Russian and American settlements, although the Americans were openly declaring that it was their 'destiny' to take it. He recognised that the Hudson's Bay Company was doing little to promote settlement, agriculture or mining, and as it was isolated, and not on the route to any other place, it had to be judged on its own merits.[60] In London Wood was in two minds:

> There is certainly much to be said for Vancouver's Island in regard to its capabilities in various ways, but the evil of it is its utter insulation from everything else. If we had a good way to it; or some ready means of communication, but in the event of being attacked I do not see very well how it could defend itself till succour arrived.[61]

A fine portrait of HMS *Trincomalee* during her second commission. The flush upperworks and gundeck paint scheme are in marked contrast to the original form and decoration of the ship when she was still configured as a frigate. There are only nine broadside guns mounted. (By courtesy of Dr Robert Prescott)

Instead he and Bruce looked at the possibility of moving the station base to Panama, which had 'the advantage of ready communication', even if it had serious disadvantages.[62] In the event the railway and telegraph solved the problem, and Esquimalt became the naval base for the Pacific Squadron.

The voyage home

After a month at anchor, preparing for sea, baptising a pair of local children and holding a farewell party for the local community, *Trincomalee* headed south. She stopped on the Mexican coast to transport treasure, for which the captain would receive a useful freight. The system was vital to international commerce in an age when piracy was still a problem; warships offered the most secure transport for valuables, and were paid a fee, fixed at one per cent of the value of the goods carried, for the security provided. The fee was then broken down, the local admiral taking one-quarter and Greenwich Hospital one-half, leaving one-quarter for the captain.[63] At Guyamas treasure was loaded intermittently for over a month, suggesting the local merchants were not ready when Houstoun arrived. Some of the treasure was discharged to the shore at Panama, for the overland passage to the Caribbean coast. While there William Williams, who had served his time, was discharged to the shore, having obtained a post on the Pacific Steam Ship Company's *Bogota.* On the passage south Houstoun attended to the domestic chores:

> Held a survey upon 1380 lbs of Bread, which was found unfit to be issued & to be so full of vermin that it was recommended to have it thrown overboard . . . which was therefore done.[64]

By mid-April *Trincomalee* had reached Valparaiso, where she met HMS *Havannah*[65] and the French frigate *Perseverance*, carrying a rear-admiral. Houstoun transferred powder and the sheet anchor to *Havannah*, and sent many spare stores ashore. In lieu, *Trincomalee* once again loaded condemned stores from the storeship *Nereus*, indicating that her commission was ending. The hold was filled with billets of firewood, and more treasure. Finally, on 2 May the ship weighed and set sail for the south. Admiral Bruce was sorry to see her go:

> Captain Houstoun is on his way to England in the *Trincomalee*, to arrive about the last of August. He is an officer of conspicuous merit and ability; one who reflects honour upon his country and upon our glorious profession.[66]

Pressing on round Cape Horn *Trincomalee* encountered no serious

58 Admiralty marginalia on Bruce–Admiralty 6 September 1856: Adm 1/5672, Y136

59 Wood–Bruce 15 October 1856: BL Add 49,566, f166

60 Bruce–Wood 22 September 1856: BL Add 49,549, f30

61 Wood–Bruce 15 November 1856: BL Add 49,566, f166

62 Wood–Bruce 31 January 1857, 17 February 1857: BL Add 49,566, ff236, 252

63 Bridge, *Recollections*, pp129-30

64 Log entry 3 April 1857: Adm 53/5841

65 Another Fifth Rate, the storeship at Valparaiso from 1843

66 Bruce–Wood 12 May 1857: BL Add 49,549, f66

problems, passing the Falkland Islands on the 24 May, although not in sight, and cast anchor in the magnificent harbour of Rio de Janiero on 21 June, where she joined HMS *Indefatigable* bearing the flag of Rear-Admiral Hope-Johnstone, HMS *Plumper* and HMS *Siren.* The storeship HMS *Madagascar* along with French, Russian, American, Spanish and Brazilian warships filled the naval anchorage. After discharging her freight and assisting to put out a fire at a foundry on shore, *Trincomalee* witnessed the arrival of the gunboat force that would serve in the Second China War, escorted by the paddle frigate HMS *Furious.* A 'distressed British Subject' was given passage home, but he did not last the voyage, dying at sea. On 29 June the boats of the squadron towed *Trincomalee* out of harbour, and she set a course for home.

By this time she had been in commission for over five years, and had spent over half her time at sea, covering some 110,000 miles. Of her original complement of 240 officers and men, 144 remained on board and would, with one exception, see out the commission. By now everyone was tired, and one officer found solace in a bottle:

> The Captain found acting lieutenant W U Miller, the officer of the watch, asleep upon his watch, and not sober, and in consequence the Captain placed him under arrest.[67]

On 29 August *Trincomalee* sailed into Plymouth Sound, saluting the flag of Vice-Admiral Sir Barrington Reynolds. The ship took on stores, and prepared for sea, only to find a recurrence of a recent problem:

> 0.15 The Captain assisted by several of the officers having in vain attempted to rouse Actg Lt W U Miller, the Officer of the Watch, who was laying on one of the Quarter-deck gun tackles; and apparently insensibly drunk, had him carried to his cabin by two Marines.[68]

Miller was placed under arrest fifteen minutes later, although he probably knew nothing of the matter for some time. On 3 September *Trincomalee* arrived at Sheerness harbour, where she saluted the flag of Vice-Admiral Sir Edward Harvey, and passed his inspection, before clearing the shell rooms and unroving the running rigging. The following the day she was towed up the Medway to Chatham by the tugs *African* and *Lizard*, securing alongside the hulk *Tartar* to clear powder and shell. Over the next six days the ship was stripped of her guns, stores, gear, rigging, and yards. On the 10th tragedy struck for the final time:

> 8.35 pm A man fell overboard out of one of the main deck ports between ship and Hulk. A strong tide running at the time, manned boats & made

> search for him, but without success. Mustered ship's company and found missing Alex McDonald AB.

Inverness-born McDonald, then 30 years old, may have been drunk or in search of drink; his record reveals that he was a man with a problem, and the hulk offered an opportunity for smuggling drink onboard. It was a sad, but hardly surprising final act to a cruise with more than its fair share of drink-related offences. On the 11th the ballast was cleared and stacked ashore, and on the 12th the ship went alongside the sheer hulk, to have her lower masts hoisted out. After Captain Edward Pellew Halstead, the Captain Superintendant of the Yard had paid the crew, *Trincomalee*'s pendant was hauled down at 6.00 pm on the 15th. Ninety of her crew, West Country men who had signed on at Devonport and entered the Continuous Service system, went back home on a naval steamer.[69] The concept of seamen belonging to one of the three Home Ports would develop, as a necessary element in the Continuous Service system. Admiral Bruce had been so impressed with the ship that he asked to have her sent back, because she had 'spacious stowage and is a heavily armed ship – good in every way'.[70] However, such praise would be to no avail.

Throughout her front-line career *Trincomalee* had played a useful, although hardly central role in the maintenance of empire. Twenty-five years in the reserve reflected the success of the British diplomacy, deterrence and naval power, while her two commissions linked the outermost reaches of the empire to the commercial and strategic concerns of London. This was a typical career, important, but not epoch-making, and in that sense, as in so many others, the ship can represent the Royal Navy and the nation it served. Not that the nation, or the Navy had done with her yet.

By contrast Houstoun had finished with the sea: he married well in 1860, and spent much of the rest of his life living at Sissinghurst Place in Kent, and sitting as a Justice of the Peace for the county. Promoted to retired rear-admiral in 1865 and full admiral in 1877, he died at his London home in Eaton Square on 17 May 1891, of bronchitis. The importance of Houstoun's work, and that of naval forces generally in the early days of British Columbia was recognised when his name was used on the chart of the British Columbia coast at Houstoun Passage and Wallace Island by Captain Frederick Richards of the survey ship HMS *Plumper*. These names joined the Trincomali Channel in the Gulf Islands named for his ship.[71] This was a high compliment, coming from so eminent a navigator, and may stand as an epitaph for an excellent officer of the Victorian navy. Houstoun's range of skills and attainments reflected the complex demands placed on captains called on to act so far from home or higher authority.

67 Log 10 July 1857 4.35am: Adm 53/5842

68 Log 1 September 1857: Adm 53/5842

69 Houstoun – Harvey 11 September 1857: LB, p354

70 Bruce – Wood 16 November 1857: BL Add 49,549, f95

71 Shardlow, T, 'HMS *Trincomalee*', in *Pacific Yachting* (October 2000), p42

Men of the *Trincomalee*

These entries have been drawn from the ship's log and muster books. While only a sample, they show how much information is available about the men of the nineteenth-century Royal Navy.

TWO DRUNKS:

William Beer: Blacksmith aged 30, born in Plymouth, 5ft 5in, fresh complexion, brown eyes, dark hair. Inoculated for smallpox, married.

Served in the Royal Navy since 1844, his last ship being HMS *Pantaloon* paid off 26 February 1852. Over the commission he would receive nine fines for straggling ranging from £1 to £1.45. Earned a good conduct badge May 1854, lost this April 1856. While he entered the Continuous Service system he lost his rating, being demoted steadily to Armourer and then Ordinary Seaman, before recovering to Armourer by the time the ship paid off.

Robert Gullett: Able Seaman. Devonport-born, 5ft 7in, fair skin, blue eyes, dark brown hair. Vaccinated, single.

Entered Royal Navy as a boy on board HMS *Impregnable*, the Devonport flagship in June 1843. Continuous Service. Last ship *Amazon*, indifferent or fair character. In *Trincomalee*'s book noted as fair, but 'ability good'.

Died on board, of a drink-related illness.

BOSUN'S MATES

John Andrews: Bosun's Mate, aged 44, born at sea, 5ft 8½in, dark complexion, dark eyes and hair. Three good conduct badges. Had been vaccinated. Single. Held a Greenwich Hospital Out-Pension No 1966.

Joined the Navy in 1818, served continuously to 1838, returned in 1841 and served until paid off from HMS *Express* in January 1852.

William Ellis: Bosun's Mate aged 47, Portsmouth-born, 5ft 6in, dark complexion, dark eyes, dark brown hair. Cut scars on left leg and hand. Vaccinated. Married. Held Greenwich Out-Pension No 1482, therefore did not enter Continuous Service.

Entered Royal Navy in 1823. Last ship HMS *Rattler* as Bosun's Mate. Vg character. Had three good conduct badges. *Trincomalee* character vvg.

The ideal type of petty officer: steady, professional, and linked to the service by a pension for wounds.

Thomas Knowles: Bosun's Mate aged 26, born at Torpoint, 5ft 8½in, dark complexion, hair and eyes. Woman and heart tattooed on left arm. vaccinated, single.

Entered Royal Navy 1845, last ship HMS *Philomel*, 1850-52, then briefly a Dockyard rigger. Took Continuous Service. Brought one good conduct badge to the ship, but lost this and his rate in December 1852 after a drunken and riotous run ashore at Valparaiso. He gained badges on 28 December 1853 and 24 December 1855, but lost both on 3 November1856. Discharged to HMS *Havannah* 22 April 1857 with a good character.

Exchanged with:
William Danniford: Bosun's Mate. Born Spilbrook Cornwall September 1826, 5ft 7½in, fresh complexion, grey eyes, light brown hair.

Joined Navy in 1847. To Pacific in HMS *Virago* in 1851, to *Havannah* in 1855, then to *Trincomalee* in 1857; one good conduct badge.

Thomas Davis: Bosun. Plymouth-born, aged 36, 5ft 6in, fresh complexion, blue eyes, light hair. Had had smallpox, married.

On ship from start. Discharged to Devonport Guardship, no record of commission.

THERE WERE THREE 'BAD CHARACTERS' GIVEN ON THE COMMISSION:

William Chadwick: Able Seaman, aged 27 born Deal, Kent, fair skin, blue eyes, brown hair. Married, vaccinated. Ship tattoed on right arm.

In service since 1846, joined ship 5 August 1852, last in HMS *Gladiator*. Continuous Service. Two good conduct badges earned, but discharged to the shore at Valparaiso with a bad character on 10 April 1856; not clear why.

John Julian: Midshipmen's Steward. Born Stonehouse, age 29, sallow complexion, grey eyes, brown hair, married.

Sent home with a bad character via depot ship *Nereus* at Callao 4 April 1853; probably theft.

Thomas Wright: Able Seaman. Born Cawsand, Cornwall, age 28, 5ft 2in, fair complexion, hazel eyes, brown hair. Anchor tattoed on right arm. Had suffered smallpox.

Entered Royal Navy ? paid off from *Queen*, with a fair character. Earned one good conduct badge, three fines for straggling, beaten 36 lashes 15 April 1856, accused two men of 'taking indecent liberties with each other' but forced to retract 13 October 1856. Discharged to *Impregnable* with bad character.

BOY

George Prince. Boy, first class. Born in Plymouth 1 May 1841, still growing, fair complexion, grey eyes, light brown hair.

Entered the service at Devonport, in July 1855 under Continuous Service terms, as second class boy. Sent out to the Pacific with a draft for the fleet. Joined *Trincomalee* as a second class boy in October, was rated as a first class boy in July 1857, and transferred back to the Devonport flagship HMS *Impregnable* at the end of the commission.

Chapter Six

A Century of Harbour Service and Youth Training

Royal Naval Drill Ship

ONCE PAID off *Trincomalee* was placed 'in Ordinary' at Chatham, as part of the Navy's reserve. However, the Crimean War had confirmed what *Trincomalee*'s experience in the Pacific had suggested, that in future all warships would require steam power, at least for coastal duties. Even as *Trincomalee* had headed for home the First Lord of the Admiralty pronounced her death sentence as a front-line warship. In 1857 he told the House of Commons that 'sailing vessels, though useful in time of peace, would never be employed again during war.'[1] Yet, while *Trincomalee*'s days in the front-line were over, she remained in fine shape, requiring only minimal repairs. In April 1860 *Trincomalee* was ordered to be fitted out as a Training Ship for the Royal Naval Reserve, which cost a mere £1492. She was commissioned in this new role at Chatham on 16 December 1860, by Commander Thomas Heard with a crew of twenty-seven mostly specialist petty officers and ratings. She was towed up to Sunderland the next month, to act as a tender to the existing drill ship, HMS *Castor*. For her new role she needed a battery of heavy guns to train the reservists, and was fitted with ten 32-pounder 50cwt guns and six 8-inch shell guns.

The Naval Reserve proved to be a critical step in making the Royal Navy national; it took warships to the major seaports, and recruited local men, who gradually lost their age-old prejudice against the service. The reservists were enlisted at 15 or 16, with parental consent, and after passing a medical examination received a bounty of £6 for their ten-year enlistment. Once over 18 they were paid at the same daily rate as ordinary seamen while undergoing annual training. The old wooden walls that served as training hulks, like the unfortunate Admiral Price's flagship HMS *President* in London, or the *Minerva* at Hull, have remained part of the local landscape–the Royal Navy's base in London is still HMS *President* although it is now ashore, while the name *Minerva* lives on in Hull as a dockside pub.

On 9 October 1862 *Trincomalee* had a brush with greatness when the Chancellor of the Exchequer, William Gladstone, an Elder Brother of Trinity House, visited Sunderland. Gladstone inspected *Trincomalee* as part of his tour of the docks. Characteristically, he found the time to make a short speech to her crew, although he was not particularly enthu-

1 Sir Charles Wood, Hansard CLXV, col 915

2 Morley, J, *Life of Gladstone* (London 1903), Vol II, p78

The training ship HMS *Trincomalee* at Sunderland, with her permanent complement of officers and men. She would be visited by Gladstone, then Chancellor of the Exchequer in 1862.

siastic about the task, noting in his diary: 'I had to address the naval men'.[2] Even so he expressed his satisfaction with the ship and the men. Then he spoke in the town about government policy on the American Civil War, before going to Middlesborough, where he spoke on commercial and social progress.

In December 1862 *Trincomalee* was elevated to the status of an independent command, and came to Hartlepool for the first time, under Commander Edward Field. Between 1862 and 1868 her permanent crew of 32 was rotated, so that 58 men are named in her muster book, but of these only 10 were from the North East, and of them only John Dodds came from nearby Seaton Carew. Three were from Sunderland, the others hailed from South Shields, Castle Eden, Whitby, Malton and York. These local men tended to hold posts not requiring naval skills, like Cook or Ship's Corporal. By contrast most of the seamen were typical mid-Victorian naval ratings, coming from the South Coast.

Commanders of HMS *Trincomalee* 1862-1895

These officers all held the substantive rank of Commander, and the majority of them left the ship on promotion to Captain.

Thomas Heard	4.1862–2.1863
Edward Field	1.1863–7.1864
Walter Pollard	7.1864–7.1867
Edward. Thomas Nott	7.1867–4.1870
Edward White	4.1870–2.1872
James G Mead	2.1872–12.1872
Richard G Kinahan	12.1872 paid off
Aretas J V Collins	1.1873–1880
Edward Pilkington	1880–1884
Henry T Clanchy	1884–1889
Wentworth T Bailey	1889–1894
Howard F May	1894–10.1895

Trincomalee recommissioned at Hartlepool in March 1868, with the four Royal Marines being replaced by locally recruited Ship's Corporals. These men required no maritime skills. One local man made a big impression on the ship, and it was far from favourable. The post of Warrant Officer Cook had been filled from December 1868 by Newcastle-born Thomas Cain, a new entry to the service. Cain left the ship in February 1869 to be replaced by West Hartlepool-born Thomas Warnaby, aged 22. Although recorded on the ship's books as bearing a good character, Warnaby was no angel. He was dismissed from the ship on 22 November. His dismissal was inevitable, since he could no longer do his duty because he had been: 'Imprisoned for 4 months by the Civil Power for theft on shore at West Hartlepool'. Warnaby was replaced by John Dodds, of Seaton Carew, who had served on the previous commission, and served until February 1871. Like several other local men Dodds was discharged to the shore to join the local Customs Service. He was followed by William Charlton, of Stranton, and then John Crawford of Sunderland, all three of whom had very good characters.

Paid off in December 1872 *Trincomalee* was modified, and fitted with new, and much heavier 6½-ton 7-inch rifled muzzle-loading guns to keep the reservists up to date with the latest service weapons; the training arc at the midships gunports dates from this period. The upper deck was also housed over at this time. In February 1877 *Trincomalee* left Hartlepool under tow for Southampton Water, where she would be moored for the last eighteen years of her naval service. By the time she was finally replaced by a new drill ship, HMS *Medea* on 12 October 1895, she was not worth moving, and was left 'in reserve' until sold for breaking up. On 19 May 1897 Read's Shipbreakers of Portsmouth Camber paid the princely sum of £1323 for the old ship, and it seemed her time had come. She would be converted into teak timber for re-use in ships, possibly as decking, or for furniture.

But before much ship-breaking could be done *Trincomalee* was saved for another spell of harbour service. The Royal Navy drill ships had set a pattern for sea training that chimed in with the manpower needs of a maritime empire and the educational and disciplinary shortcomings of underprivileged urban boys. Taken afloat pauper boys could be given their basic training, at an early age, in the safety of a harbour, before transferring to sea-going vessels. This solved a social problem ashore, saved training time and expense for any future employer, and ensured that the new hands were useful from the outset. The Marine Society had pioneered this form of training in 1786, and other philanthropic bodies were inspired to follow suit in the latter half of the nineteenth century. While most have fallen away over time, the Marine Society continues to help young people to enter the Royal and Merchant Navies.

3 Littlewood, K & Butler, B, *Of Ships and Stars: Maritime Heritage and the Founding the National Maritime Museum, Greenwich* (London 1998), pp35-9

The Cobb era, 1897-1932

The man who saved the ship. Geoffrey Wheatley Cobb, seen here shortly before his death in 1931, was determined to build on the naval heritage of the nation, and train boys for a career at sea. His energy, and funds, saved the *Trincomalee* from the ship-breakers in 1897, and kept her usefully employed for a generation.

The ship's saviour was Geoffrey Wheatley Cobb (1859-1932). Inspired by his father, who had combined a legal career with local antiquarian and restoration interests, Geoffrey Cobb had a passion for the sea. By the early 1890s he was independently wealthy, having secured a share in a Rhondda coalfield. His wealth enabled him to save the old wooden sailing line of battle ship HMS *Foudroyant* in 1892; she had been Nelson's flagship in 1799-1800, and spent many years as a gunnery training ship. He planned to run her as a working ship, touring coastal resorts under tow and training boys. Having paid £5500 for the hulk, and restored her for another £3400, he seemed unaware that a large square rigged ship was a particularly dangerous means of transport, and never more so than when close to a lee shore. Anchored off Blackpool she was driven ashore and wrecked by a gale on 16 June 1897.[3] At the time Cobb had only six competent hands in his crew, and twenty boys in a ship that needed ten times as many men to handle under sail. No-one was hurt, but the ship was beyond salvage, and

The original two-decker ship of the line HMS *Foudroyant*, famously the flagship of Lord Nelson, being dismantled before Wheatley Cobb rescued her in 1892. Nothing of the original upper deck remains and shows how much of the ship was reconstructed.

Despite the extensive demolition Wheatley Cobb had the *Foudroyant* rebuilt and restored to her sea-going condition, using original building plans. She then set off under tow on a tour to the coastal resorts, to raise funds and recruit trainees.

A disaster at Blackpool. Anchored off a lee shore and then driven ashore by a gale on 16 June 1897 the *Foudroyant* was soon beyond repair. The ease with which her guns tore through the hull suggests the repairs were not as sturdy as the original structure. Although the ship was broken up where she lay, many of the guns, and other materials were salvaged.

only fit for breaking up.[4] Her timbers were converted into furniture, table tennis bats and even collar studs by enterprising northern businessmen.

Despite the loss of a national treasure Cobb wanted to carry on, and quickly asked the Admiralty for another ship. They directed him to Read's, who sold him the *Trincomalee*. Cobb had her towed over to East Cowes on the Isle of Wight, where she would spend the next five years being refitted for her new role. Timbers already removed were replaced, but unfortunately not with teak, while a new poop was built to house a large wardroom, and a false forecastle to accommodate bathrooms and heads for the trainees. Some delay may have been caused by the death of his father in December 1897, leaving Geoffrey to take over Caldicott Castle and other property. In addition, the ship was frequently moved, as Cobb started a life-long career of arguing with the harbour authorities about moorings and harbour dues. This time he wanted to pay at the yacht rate!

In September 1903 the *Trincomalee* was towed to Falmouth, but she arrived on the 19th as the *Foudroyant*, a ripe source of confusion. Cobb had renamed his relatively undistinguished new vessel after her famous predecessor. In the Official Register of British Ships she became '124603 *Foudroyant* No 6 1907 Port of Falmouth'. On arrival the new *Foudroyant* was docked until early November. Although the training programme had started, Cobb was soon on the move, this time towing the ship to Milford Haven in June 1904.

Once in Milford Haven the ship spent a year moored close to the Naval Dockyard at Pembroke, before moving to Milford in May 1905. Here he loaded guns and stores salved from the original *Foudroyant*. Cobb's mission was widely praised, both as a relief to inner city poverty, and as an aid to the maintenance of naval mastery. The motto 'Remember Nelson' was the first thing to be seen on boarding the ship, and was doubly appropriate, being the signal flown by the great man's protege Sir William Hoste as he led a frigate squadron into battle off Lissa in 1811.

In September 1905 Cobb took the ship back to Falmouth, with several Milford boys among his complement. On Trafalgar Day (21 October) 1905 the *Foudroyant* was dressed overall with appropriate flags for the centenary. The less agreeable side of shipboard life surfaced the following year. In April 1906 Edward Lashmoor absconded with his blue serge suit, blanket and other kit items after sixteen months on board. He was quickly apprehended, and given fourteen days in gaol for his crime. Fortunately the other boys made amends by showing up particularly well in the local regatta a month later, and Cobb's work continued to receive wide local support.

That *Foudroyant* was an efficient outfit was entirely down to Cobb,

4 Birbeck, T T, *The Foudroyant* (Chepstow 1966), pp107-14

who lived on board as owner, commander and training supervisor, with a small team of professionals. The boys were entered without charge, so the entire project was run on his funds. With the ship full to capacity and more entrants available, he began to look for another ship. His friend the marine artist W L Wyllie drew his attention to HMS *Implacable*, an old 74, captured only a month after serving at Trafalgar as the French *Duguay-Trouin*. After an active career with the Royal Navy lasting into the 1840s she became a training ship, until her final task, as the boy's training ship at Devonport came to an end in 1908. At a Royal Academy dinner in May 1909 Wyllie circulated the guests, the usual Edwardian collection of eminent men from all walks of life (including the great imperial poet, storyteller and navalist Rudyard Kipling), with a round-robin, which was then sent to the First Lord of the Admiralty, asking for the ship to be given to Cobb, who would cover all the costs. Eventually Edward VII intervened and the ship was duly passed to Cobb on indefinite loan.[5]

In 1912 the *Implacable* was towed to Falmouth to join the smaller *Foudroyant*, and the two ships provided initial seamanship training to young men before they entered the Royal or Merchant Navies throughout the First World War. However, by 1925 even Cobb's coal-fired generosity was unable to sustain the rising costs of the loaned vessel. With the help of Admiral of the Fleet Earl Beatty, Cobb set up the *Implacable* Committee, essentially a group of his friends, to raise funds to maintain the large ship. With support from the shipping magnate Sir James Caird the old 74 was repaired. This left Cobb free to devote his efforts to training on board the *Foudroyant*. In 1927 yet another dispute with harbour authorities, this time about *Foudroyant*'s mooring, saw him move her back to Milford, while *Implacable* remained at Falmouth under the direction of her Committee. Cobb died in 1931, having devoted close on forty years to the first-hand provision of sea training for the disadvantaged as the basis for a better life and a larger supply of seamen. It was a remarkable example of late Victorian public-spirited philanthropy. With him an era passed. After 1918 the state proved rather better at dealing with inner city poverty.

Suddenly finding herself the owner of a wooden warship, and the custodian of another, Mrs Cobb consulted Lt Col Harold Wyllie, the son of the artist. Probably on Wyllie's advice she had the two ships moved to Portsmouth, where they were re-united under Wyllie's direction. Mrs Cobb had tried to sell the *Foudroyant*, to fund the running of the larger ship, but these plans fell through, and she made over the ownership of the *Foudroyant* to the *Implacable* Committee. The two ships were now the sole responsibility of the Committee.

The Chairman of the Committee was an old friend of Cobb, Sir Owen Seaman, Bt, editor of the satirical magazine *Punch*, although much of the

5 Ibid, pp41-2

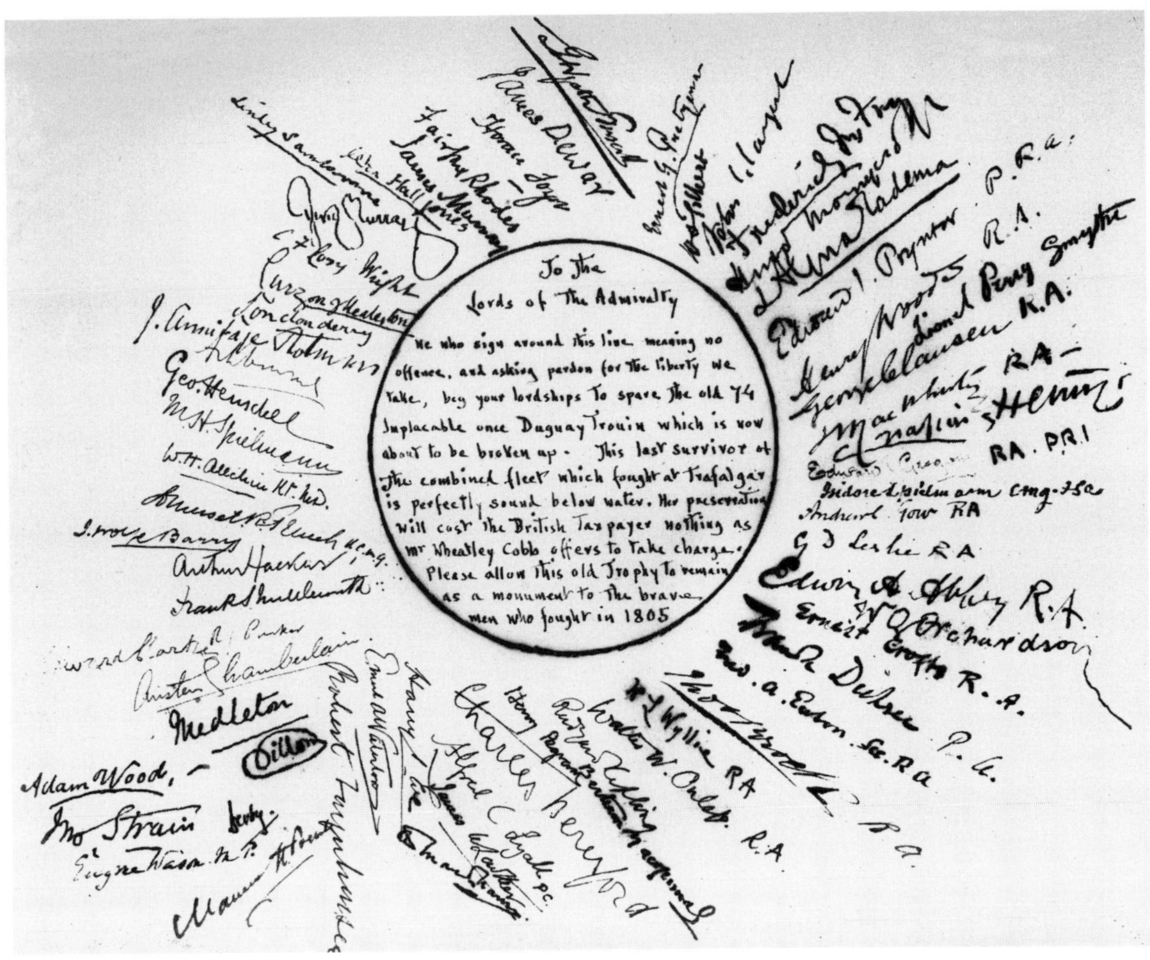

To the
Lords of the Admiralty

We who sign around this line, meaning no offence, and asking pardon for the liberty we take, beg your lordships to spare the old 74 Implacable once Duguay Trouin which is now about to be broken up. This last survivor of the combined fleet which fought at Trafalgar is perfectly sound below water. Her preservation will cost the British Taxpayer nothing as Mr Wheatley Cobb offers to take charge. Please allow this old Trophy to remain as a monument to the brave men who fought in 1805

Devised in imitation of the sailors' traditional method of addressing their superiors, this 'round-robin' letter was signed by many of the Great and the Good and sent to the First Lord of the Admiralty.

impetus came from the Secretary, Geoffrey Callender, later Director of the National Maritime Museum. The other committee members included naval officers, both serving and retired, an Elder Brother of Trinity House, artists, broadcasters, explorers and an adequate supply of the great and good, who lent their names, rather than any expertise, to the project. The Committee met nearly every month somewhere in London, often at Trinity House, and occasionally on board the ships. Seaman died in 1936, by which time the Committee had become part of the Society for Nautical Research, and as Callender was the Chairman of the Society he could not also chair the *Implacable* Committee, so he secured Vice-Admiral Humphrey Hugh Smith as Chairman.

Meanwhile Harold Wyllie overhauled the training objectives of the ships. The original clients, destitute boys, were replaced by boys and girls of a rather higher class, taking short residential training courses. The ships would act as a floating adventure holiday centre. The children were accommodated on board *Foudroyant* and used facilities on both ships.

Foudroyant, ex-*Trincomalee* lying at Falmouth, as a training ship. The two-level stern gallery and modified gunport arrangement imposed by Cobb are obvious.

The young trainees were funded by schools, parents, and nautical organisations like the Sea Scouts and Sea Rangers. At the same time Wyllie planned a long-term refit for the *Implacable*.

A contemporary advert for the ships set out their role:

> ***FOUDROYANT*** is used today for the sea-training of the younger generation. Every year hundreds of boys and girls spend unforgettable weeks on board, learning the elements of seamanship and benefiting greatly from their brief experience of nautical comradeship and discipline.
>
> During the summer months from March to October, the ship can accommodate boys or girls from 11 years of age upwards, either in parties or independently, for periods of either one or two weeks, or for week-ends only. The course of training includes the opportunity for learning to handle boats under oars, sail and power, and instruction is given in signalling, knots and bends, compass work and swimming. Facilities are given by the naval authorities for visits to HMS *Victory*, and to modern warships of all kinds as opportunity offers. There are also lectures, film shows, concerts, competitions and regattas from time to time.
>
> Special training programmes can be planned by arrangement.

The new residents did not always find the nautical life to their taste, and recorded their thoughts in verse.

All my Trials!

My family just doesn't like me
They wanted me out of the way
They sent off to *Foudroyant*
The slaveship of Portsmouth Bay

And now I am on the *Foudroyant*
The life here just ain't very gay
The hammocks ain't fit for a slum life
The slaveship of Portsmouth Bay

The food is the piggies left overs
We get 'happy weekend' everyday
The tea is the last meal's dish water
The slaveship of Portsmouth Bay

I can't say much for the cutter
It threatens to sink every day
The hole in the bottom don't 'elp us
The slaveship of Portsmouth Bay

And now I am leaving *Foudroyant*
They're dumping me off here today
You'll see me back here next summer
In spite of what I say

Anon (undated poem by pre-1939 trainee).

Gun drill. Barefoot crew haul on the tackles, under the supervision of Wheatley Cobb himself. The complement in the pre-1914 era consisted of boys and young men in training for a career at sea. The variety of ages is obvious. (National Maritime Museum, London)

As the poet observes, conditions on board were hardly ideal, even by the standards of the time. However, the young are highly adaptable, and most found the change to be a positive experience. The ships needed a major overhaul, but had to balance scarce funds between training and education, staff costs, and maintaining the ships. The regular income of the ships only covered day-to-day expenditure, so any long-term refurbishment had to rely on fund-raising. In June 1937 *The Times* supported one such appeal by printing a letter signed by seven Admirals of the Fleet, which laid particular stress on the need to introduce the youth of the country to the sea. The letter pointed out that 'the masses of people who depend for existence on sea-borne food supplies, would, without sea services, under war conditions, be reduced to famine in a fortnight. The *Implacable* and *Foudroyant* at Portsmouth have for years supplied a unique corrective.' While the basic economics of maintaining old wooden ships have not changed, the message has undergone a considerable shift of emphasis!

Between 1932 and 1939 some 10,000 young people took up training courses on board the two ships. They learnt elementary seamanship and practical boat handling, with much of the day spent in the ten sailing, eight rowing and two motor boats that belonged to the two ships. The daily routine was regulated by a set of Standing Orders derived from those used by Captain William Parker when he commanded the frigate HMS *Amazon* in the Mediterranean in Lord Nelson's fleet between 1803

Wheatley Cobb had ensured that the *Foudroyant*, ex-*Trincomalee* was soon joined by another historic ship, the old 74-gun ship of the line HMS *Implacable.* Previously the French *Duguay-Trouin* she had fought at Trafalgar, and been captured a fortnight later. Although scuttled in December 1949, her tragic loss was the spark that galvanised post-war attempts to preserve historic ships, and helped ensure that the same fate did not befall the *Trincomalee.* The figurehead and stern gallery of the *Implacable* are now featured at the National Maritime Museum.

and 1805.[6] Parker was an outstanding officer, but he was also St Vincent's nephew, Nelson's protege and, at the end of his career, the admiral who nominated John Fisher for the Royal Navy.

Foudroyant and *Implacable* at war

On 3 September 1939 Britain was once again at war with Germany, but this time the daily routine of the ships would be affected to a far greater extent, both by the threat of air attack, and the changed nature of their work. In 1914-1918 they were supplying shore-trained seaman recruits, who were very attractive to the Royal and Merchant Navies, whereas their current products had less obvious wartime uses. Furthermore, many of those involved in running the ship were required elsewhere. Colonel Wyllie returned to the Air Force, and Captain Clement Brown RA, the Hon Treasurer and for the duration Hon Secretary also, was recalled to service in 1943, despite being blind in one eye. Even so he found the time to run the business affairs of the ships. Chief Officer Michael O'Loughlin lived on board, alone and under the constant threat of air attacks. This threat was very real with Portsmouth Dockyard only a mile away. Committee meetings dwindled from monthly to annually, and few were able to attend. Vice-Admiral Smith, although retired and 65 years of age, went back to sea, as a Convoy Commodore, but tragically drowned when his ship was sunk by enemy action in September 1940. His Commodore's pendant still hangs in Portchester Castle Church, in sight of the mooring of the two ships.

For the first nine months of war day training had been provided for local sea scouts, but the fall of France put Portsmouth in the front line. With the Luftwaffe only fifty miles away the Committee, now led by Geoffrey Callender, accepted that training could not continue and offered the ships to the Admiralty. Initially they were used for storage. In August 1940 *Foudroyant* was on the receiving end of war, for the first time, when a bomb hit the port gunwale, smashed through the heads and exploded in the harbour mud between the two ships. An impressive column of mud and water lifted both *Foudroyant*'s bow, and *Implacable*'s stern clear of the water, but neither ship suffered any serious damage. Even the glazing in the stern galleries of the *Implacable* survived. Despite their exposed position the ships escaped further damage.

In early 1943 *Implacable* was adapted for use as a naval training ship, and in June resumed her place with her wooden stable-mate to form a new naval unit, HMS *Foudroyant*. This choice reflected the fact that the Royal Navy had already re-used the name *Implacable* on a brand new fleet aircraft carrier. Chief Officer O'Loughlin was commissioned as a lieutenant into the Royal Naval Volunteer Reserve (RNVR), while Col

6 These were probably drawn from Phillimore, A, *Life of Admiral Sir William Parker* (London 1876), Vol I, pp192-205

Wyllie was transferred from the Air Ministry as a lieutenant-commander RNVR to take command and act as Director of Training at the request of the Admiralty. The new unit provided instruction in flag and light signalling and seamanship for new entry naval ratings, many of them specially selected from the Sea Cadet Corps for communication duties, and referred to as the 'Bounty Boys'. The two ships carried on in this role until the end of the war, when they were closed down and reduced to a care and maintenance status until their future could be determined.

Post-war readjustment

When the *Implacable* Committee met in July 1945 to consider the post-war situation, they faced major problems. When Geoffrey Callender died the following year, they also needed a new chairman. Admiral Sir Percy Noble, wartime Commander-in-Chief Western Approaches, accepted the post. The main issue was to settle the future of the training programme, and the ships in which it had been conducted. The Admiralty was prepared to release the ships; they had, after all, now been obsolete for a century. Unfortunately neither was in very good condition, and there would be no compensation due for the damage done to the *Implacable*, which was still Admiralty property. After hearing an estimate that it would cost of £200,000 to restore her, the Committee declined the Admiralty's offer to return her, and Sir James Caird declined to make funds available for restoration.[7] Other options for her future were considered, including towing her round to be preserved at Greenwich, while the French Navy had expressed interest in her return. Eventually she was sacrificed to the austere economic conditions of the age, being towed out into the Channel and ceremonially scuttled on 2 December 1949, under the flags of the two countries that had owned her.[8] The loss of this historic veteran stimulated a much greater interest in the preservation of historic ships, in large part led by Frank Carr, the new Director of the National Maritime Museum. The Museum managed to save the figurehead and a proportion of the stern decoration, and these items are now prominently displayed at Greenwich.

The *Foudroyant* was less badly damaged, and the Admiralty offered to return her with some compensation, although it was not enough for the task of repairing the ship. The Committee met on 30 July 1947, with several dockyard experts attending, to advise on the best way forward. After a long and often heated discussion Admiral Noble proposed that the ship be disposed of as soon as possible, to conserve capital and income until the time was right to launch a new appeal to the public, and secure a more modern vessel for the training role. The motion was defeated by eight votes to six, and the Committee resolved to carry on with a training programme directed by Col Wyllie for a period of six months, after which a further report would be considered. For obvious reasons the Committee was renamed the *Foudroyant* Committee around this time.

In August 1950 an Admiralty warrant, signed by Earl Mountbatten, authorised the ship to fly the Blue Ensign with the distinguishing mark of a flash of lightning with a red capital F in the fly for such time as she should be employed for the vocational training of boys ands girls in seamanship. The same year Admiral Sir Clement Moody replaced Admiral Noble as Chairman of the Committee.

In the early 1950s the educational role of the ship was emphasised by appointing an education officer, while local and national education officers joined the Board of Governors. This strategy paid off handsomely in 1951-53 when the reports sent in by Inspectors from the Ministry of Education led to a Government grant, which would be paid until 1986.

The *Foudroyant* Trust, 1959-1992

In 1959 the *Foudroyant* Trust was set up as a Limited Company under a new Chairman, Frank Carr, who would hold office until he retired from Greenwich in 1967. The new arrangement avoided the danger of Committee members becoming individually liable for the debts of the ship. As ever they comprised a mixture of the professionally concerned, those with a personal interest, and others who could lend weight and influence. Fund-raising, local and national lobbying, newspaper support, links to other organisations and from 1974 even the descendant of a former Captain, Commander Richard Warren RN, helped to keep the ship in business. The new status also necessarily ended the long term official relationship with the Society for Nautical Research, although personal contact was maintained at a high level.

On board the ship training remained popular, with around 2000 young people getting a taste of sea life every year. However, the fabric of the ship, from the porous pine upper deck put on after her partial demolition half a century before, to the leaky hull, were showing the ravages of time and inadequate funding. Nothing lasts forever, and wooden ships are more perishable than most things.

When Frank Carr stood down in 1967, he was followed into the chair by Admiral Sir Wilfred Woods, a former Commander-in-Chief Portsmouth, who would serve until his death in 1975. Thereafter the Governors waited three years before appointing a new Chairman. Their choice fell on Captain David Smith RN, who had taken his seat as an Elder Brother of Trinity House and became a Trustee two years previously. Captain Smith immediately instituted a major review of the ship and the training role. Afloat repairs were organised, and dry-docking in 1979

7 Littlewood & Butler, *Of Ships and Stars*, pp131-2

8 Lambert, A D, *The Last Sailing Battlefleet: Maintaining Naval Mastery 1815-1850* (London 1991), pp 94 & 119-21 for a series of photographs taken at this time

revealed that the hull was sound. After minor repairs the *Foudroyant* was able to return to her berth and resume training. However, the cost of this work forced the Trust to liquidate assets.

In 1976, concurrently with joining the *Foudroyant* Trust, Captain Smith had also joined the Council of the Marine Society, a charity that had supported the training and education of young people for sea careers since the mid-eighteenth century. This link helped to integrate the work of two bodies with a shared interest. The Marine Society proved to be a generous supporter of the ship and the work she carried out. In 1981 this support consisted of £50,000 worth of equipment and supplies. The Society also sponsored a fund-raising appeal for the Trust. This was greatly appreciated by the Trust, which duly recorded its thanks. The obvious results were new teaching equipment, six dinghies, galley fittings and improved habitability. Unfortunately deteriorating soft timber in the ship's side had to be replaced at a cost of £25,000.

The Marine Society contributed an interest-free loan of £300,000, over seven years, and a further £750,000 was raised from the stock market. The income available to this split level trust known as the Marine Adventure Sailing Trust (MAST), was to support 'Sail Training whenever it arose'. The two main beneficiaries were *Foudroyant* and the Sea Cadet Corps vessel *Royalist*.

The basic problem for the Trust was that it cost over £100 to provide a week's training, while they were only able to charge £75 for the service, and that was a marked increase on the £55 charge levied the year before. With the country sliding into recession some 240 places were cancelled in

A taste of the sea. Young trainees enjoying messing conditions in 1966 that look very similar to the great days of sail.

1981 by hard-up local authorities and other groups. This caused a cash-flow crisis, and forced the Trust to lay off staff. Fortunately an anonymous donor provided £20,000 and allowed the ship to run as normal, and uniquely to offer free places to local authorities and children's charities. Other fund-raising continued on an annual basis, with strong local support.

The cost of running such an old hull forced the Governors to consider purchasing a more modern vessel–the redundant Trinity House vessel *Patricia*, which would be available for £80,000 in mid-1982, was an obvious candidate. As the Marine Society was unable to help, the idea was dropped. Instead, the main focus was now placed on the *Foudroyant* Appeal of 1983, to raise £250,000 to preserve the ship so that she could continue to provide an introduction to maritime heritage for the young. Encouraging support was received from the Marine Society and other prominent institutional and individual backers, including Countess Mountbatten and Admiral Lord Lewin. Hampshire County Council presented the Trust with a yacht, and a grant to maintain her. This greatly enhanced the sailing experience of the trainees, who could now leave the harbour, work up in the Solent, and cruise to France and the Channel Islands.

In 1983 the future of the Georgian section of Portsmouth Dockyard was under consideration, with the creation of a Heritage Area being strongly backed. The Chairman ensured that the Government did not ignore the place of *Foudroyant* in this process, with a favoured solution being to place her in No 1 dock adjacent to HMS *Victory*. However, it gradually became clear that *Foudroyant* was not going to be invited to the party, because the consultants tasked with devising the new scheme did not consider she would generate adequate income for the site as a whole. By 1984-85 the Ministry of Defence was anxious to move out of the older section of the dockyard, but the Portsmouth Naval Heritage Project was unwilling to see *Foudroyant* enter the site. They did not want an unsightly hulk spoiling the carefully manicured location, and even if fully restored she would not be allowed to charge admission, or share any general income.[9] These terms were effectively a rejection, and the Governors decided to continue training in the harbour.

In 1984 1337 trainees were received on board, while a grant of £60,000 from the Marine Society, and other smaller sums kept the ship running. The following year a work to rule by teachers led to a notable downturn in trainee numbers, and by 1986 it was clear that schools activity was unlikely to recover. Only 808 trainees arrived that year, forcing staff cuts, despite continued external support. The shortage of trainees forced the price of courses to rise from £105 to £150 a week for 1987, while the Chairman warned the Governors that unless demand increased the future

9 Portsmouth Naval Heritage Trust letter of 26 September 1984

of training would have to be reconsidered. On 10 October 1986 an extraordinary General Meeting of the Board of Governors was held, and unanimously decided to suspend training and reduce the ship to care and maintenance by January 1987. Negotiations were to be opened with any body able to form a viable preservation plan. A number of options were considered, from carrying on the training mission with a restored ship, to moving to Chatham, Bristol, London, or–courtesy of the Indian Navy–back to Bombay.

By late January 1987 the preferred option was to move the ship to Hartlepool for restoration. This prompted a dramatic increase in local interest. However, action had to be taken immediately, funds were running out, and there was no income. The boats were given to other sea training charities, and the ship surveyed for a passage to the North East. The hull was deemed unsafe for towing, so the *Foudroyant* would have to suffer the indignity of being carried. After liquidating the last assets, and securing a cheque for £30,000 from the Thornton Foundation, the Dutch heavy lift barge *Goliath Pacific* which happened to be passing, was chartered to carry *Foudroyant* to Hartlepool. On 22 July the barge came into the harbour and flooded down; without loss of time the ship was towed into position, secured and then lifted clear of the water. On the 23rd she was towed out of the harbour she had occupied for the past fifty-five years. Crowds of spectators witnessed her leaving, but no-one realised that she would never return. By the time she cleared the harbour the Chairman had to report that there was nothing left in the bank. He also thanked the Indian Navy for their interest and promised that she would be restored as a monument to the men who built her, as well as all those who had served in her. In reply the Chief of the Indian Naval Staff wished the project well. Another letter received on the day the ship left Portsmouth came from Sir John Smith. Sir John had founded and funded the *Warrior* Preservation Trust, which had restored the pioneer ironclad HMS *Warrior* over a period of years at Hartlepool. With that heroic project now complete the Trust had no further need for the facilities and staff at Hartlepool. His organisation had been closed down, but Sir John generously devoted £25,000 towards *Foudroyant*'s uncertain future. This money ensured the ship would be able to meet her dues on arrival, and pay for time in care and maintenance; there was at least some money now in the bank.

The *Pacific Goliath* arrived in the River Tees on 27 July, and *Foudroyant* was then un-docked and towed across to Hartlepool for a civic reception. After an absence of a hundred and ten years she had returned to one of her old home ports, ready to be restored. After one hundred and twenty-five years as a training ship it was time to save the ship. The task would require skill, time and above all money.

The Restoration of HMS *Trincomalee*

Chapter Seven

THE RESTORATION of HMS *Trincomalee* was a triumph of human ingenuity over the ravages of time. It stands as a testament to the enduring ability of the human spirit to rise to a challenge, in this case that of re-creating the skills and understanding of the early nineteenth century in the last years of the twentieth.

Choosing Hartlepool, Strategic Review and a Development Plan

Before any substantial relic of the past is restored those responsible have to consider whether it is worth preserving, if the job can be done, and how the final result will be supported. The *Foudroyant* Trustees had never doubted that they were responsible for a historic artefact of immense value to the nation, a trust that they should discharge by preserving her for the future. Ships of this very class had helped to defeat the challenge of Napoleon, and to police the British Empire for half a centu-

The ship, still at that point known as *Foudroyant*, being towed into Hartlepool docks on 29 July 1987. Because of uncertainty about the state of the hull, the ship had been transported from Portsmouth on a barge, which was flooded down off Hartlepool and the '*Foudroyant*' floated off prior to being towed into the docks. When the ship was eventually dry-docked serious decay in some of the lower frames proved that the decision had been prudent and far-sighted.

ry. Furthermore, she was a living symbol of the interdependent, integrated, commercial basis of that empire, one that linked past achievement with current commonwealth partners. However, by the time *Foudroyant* left Portsmouth in July 1987 she was an almost unrecognisable hulk, in poor material condition.

On her arrival at West Hartlepool the ship was tied up alongside the old coaling pier, recently vacated by HMS *Warrior*,[1] amidst an almost apocalyptic scene of post-industrial decline. The industries that had built Hartlepool in the nineteenth century, coal and shipbuilding, industries that made it a great port and worthy of a drill ship, were all gone, and nothing had taken their place. The *Warrior* project had given the area a focus and employed a large number of skilled men, but she had gone, and the project team was unemployed. But at least they were available, if the money could be found.

However, *Foudroyant* could not offer employment; she just lay alongside as a dormant hulk waiting for decisions to be taken, and money to be found. Before the Trustees could address the challenge of restoration they had first to ascertain the scale of the task. To this end they had commissioned a report to establish the historical context for any restoration, determine her current condition, and consider future uses. This was to provide the information on which to base the search for outside funding. The necessary two-stage investigation was funded by Hampshire County Council. The first report 'A future for *Foudroyant*–a strategic review' was produced in February 1988. The Board accepted the recommendations it contained:

- the ship should be restored to her original configuration
- the ship should not return to her previous training profile, but should pursue one that provided a sophisticated, diverse and professional educational service
- that No 1 Basin in HM Naval Base Portsmouth would be the best long-term location
- the immediate object of the Trust should become that of preservation of the ship.

The Trust had then commissioned the follow-on development study, conducted jointly by the Trust Management Team and their Consultants. The task was to consider alternative locations in comparison with Portsmouth. This exercise quickly resolved any remaining uncertainties, and focused the project. After considering thirty potential locations around the coast of England and Wales, six sites were deemed worthy of further examination. Liverpool, Manchester and London Docklands ruled themselves out by failing to offer any capital contribution toward the restoration. The newly established Chatham Historic Dockyard offered a rent-free berth, but neither the Dockyard nor the town could provide financial assistance or skilled labour to support restoration, so this generous offer had to be declined. This left Plymouth, Portsmouth and Hartlepool. Plymouth had a historic naval location, but the ship would have had to be restored in the privately run Devonport Dockyard, and relocated at the Trust's expense. These costs greatly exceeded the value of the financial offer. Portsmouth remained the preferred location, as Councillor Emery-Wallis, Chairman of Hampshire County Council, was informed in April 1989. At the same time he had been left in no doubt that the future of the ship was the priority. Hampshire offered £225,000 over three years. However, the County's vision was not shared by the City, while the Heritage Dockyard partners were far from happy at the prospect of sharing their site with another ship that had the potential to become a major attraction.

The under-whelming response of the Naval Dockyard towns left the field clear for Hartlepool, which had hitherto only been seen as the restoration location. In September 1989 the Borough Council made a strong case for her to remain, as part of the town's renaissance after the industrial decline of the 1980s. They envisaged the ship being a central attraction, not only as the oldest frigate in Britain but also as a ship with a strong local connection. This approach reinforced a dialogue about the ship's future between the Trust and Teesside Development Corporation (TDC) over the past year. In late August the TDC recommended that the Trust be assisted with a grant of £1 million, spread over five years, provided the ship was restored and located at Hartlepool for not less than fifteen years. In addition she would have a berth alongside, and access to a dry-dock free of charge. After two years of planning it was time to consider the balance of advantage. Like all judgements, the final decision could not please everyone.

On 20 October 1989 the Trustees were given all the information, and advised that before any commitment was made they should seek a financial pledge of at least £2 million from one of the short-listed locations. The three interested parties were invited to reconsider their options within the next four weeks. On 1 December an extra-ordinary meeting was convened, to hear that the two Naval Dockyard towns were unmoved, while Hartlepool had met the target but stipulated that the Trustees must undertake to leave the ship in the harbour when restored. The Board was unanimous in accepting the offer. Before the meeting closed attention was shifted to the security arrangements at the current location, which were being reduced, and with the co-operation of the Port Authority a rent-free restoration berth was provided, until the dry-dock became available. The new arrangements between the Trust, the TDC and the Borough Council were given legal form over the next two months.

1 Lambert, A D, *Warrior: Restoring the World's first Ironclad* (London 1987)

At the end of the decade the ship cut her links with Portsmouth, the South Coast and the Naval Dockyards. While there were some who regretted the move to Harlepool, the prospect of a new start in the revitalised North East was alluring. Here the ship would find a whole new hinterland, one that she would not have to share with other historic warships.

The restoration years, 1990-2001

The restoration of HMS *Trincomalee* began on 1 January 1990. With adequate funding and a berth secured it was time to recruit the nucleus of the workforce. The sale of the Trust's last asset in 1988, a launch named *Hanway*, funded the one-year appointment of a Director to prepare for the restoration, and by the end of the month he had been joined by a Ship's Engineer/Electrician, two Shipwrights and a part-time Project Manager. A Technical Officer was also required for research, drawing office and technical work. All five of the appointees had worked on the *Warrior* project. Now they would have to refine their skills in reverse, having started out in modern steel ships, then worked on iron, they would now be working in wood. Access to much of this knowledge could be had from historical consultants, and their advice proved useful in the early stages of the work.

The decision was taken to revert to the original name of *Trincomalee* and to fit out the ship as she would have appeared if commissioned when first built in 1817. Once restoration began in 1990 the first job was to clear the upper deck of the various accretions and return the above-water appearance to the classic frigate profile. The ship's original iron ballast was removed, and 'pigs' can be seen stacked to the left of the gate. Support facilities in these early days were not very elaborate.

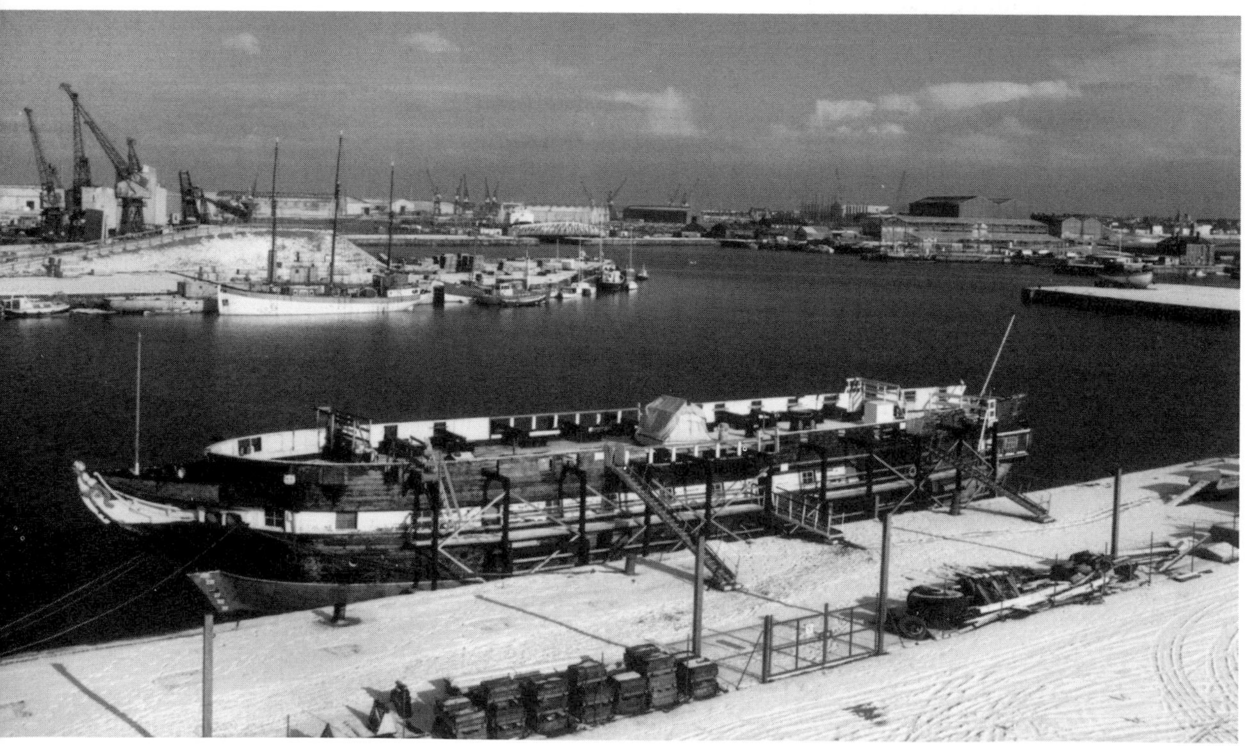

Five-year funding was provided by the TDC and Hartlepool Borough Council, at £200,000 and £50,000 a year respectively. The money was made available immediately, before contracts had been signed, in return for a gentleman's agreement not to move the ship from the port. The berth and workshop space were provided free, as was an old dry-dock. This had long since been filled in and built over, but it was to be cleared and refitted. The financial value of these facilities would be hard to compute, but they gave the project a vital step forward, enabling any funds to be devoted to the labour and materials of restoration. With a clear objective, money in prospect, a suitable location and labour being recruited the mood was buoyant.

On 28 March 1990 the Chairman announced that the ship would revert to her proper name, HMS *Trincomalee*, after a century masquerading as the *Foudroyant*. This was the only appropriate name for a ship that was going to be restored to her original condition as a sailing frigate of the early nineteenth century.[2] However, close on a century of maritime training will remain one of the proudest elements of the ship's history, and will be one of the central stories recorded in her exhibition and display. The many ex-*Foudroyant* trainees will find much to remind them of past days.

At this stage the Charity Commissioners advised that it would be inappropriate for the existing Trust to manage a ship restoration project, and that a new Trust, to which all assets were surrendered, should be formed. The *Foudroyant* Trust became dormant, and a new HMS *Trincomalee* Trust was formed, with the same trustees. This took effect as soon as the legal formalities could be arranged.

By great good fortune the Trust was able to secure Bill Stevenson as part-time, later full-time, Project Manager. A locally trained shipbuilder, Bill had worked on the *Warrior* and was working for the borough, restoring the old Humber paddle steamer *Wingfield Castle* in 1990, a task that was coming to an end. By arrangement he was gradually released to the *Trincomalee*. His experience and skills laid the foundations of the successful restoration. Nowhere was this more significant than in recruiting staff for the tasks at hand. Bill created a highly effective team initially consisting of Technical Officer Keith Johnson, Chargehand Les Gilfoyle, Ship's Engineer/Electrician Brian Smith, five Shipwrights and two office staff.

Before restoration could begin the ship and the facilities had to be prepared, with light and power on board, workshop space ashore, offices and all the necessary support for effective work. New gangways were built to allow the easy removal of redundant stores, and other unnecessary equipment from the ship. The first major step was to take down the non-original cabins, partitions and clutter that had accumulated during the years of harbour service. These included plumbing, wiring, heating systems and other fittings incidental to twentieth-century residential life.

2 It was decided not to reverse the major structural work of the 1845 rebuild, so there are areas, such as the stern, where the ship is, like *Victory*, configured in the form in which she saw service, not as completed

The next stage was to remove the interior cladding of the gundeck, which disclosed the remains of at least three different arrangements of the gunports, a legacy of *Trincomalee*'s service as a drill ship. Without further ceremony the false forecastle, which had contained the bathrooms, showers and heads of the training ship era, was taken off, together with the stump mast and the large poop cabin. Removing these unsightly excrescences left the ship somewhat reduced, but rather closer to the condition in which she left naval service in the 1890s. The task would now be to restore her to the condition she had been in when she entered naval service in the 1810s.

With the ship lightened, and tied up alongside in a safe haven, there was no need to keep her down to her flotation marks. Ballast could be removed, so the chain cable from the fore-peak, and about two-thirds of the 80 tons of pig iron from the bilge was taken out, inspected and stored for future re-use. As a result the mastless hull now floated high in the water, which allowed platforms to be built for access to the defective outer topsides. Here the bulk of the modern repair work, mainly carried out with inferior timber, would have to be stripped back to the original futtock frames. Work on the ship was supported and informed by the technical research programme directed by Keith Johnson. His research and graphic work charted the removal of defective timber, and ensured that new information coming from the ship was integrated into an increasingly detailed understanding of the ship's structure. A full structural plan of the ship as she was, rather than as she had been when built, would be produced to set alongside the original building drawings.

The scale of the project was now attracting attention from the media, and also the Department of Employment, through their Hartlepool Task Force. At the request of the Department an employment training scheme was set up, funding two shipwright instructors, three apprentices and ten trainees at a cost of £130,000. Welcome publicity was generated when Douglas Hogg, Minister for Employment, announced the scheme on board the ship on 12 June 1990. The trainees built a new workshop, and fitted it out with machinery and workbenches.

The second year of the restoration, 1991, followed the same pattern, clearing and cleaning out the ship, finishing the workshops and offices and getting ready for a restoration effort that was then expected to occupy at least six or seven years. After that the fully rigged ship would remain afloat in Hartlepool docks. The timing of any work below the waterline would be determined by the availability of the re-excavated dry-dock, which was not expected to be open for another two years. Consequently the project would initially have to concentrate on the topsides, the area in the worst condition.

The gunports of the *Trincomalee* had been heavily modified over the

Because the dry-dock was not available but funding was, the Trust took the courageous and radical step of restoring the above-water hull before working on the ship's bottom. The topside had been repaired at various stages in the ship's history with timber inferior to the teak of the original construction, and much needed replacing. In this September 1991 view many of the midships toptimbers have been removed.

previous 150 years. In the 1840s the upper-deck battery had been reduced from 16 to 8 and the gundeck from 28 to 18 guns, with considerable modification of the gunports. In the 1870s larger guns were fitted, and some gunports were further widened. Finally, when Cobb took over he had an approximation of the original frigate arrangement re-instated. Only the first of these modifications had been conducted with skill and seasoned timber; the rest were cheaply executed in softwood, or merely cosmetic makeovers. Worse, the ship-breakers had already begun to remove the teak topsides before Cobb bought the ship. These planks were replaced with inferior softwood, which had allowed water to penetrate into the frames.

Restoration began by stripping away the topsides from the weather-deck down to the sound teak planks just above the copper sheathing. Once the frames were exposed they could be assessed, and plans made to replace the defective timbers; only when the structure of the ship had been repaired could the planking be replaced. Inside the ship the removal of the ballast revealed sound timber. Of equal importance, regular measurements showed that the ship's timbers were not showing signs of movement. With the ship higher in the water leakage was much reduced, and the hold began to dry out. When it did the timber was largely free from the smell of decay. Clearly the hull was strong, giving the project a sound basis from which to work. Some ballast was shifted to the port side, to correct a permanent 2-degree list to starboard. New pumps were installed, together with fire alarms and lighting to enhance the safety of the ship. Research and planning was also begun on the ship's crowning glory, her three masts and full sailing rig.

Although she presented a rather unsightly profile to the world, *Trincomalee* was surrounded by the redevelopment of Hartlepool Docks, a process that would transform the area into a yacht marina, shopping centre and housing. It was already evident that the great leisure opportunity of the modern age would be watching skilled labour at work, and the ship was opened to the public, as far as was consistent with the dangers of the work environment, and the convenience of the tradesmen.

In 1992 the *Trincomalee* Trust was restructured as a private limited company, and, following advice from the Charities Commission, the objectives were modified. The management was restructured, with the post of Director lapsing. This left Bill Stevenson, now restyled Restoration Manager, responsible for local management and restoration, reporting directly to the Chairman. The ex-Director, Tony Bridgewater, was re-employed on an annual contract as the Development Officer, primarily charged with fund-raising and working with the Chairman. The financial aspect of the project was vital, and the Trust was already in discussions with English Heritage and the National Heritage Memorial Fund. It was hoped that both bodies would become major donors.

By May 1992 preparatory work was sufficiently advanced for hull restoration to begin. Over 50 tons of high grade West African Opepe hardwood and suitable fixings had to be purchased, together with heavy woodworking machinery. In addition shore-side equipment was required, like a fork-lift truck, to enable the small workforce, which totalled only twelve at this point, to make the best use of their time and skills. It was in this area, labour saving, that the late twentieth-century shipwright had a real advantage over his early nineteenth-century predecessor. With sheltered staging erected along both sides, the restorers could work effectively in almost all conditions, even though the ship was still afloat. At this time it was intended to leave the more complex bow and stern areas until the ship was docked.

Once work began the labour force expanded to some forty skilled hands. The ship was stripped out, cleaned and repaired in twenty-foot stages, working forward from the stern with both sides being opened together. The first task was to inspect, and in most cases remove, the upper-deck frame timbers where the softwood planking and leaky plumbing had allowed fresh water to collect in the linings and rot the teak timber. Only four original frames were sound; the other 140 were copied onto individual plywood templates, removed, and replaced by new one-piece frames cut from the Opepe timber. Even with a large bandsaw cutting each new frame occupied four men for three hours. The frames were then fixed in place using stainless steel bolts, rather than the original mix of iron spikes above the waterline, and copper bolts below. The original gunport layout was reconstructed from the *Leda* class drawings, while the 3- to 4-inch thick outer planking was bent onto the curved hull using special tools devised for the task by the project shipwrights, and then bolted to the frames. Finally, the internal linings were replicated in hardwood, allowing discreet access for modern electrical and electronic cabling for power, alarms and information. At the same time a two-man team restored the troublesome upper-deck planking, another softwood disaster area–defective timbers were removed, and replaced by hardwood sanded to conform to the wear patterns of the remaining teak planks. The whole deck was then re-caulked using the traditional method of stuffing the seams with oily yard, topped off with molten pitch.

By autumn 1992 nearly half of the upperworks had been restored, but the evidence of progress was unmistakable. The training workshop was also producing results, completing the first of twenty-eight 18-pounder gun carriages. A wooden building donated by the TDC was adapted into a visitor centre to cope with the steady increase in numbers, and by the end of the year 3500 people had paid to visit the ship, adding £860 to the funds. On 9 June HRH the Duke of Edinburgh awarded the project his patronage, an honour that reflected his long-term interest in the ship and her future.

By the following year it was time to take a longer view of the project. The HMS *Trincomalee* Trust (Registered Charity No 1007784) set out its objectives:

- to restore, refurbish, improve, maintain and preserve HMS *Trincomalee*
- to provide facilities of an educational or cultural nature to improve the public's awareness and appreciation of the ship's historical past

By April 1993 much of the midships area of the upper hull had been replaced. Seasoned teak proved unobtainable at a realistic price, but high quality African Opepe was chosen as an acceptable substitute on the recommendation of the British Timber Federation. In the left foreground is one of the dummy 18-pounders on a carriage fabricated in the Trust's workshop.

- to provide recreation and public enjoyment by the promotion and explanation of matters concerning Britain's naval heritage
- to provide training in seamanship and projects and activities to the public of a general educational nature.

Visitor numbers continued to rise, reaching 14,000 in 1993, requiring two part-time guides. The youth connection of the old ship was restored when the local Sea Cadet Unit was renamed TS *Trincomalee*; these young people served the ship as an honour guard and band for official events and ceremonies. These included a Royal Visit. On 18 May 1993 the Queen and Duke of Edinburgh visited Hartlepool in the Royal Yacht, and after the Queen had opened the gateway of the projected Heritage Quay area, the Duke conducted a thorough inspection of the ship, meeting the workforce and others connected with the project.

As Phase 1 of the restoration, work on the above-water hull, was completed, Phase 2, the masts, was already underway. This work was greatly assisted by grants of £150,000 and £300,000 respectively for 1992-93 from English Heritage (EH) and the National Heritage Memorial Fund (NHMF). Advice on selecting the most appropriate types of timber for specific uses was generously given by the Timber Research Association. By the close of the 1992-93 financial period the project had expended some £1.6 million, and projected additional costs of £3.1 million to complete the task. Work on fund-raising and local awareness continued, while a 'Friends of HMS *Trincomalee* Association' was set up to encourage 'Old *Foudroyants*' and 'new *Trincomalees*' to support the ship in a variety of ways.

The continued delay in opening the dry-dock led the team to begin

To reduce long-term maintenance costs the masts and yards were fabricated from tubular steel, a common solution for non-sailing historic ships. However, the correct external appearance of the spars was carefully contrived, as can be seen in this view of the fore mast, the fore top and the housed fore topmast. The tubular masts also act as ventilators for the hold.

Miles of rigging was required to support the masts and spars, and this was also prepared in the Trust's workshop. Some forgotten skills needed to be relearned: here, for example, the shrouds (the substantial ropes that support the masts laterally) are being 'wormed, parcelled and served'. This comprises winding small-diameter rope into the groove formed by the twisted strands of the shroud (worming); then covering the shroud with tarred canvas (parcelling); and finally putting on a tight whipping with spun yarn (serving).

work on the bow and stern in 1994, although the ship was still afloat. The frames in these areas were in far better condition, as rainwater had not been able to penetrate the linings. To mark the progress of the restoration, parts of the side were painted black and white frigate-fashion. The stern posed a major problem, since it had been essentially rebuilt in 1846, largely to conform to contemporary thinking on armament. This structure had survived the various modifications inflicted elsewhere, and after much discussion it was decided that it should be retained. It was thought better to have an original 1846 stern than a replica of the 1817 version, especially as the timbers were sound and the cost of any such change would be considerable, in time, materials and labour. That the ship saw all her active and harbour service in this configuration was also important. Furthermore, to the uninitiated the difference was neither obvious nor unsightly.

Work on the rig progressed. The main mast alone would be 160 feet (49 meters) long, with the three-ton maintop platform mounted over 60 feet above the deck. It was decided that the Trust workshops would fabricate the twenty-seven separate masts and spars in galvanised steel, rather than the original pine, since steel tubes would be far easier to maintain. The standing and running rigging posed further problems, with miles of rope and over 1000 blocks to be fitted.

To carry out this work the Trust used a workforce of thirty-two locally-recruited skilled men, with support staff. This made the project a significant employer. Inspection by EH and the NHMF demonstrated that the project was on time, and on budget, consistently producing work of the highest standard. One month was taken up shifting the base of operations about 300 yards to meet local development needs, but the opportunity was taken to improve and upgrade the workshop, which improved output. The TDC continued to provide land free of charge.

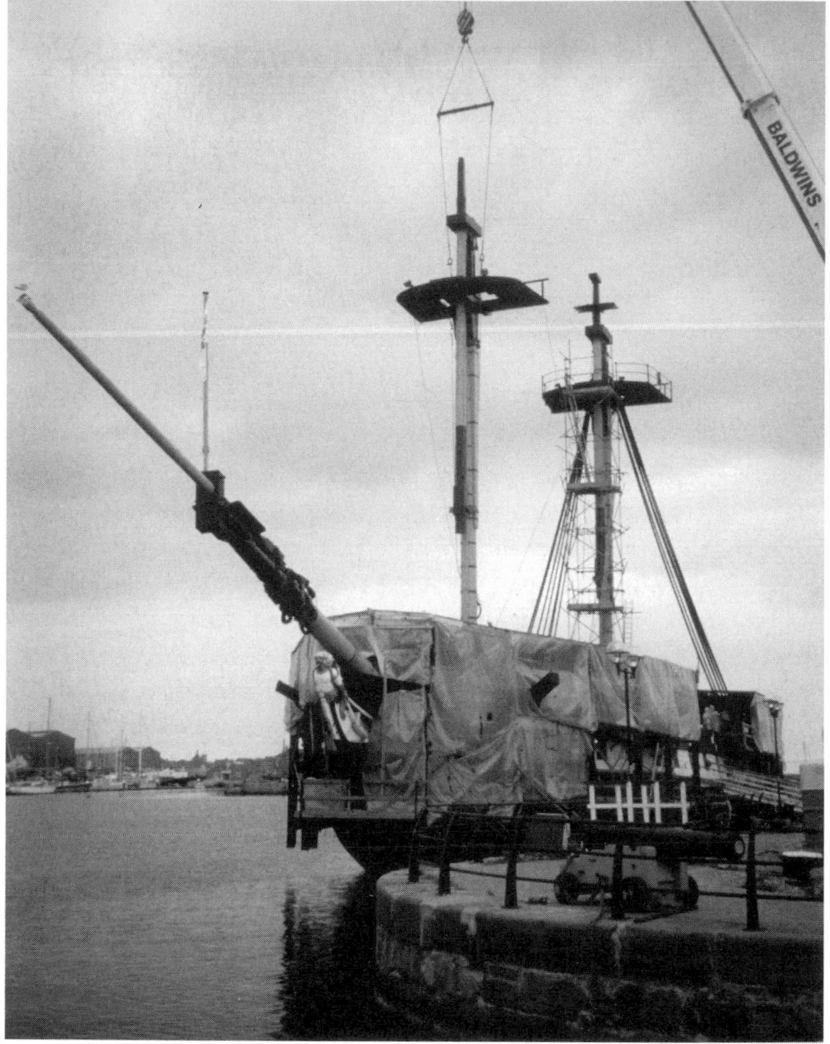

In the public imagination the principal feature of a sailing ship is its masts and yards. This made the stepping of masts a relatively high priority. Here the fore mast is being gently lowered into the hull on 30 August 1995, following the installation of the bowsprit earlier in the day. The main mast had been stepped in May and the final lower mast, the mizzen, was stepped in the following February.

Further financial support was secured when the Inland Revenue allowed the Trust to recover Gift Aid on major donations. In addition to the major benefactors already noted, the European Regional Development Fund made a significant contribution, and smaller, but no less welcome help came from the Esme Fairbairn Trust, Hartlepool Business Group, the Peacock Trust, The Spooner Trust, and other donors. (See Appendix 6 for a list of major donors to the project.) The economic situation, as the country began a slow recovery from recession, made private fund-raising particularly difficult. By the end of 1994 some £4 million had been raised, leaving an estimated £2 million to complete the task, but any estimates were still highly provisional, as the underwater hull had not been examined! Visitors for the year passed 20,000, including HRH the Princess Royal accompanied by the Lord Lieutenant of Durham. In consequence the local authority funded guides were transferred to the project.

In 1995 the restoration of the above-water hull was completed from bow to stern, ending Phase 5. Inner linings, fittings and other work continued, beginning to transform the hull into a fully fitted ship ready for service. To provide the motive power new masts were fabricated, with the main mast being stepped on 16 May 1995, the fore mast and bowsprit on 30 August, and the mizzen on 21 February 1996. *Trincomalee* was now shipshape, for the first time in over a hundred years.

More pressing was the financial position. Early in the year contingency plans were drawn up for the project to be mothballed, in case the money ran out. The decision on a large application to the European Regional Development Fund was delayed in Brussels, leaving the income dependant on Gift Aid, and a combination of large and small donors. Not only was the completion of the project in doubt, but the future of the ship, if she was completed, was also in question. Fortunately, the European application was successful, securing a total of £0.65 million in April 1995, enough to keep the project going until the autumn of 1996.

This was critical, because the original grants from the Teesside Development Corporation, and the National Heritage Memorial Fund ended in June 1995. For the longer term the Trust needed to find a new, large-scale supporter, and having already secured generous funding from all existing bodies it was time to approach the new Heritage Lottery Fund. Funded by a new national lottery this body offered hope to many charitable causes. Fortunately the Lottery proved highly successful, raising large amounts of money for 'good causes', although the choice of projects and distribution of funds did not escape criticism. On 27 September an expert panel representing the Lottery Fund visited the ship, and after receiving supplementary information the Fund made an initial grant of £0.95 million to support additional above-water restoration, with payments phased between October 1995 and March 1997. This money would also cover the cost of an underwater survey. The Lottery Fund was made aware of the financial position of the project, and indicated that it would consider further applications for support. The European Regional Development Fund was also willing to consider further bids. The Heritage Lottery Fund also employed a consultant naval architect, Fred Walker, to represent their interest in the project. His impartial advice would be greatly appreciated.

By early 1996 the restoration had reached a stage where the long-term future had to be considered, and the TDC funded a study of the shore-side infrastructure necessary to support a visitor attraction, educational facility and maintenance workshop. The study was based on the assumption that the ship would be based outside the Historic Quay area, with her own facilities. To this end the Development Corporation had offered up to 1.5 acres on the south side of Jackson's Dock.

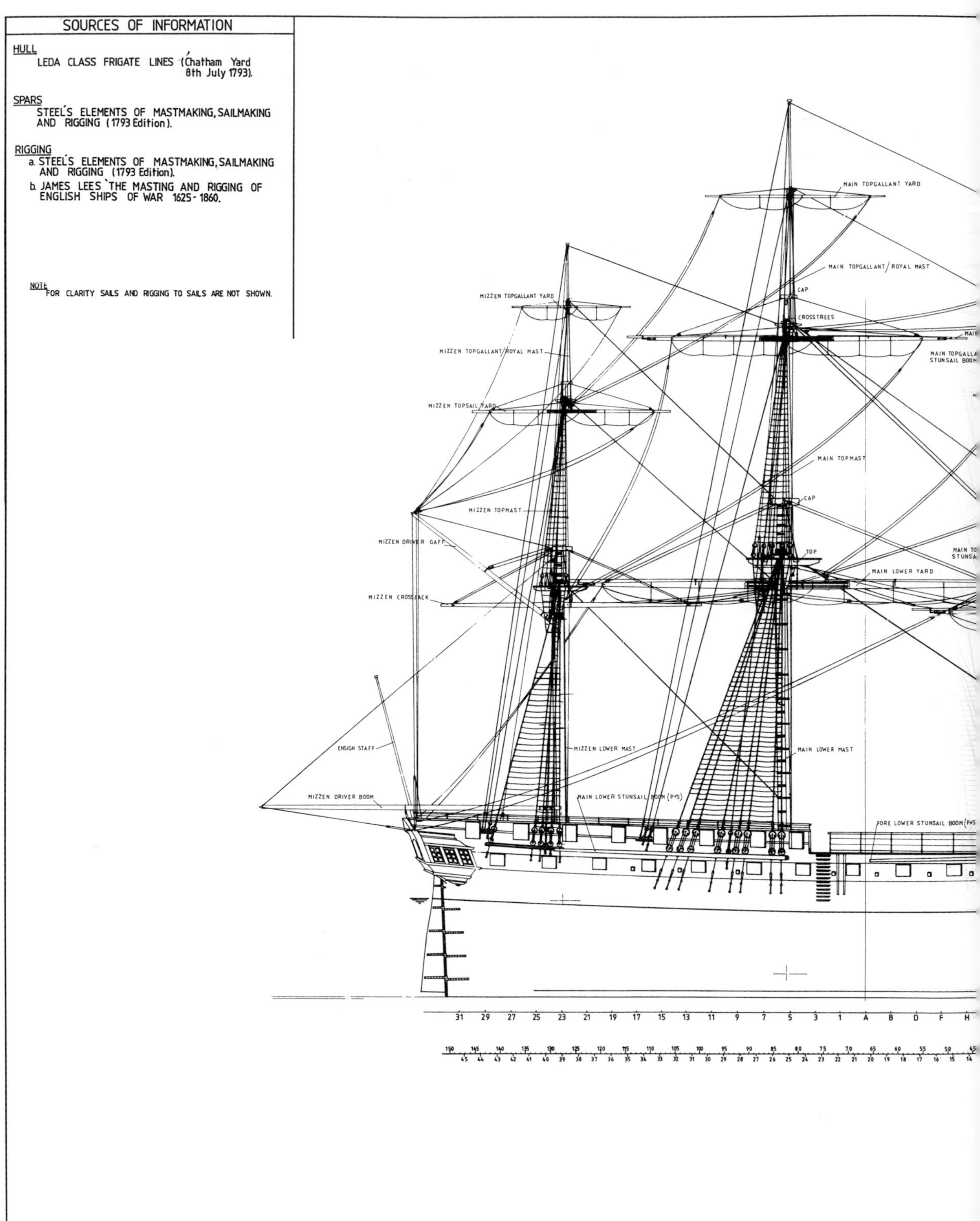
SOURCES OF INFORMATION
HULL
LEDA CLASS FRIGATE LINES (Chatham Yard 8th July 1793).
SPARS
STEEL'S ELEMENTS OF MASTMAKING, SAILMAKING AND RIGGING (1793 Edition).
RIGGING
a. STEEL'S ELEMENTS OF MASTMAKING, SAILMAKING AND RIGGING (1793 Edition).
b. JAMES LEES 'THE MASTING AND RIGGING OF ENGLISH SHIPS OF WAR 1625-1860.
NOTE
FOR CLARITY SAILS AND RIGGING TO SAILS ARE NOT SHOWN.
MAIN TOPGALLANT YARD
MAIN TOPGALLANT/ROYAL MAST
CAP
CROSSTREES
MIZZEN TOPGALLANT YARD
MIZZEN TOPGALLANT/ROYAL MAST
MIZZEN TOPSAIL YARD
MAIN TOPMAST
CAP
MIZZEN TOPMAST
MIZZEN DRIVER GAFF
TOP
MAIN LOWER YARD
MIZZEN CROSSJACK
ENSIGN STAFF
MIZZEN LOWER MAST
MAIN LOWER MAST
MIZZEN DRIVER BOOM
MAIN LOWER STUNSAIL BOOM (P+S)
FORE LOWER STUNSAIL BOOM (P+S)
31 29 27 25 23 21 19 17 15 13 11 9 7 5 3 1 A B D F H

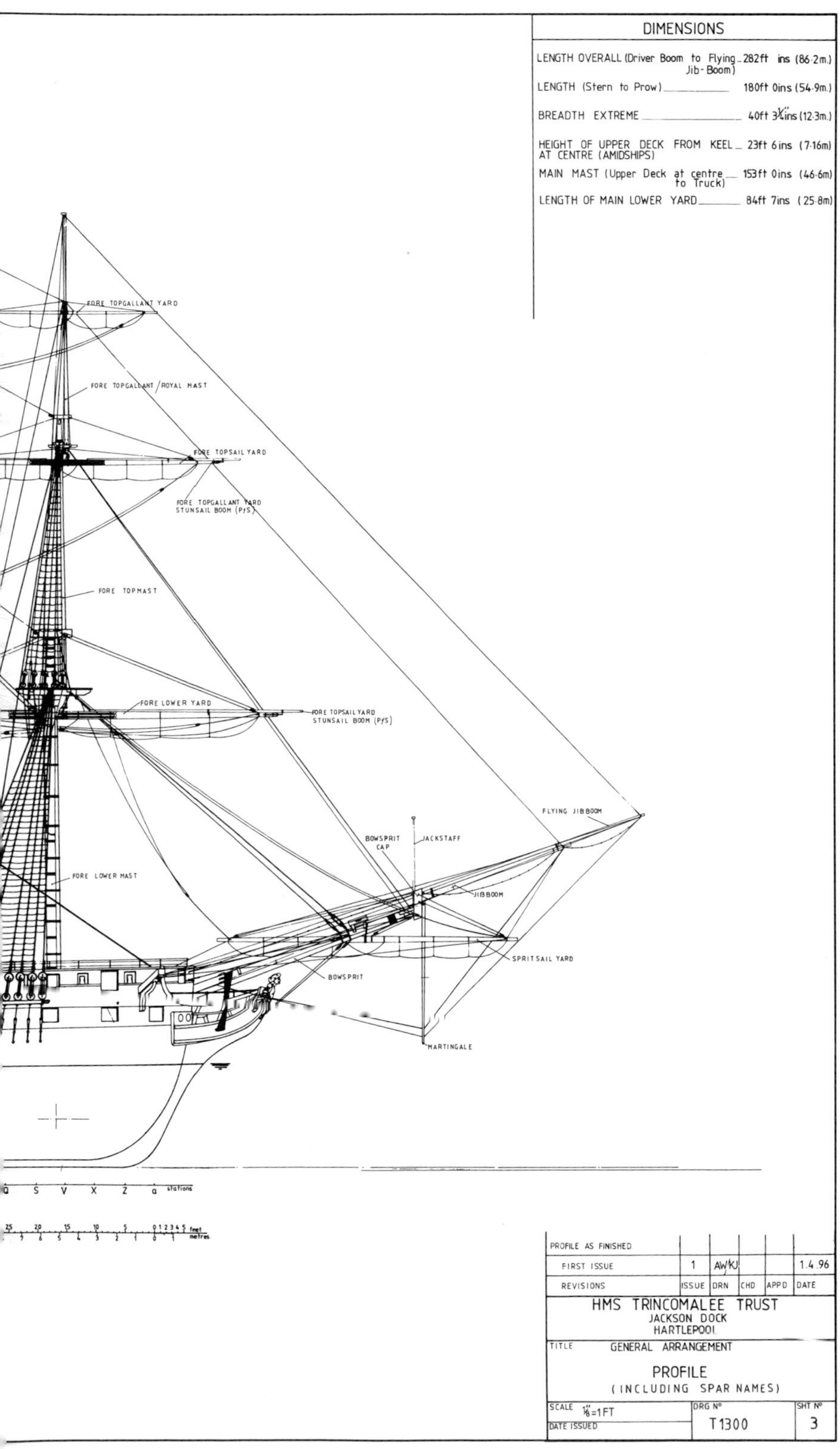

A considerable research effort went into establishing the details of frigates of about 1817 so that the ship's restoration would be as accurate as possible. The end result was a set of highly detailed plans on which each aspect of the work could be based. This profile drawing shows both the general appearance of the hull, with the true positions of the gunports, and the full set of masts and spars.

By the middle of 1996 the standing rigging was taking shape, and the working platforms had been removed from the hull. With the masts stepped and yards braced the ship became less stable. Had she been going to sea more ballast would have been installed to compensate, but her destination was a dry-dock, with a depth limit. Inclining experiments determined the minimum addition of the original iron ballast to preserve stability without increasing her draught. In August *Trincomalee* entered the restored dry-dock at the centre of the Historic Quay area, a complex task

July 1996: all masts stepped and the upper hull restoration complete. This was the first time the ship had been fully masted for over a hundred years. The ship is ready to be moved into the dock at the centre of the Historic Quay area (just visible at the stern of the paddle steamer moored ahead of *Trincomalee*.

Water seeping into the exposed open-grain at the heads of some frame timbers had produced serious decay. These frames needed replacement, and as can be seen here, this involved working substantial pieces of Opepe timber.

During 1998 work continued on the lower hull, with any defective frames being removed, and replaced, new outer planking as required, and then re-caulking the entire outer hull. The copper sheathing, which had been in place since 1846, had to be removed to inspect the lower hull, and was, unsurprisingly, much degraded by 150 years in a variety of fresh and salt water environments. The whole ship would need to be re-coppered. This centuries-old task was conducted essentially as it had been two hundred years before. Once the hull was complete it was coated with Stockholm tar, followed by a thick coat of bitumen, with a layer of silicon-impregnated felt being fitted over the molten bitumen before it cooled. Finally the copper sheets were nailed on using a pattern employed by the dockyards in the days of the wooden walls. Each sheet is 48 inches long, 14 inches wide and 1.2 millimetres thick. They were secured with specially-made copper alloy nails Despite the original

Contrasting old and new timber in the frames of the lower hull. Thanks to power tools a much smaller modern workforce was able to match the impressive accuracy and finish achieved by their nineteenth-century predecessors.

methods and materials the purpose of the coppering is rather different on the restored ship. Originally the copper was used to keep the hull free of marine growths, to preserve speed. The modern method was developed to preserve *Trincomalee*'s watertight integrity over a long period of stationary harbour duty.

To support the final phase of work a fresh appeal was launched with a press release on 29 September, backed by an open letter from the Patron, HRH the Duke of Edinburgh. The ship was nearing completion, but the interpretation, education and support facilities were not ready. The Heritage Lottery Fund supported the development of education and interpretation strategies, but the shore-side buildings seemed to be best provided in partnership with private sector developers. The new plan was for a ground floor visitor and interpretation centre in a new building otherwise given over to residential use. Even with the help of the Commission for New Towns (successors in title to the Teesside Development Corporation and therefore owners of the freehold), the Charities Commissioners and the Planning authority, this process took time, and time was becoming an increasingly scarce commodity. The Conservation Plan, approved in September placed the ship in her historical context, and was then submitted to the Lottery Fund. After a lengthy development phase, extended by the complex process of reconciling the requirements of the concerned parties, plans for the visitor centre collapsed in April 2000. This left the ship without shore-side facilities, for revenue earning, or maintenance. This situation was the more to be regretted because excellent progress had been made in discussions with the National Maritime Museum for a museum/interpretation facility.

Work on the lower hull had been completed by 21 October 1999, Trafalgar Day. The event was marked by a traditional Indian Silver Nail ceremony, which the ship had last experienced on 19 May 1816, shortly after her keel had been laid in the Bombay dock. On this occasion the nail had been crafted and presented by silversmith Daphne Smith, the wife of the Chairman, and she had the honour of driving it home with the Ship Superintendent Les Gilfoyle, while the blessing was provided by a Zoroastrian Priest (as in the original naming ceremony), accompanied by two Chaplains from the Missions to Seamen. The Mayor of Hartlepool and the Lord Lieutenant of Durham were among those attending. This event marked the formal end of the underwater restoration. Plans were now made to re-float the ship early in the year 2000.

Further afield the news was less satisfactory. The National Historic Ships Committee had announced that their register of over 1500 historic ships would be assessed to establish a 'core collection' of vessels deemed to be of national importance to cover the widest spectrum of maritime activity and technology. This collection was highly significant, because it

While the restoration of the hull was underway the Trust's workshop was steadily turning out replica fittings to give the ship its final authentic appearance. Four of the 32-pounder carronades on their characteristic slide mounting are shown here after painting. Some of the round shot can be seen to the left.

would inform all future preservation strategies. The Trust had been told that the frigate would be in the collection, yet when the list of thirty-four named ships was published on 1 November 1999 *Trincomalee* was excluded – because she had not been built in Britain! It is hard to understand how the criteria for this list could have been so badly drawn up as to exclude her. *Trincomalee* was built in Bombay for the Royal Navy under an Admiralty contract placed with the Honourable East India Company, a British company established by Royal Charter, in territory belonging to the British Crown. Her exclusion demonstrated a compete lack of comprehension of the nature of the British Empire, and of modern Britain. Perhaps it was fortunate *Implacable* did not survive to be treated in the same way, for the sin of being a French prize! Reaction among all those who knew the *Trincomalee*, expert and enthusiast alike, was universally critical. Those who worked on the ship, and all her local supporters, were incredulous. The Chairman of the NHSC, Admiral of the Fleet Sir Julian Oswald, while unable to change the criteria, did recognise their failings when the Committee later accepted that HMS *Trincomalee* 'despite not being eligible within the criteria to be included in the Core Collection only because she was built outside the United Kingdom, is accepted by NHSC as an historic vessel of acknowledged national maritime significance to the United Kingdom.'

On 3 May 2000 the *Trincomalee* was floated in dock, so that inclining experiments could be conducted to determine her stability, and she has remained afloat ever since. Most of the work now consisted of fitting out the ship to 'prepare her for sea', so that visitors could experience as much of the life of an earlier age as possible. With the delay to the visitor centre project the Chairman informed Trustees that it would be necessary to defer moving the ship out of the dock at Hartlepool Historic Quay for the foreseeable future, while a new development partner was being sought . With this decision taken Captain Smith handed over the office of

The ultimate aim of the display was to give the visitor an idea of the ship as ready for sea and complete in every detail. To this end drawings were produced to work out the positioning of even the smallest piece of equipment, as demonstrated by this drawing of an 18-pounder gun and the photograph of the gun in position and complete with all its tackle.

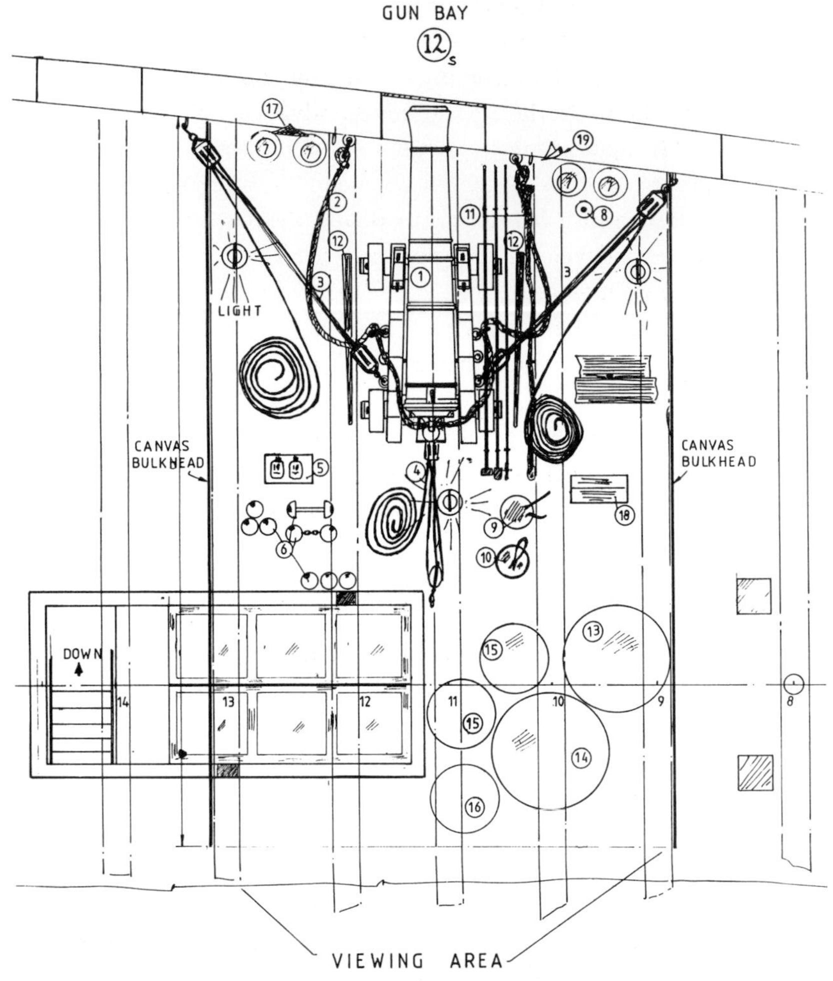

Chairman to Colonel Michael Stewart on 8 June. Michael Stewart, a Trustee since 1993 and the Vice Chairman since 1997, was a wide ranging businessman, being a Director of several companies including the Tees and Hartlepool Port Authority. He has the advantage of living and working locally. His appointment brought a strong business emphasis to the project. As a mark of his successful leadership of the Project for over two decades Captain Smith was invited to assume the new office of President.

With the shore development postponed the Trust had to face a severe shortfall in revenue once the Heritage Lottery Fund grant terminated in November 2000. HLF appreciated that the restoration phase had to include interpretation within the ship, and that temporary facilities were required at the Historic Quay to give visitors a better understanding of the history of the ship and the many worlds that she inhabited. Therefore HLF agreed that a portion of the unexpended funds from the restoration phase could be used to support an interpretation strategy, provided the work was complete by the end of April 2001. The Trust had produced an education and interpretation strategy, and began working with designers Brennan & Whalley to finalise the onboard interpretation of the ship. At the same time the large scale electrical contract, which would carry power, light, fire detection, ventilation and CCTV, was completed. On 1 November HRH the Duke of Edinburgh made a morale-boosting visit to the ship to inspect the finished product.

Although it had been necessary for the Trust to reduce its workforce in May and November 2000, with the project close to completion, the remaining staff were heavily involved in the interpretation phase. The concept was that the ship should be seen as she might have appeared in her prime, with the crew having but recently taken their well-earned leave. Trust staff worked closely with specialist contractors as the ship was prepared for display. Notable tasks were the introduction of an audio guide, the reinstallation of the wheel and capstan, furnishing the captain's cabin, ward room and mess deck, together with the provision of shot racks and rope tackle for the cannon. These finishing touches were rounded off with a sympathetic lighting treatment, that would ensure visitor safety, without detracting too much from the enclosed feeling of a Nelsonic frigate. Modern light fittings were hidden in period battle lanterns. The most remarkable element of the visitor experience is another first for a restored wooden warship: *Trincomalee* has been fitted with two platform lifts, linking the gun deck, which has ramped gangway access, with the quarterdeck above, and the mess deck below. The lifts used existing openings in the ship, making no structural demands on the fabric. As a result disabled visitors can visit the three major decks, only the orlop and hold remaining inaccessible to them. It was appropriate that the final detail should be the fitting of two fine stern lanterns. The

Looking forward along the quarterdeck. At the break of the waist there is a conventional companionway with ladder (left of the main mast) but the almost identical canvas-covered structure to the right is a cunningly concealed wheelchair lift. A further lift between decks allows disabled access to almost all of the ship.

shore-side interpretation of the ship was housed in a temporary quayside building, which doubled as a reception and souvenir outlet.

The final inspection of the restoration work was carried out on behalf of the Heritage Lottery Fund, the main funding body, by Fred Walker in early April 2001, just weeks before the grant ceased. His report concludes:

> . . . it is with great pleasure that I am able to confirm that the *Trincomalee* is in near perfect condition. She is a great credit to Hartlepool and indeed to the whole United Kingdom.
>
> The Heritage Lottery Fund should feel that in this particular exercise, they have made a significant contribution to the recording and understanding of maritime affairs in Britain and contributed generously to one of the finest restorations in the whole world.

The end of April 2001 marked the end of the restoration, and of the Heritage Lottery Fund grant that had been so beneficial to the completion of the task. Despite the Trust's efforts to secure further suitable projects during the preceding year none had been forthcoming, and the Trust had to pay off many of its workers, retaining only a small maintenance team, ship guides and administrative support under the General Manager. Although all concerned had expected this reduction in the numbers employed, it was particularly sad to see the end of such a strong and successful team.

It was appropriate that the National Historic Ships Committee's earlier recognition of the significance of HMS *Trincomalee* should be confirmed at the international level. In April 2001 the World Ship Trust, the international organisation which supports maritime projects, announced that they had made two awards, one to the ship, and one to the former Chairman and now President of the Trust. The two citations could not be clearer:

> The Trustees of the World Ship Trust make this Maritime Heritage Award to HMS *Trincomalee* in recognition of the outstanding restoration and preservation of this historic ship. HMS *Trincomalee* is an inspiration to all who seek to restore and preserve the maritime heritage of the world.
>
> The Trustees of the World Ship Trust have great pleasure in making this award for individual achievement to Captain David T Smith, Royal Navy who through his personal and enthusiastic leadership as Chairman and Chief Executive of the Board of Governors ensured that the restoration and preservation of HMS *Trincomalee* has been an inspiration to all who seek to preserve historic ships and the maritime heritage of the world.

These citations by the World Ship Trust are the first major public acknowledgement of the valuable contribution to maritime heritage made by the project. It was fitting that the awards should be presented by an old friend of the Project, HRH the Duke of Edinburgh, in the Throne Room at Buckingham Palace on 29 November 2001. Captain Smith was also awarded the OBE in the New Year's Honours List of 2002 for his services to HMS *Trincomalee*. Another recipient was Brian Dinsdale, a stalwart supporter of the project as Chief Executive of Hartlepool Borough Council, for his services to regeneration in Hartlepool.

Between 1987 and 2001 the decayed hulk of the old TS *Foudroyant* that arrived in Hartlepool had been transformed into the fully restored frigate HMS *Trincomalee*. Her restoration had been completed on time, within budget, and to universal acclaim. In fulfilling the task they set themselves in 1986 the *Foudroyant* Trustees had reason to be grateful for the generous support of local, regional, national and European bodies, individuals, grant making trusts and a loyal paying public. With this support the project workforce provided the human resources of skill and experience, determination and flexible management to do the job. The project has set a standard for the restoration of wooden ships that will be hard to equal.

HMS *Trincomalee* is the oldest ship afloat in Britain, and nearly two centuries after her construction she retains over sixty per cent of her original hull fabric. The durability that underpins this fact is testimony to the skill of her builders, and the quality of her materials; that so little of the fabric had to be replaced reflects the skilled and sympathetic restoration. Bombay and Hartlepool can take pride in their ship.

Epilogue

While the restored HMS *Trincomalee* makes an imposing, award winning sight, the accumulated statistics are equally impressive. The restoration took eleven years, around three-quarters of a million man hours, supported by the Trust raising ten and half million pounds, about eight million of which was invested in the local economy in wages and purchases.

There is also a long term conservation plan for the ship, as all wooden structures, however well restored, need constant care and maintenance. It was recognised that the best source for the necessary funds would be the visiting public, if they could be made aware of the ship. Here the Teesside Development Corporation had stepped in, recognising the potential role of the ship in regenerating the town and the area. The ship would serve as an icon, linking the shipbuilding past with the marine leisure based activities of the present and future. With this vision in place the ship was restored against the backdrop of a remarkable change in the town, with a multi-million pound marina, business and residential developments. In this positive environment the Trust has planned for the future, with new partners, and new challenges. HMS *Trincomalee* will play a major role in the education, tourism, leisure and economic opportunities of the region.

However, the Trust had first to overcome the serious loss of capital grants after April 2001 if it were to sustain the restoration and continue the public operation and appropriate maintenance of the ship. Hartlepool Borough Council helped with office accommodation, storage space and a revenue grant in 2001. In addition the Trust's fund raising efforts in the charitable sector also began to produced encouraging results.

Throughout this period the Trust was in discussion with a developer, introduced through English Partnerships, who had inherited the responsibilities of the former Teesside Development Corporation. The aim has been to create a partnership that will enable the long-awaited Visitor Centre for the Trust to be built on land close by at Jackson Basin. The Centre would provide the space for exhibitions and displays about the ship, and the many worlds that she has inhabited. These could combine a core of permanent material with opportunities to focus on specific aspects of her career. To make the most of this opportunity discussions have continued with the National Maritime Museum, with the aim of bringing artefacts and exhibitions from the Museum to the Visitor Centre to supplement the Trust's existing collection. The presence of a major national museum would lend status to the further development of the region. The records generated by the restoration have been lodged with the University of Teesside, through the good offices of the Vice Chancellor, where they are stored under ideal conditions, ready to guide those who would follow in the footsteps of the Trust.

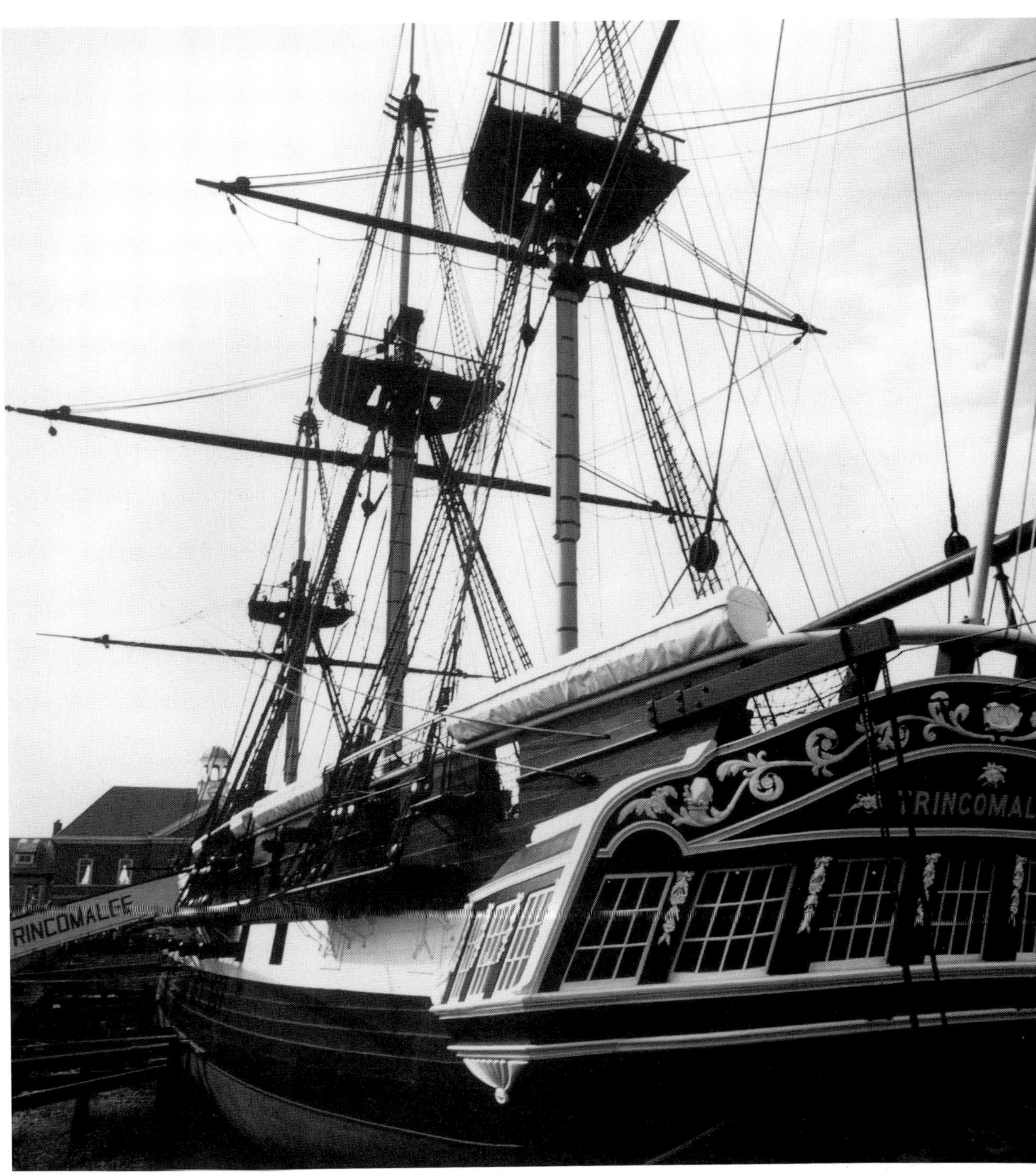

With the restoration work complete, the ship was refloated and the lower yards crossed. The topsail and topgallant yards have been made, but in order to preserve the ship's stability they will not be shipped until the *Trincomalee* is permanently moored in the Jackson Basin and can be ballasted deeper. The quality of the decorative work on the stern and quarter galleries makes it obvious why the project has won a prestigious award from the World Ship Trust – and the praise of the whole ship preservation movement at large.

Ultimately it is planned that the ship will be undocked, and moored in Jackson Dock, close by the completed Visitor Centre. Access will be along a fixed jetty. This location will make HMS *Trincomalee* visible from all angles. Once in place visitors will be able to stand back and marvel at a fully fitted wooden warship, one of the finest achievements of human ingenuity. Few artefacts so clearly demonstrate the intellectual sophistication of mankind as this structure. Although made by hand, from thousands of pieces of wood, using techniques developed over centuries, it was durable enough to brave the oceans of the world and survive nearly two centuries afloat. *Trincomalee* will allow succeeding generations to marvel at the prowess of their precursors.

The ship's current home is the Historic Quay. Although an entirely modern development this 'outdoor museum' is devoted to the shoreside infrastructure that supported seafaring in the age of sail, so is a perfectly appropriate environment for *Trincomalee*. The one disadvantage is that the complete ship cannot be seen and appreciated from any distance, but this will be remedied when she is eventually moored in the basin outside, with access across a jetty from a new purpose-built visitor centre.

Furthermore, HMS *Trincomalee* offers a unique opportunity to revisit the world of the Nelsonic frigate, the very stuff of fiction, made famous by Marryat, Forester and O'Brian. Together with a linked museum and exhibition space in the shore-side Visitor Centre the ship will open up new vistas for the visitor, making connections with the many worlds that have touched the ship, and that have been touched by her. Over time it is hoped that these worlds will be the focus of specific exhibitions, drawing on every facet of her story, from Bombay shipwrights and Malabar foresters to the generations that swung a hammock under her deck, and the skilled team that brought her back to life.

This is not just the story of a ship, it is also the story of the people who have made her a thing of life for two hundred years. The future for HMS *Trincomalee* is bright.

The HMS *Trincomalee* Trust has a web site that provides information about the ship and the continuing developments. The address is: www.hms-trincomalee.co.uk

Appendix 1

The Royal Navy's Indian Battlefleet, 1803-1850

(These ships were built at Bombay, unless otherwise indicated)

74-GUN LINE OF BATTLE SHIPS

Akbar built at Prince of Wales Island (Penang): laid down 1807, cancelled 1809, never completed

Minden launched 1810: hulked 1842 as a seamen's hospital at Hong Kong, sold 1861

Cornwallis launched 1813: screw blockship 1855, hulk 1865, broken up at Queenborough 1957

Wellesley launched 1815: hulked 1862 Chatham, 1868 school ship, sunk by enemy bombs 1940

Melville launched 1817: hulked 1857 as a hospital ship at Hong Kong, sold 1873

Malabar launched 1818: hulked 1848 as a coal depot at Portsmouth, sold 1905

Carnatic launched at Portsmouth in 1823, but built from Indian frames and timbers: hulked 1860 as a coal depot, floating magazine for War Office 1886, returned 1891, sold 1914

Hastings built at Calcutta, purchased 1819: steam blockship 1855, Coastguard 1857, hulk as a coal depot 1870, sold 1885

Imaum presented to RN 1836 (originally built as the *Liverpool* for the Imaum of Muscat): receiving hulk at Port Royal, Jamaica from 1842, broken up1862-66

80-GUN SHIPS

Indus launched at Portsmouth in 1839, built from Indian materials: hulked 1860 as harbour flagship at Devonport, broken up 1898

Hindostan launched at Devonport 1841, built from Indian materials: hulked at Portsmouth 1884, to Dartmouth 1905 as part of the *Britannia* training ship, broken up 1921

84-GUN SHIPS

Ganges launched 1821: hulked 1857 as training ship at Portsmouth, training ship at Plymouth 1866, broken up 1929. Gave her name to the Boy's Training Establishment at Shotley in Suffolk.

Asia launched 1824: British flagship at the Battle of Navarino 20 October 1827, hulked as harbour flagship at Portsmouth 1859, broken up 1906

Bombay launched 1828: screw ship 1861, destroyed by fire off Montevideo 1864

Calcutta launched 1831: hulked at Portsmouth 1863 as part of the gunnery training establishment HMS *Excellent*, sold 1906

NEW 80-GUN SHIPS

Meeanee (ex-*Madras*, renamed 1843) undocked 1848: screw ship 1857, floating hospital for War Office 1867, quarantine hulk Hong Kong 1886, broken up there 1905

FRIGATES

Salsette launched 1807: hulked 1831

Doris (ex-*Pitt*) launched 1805, sold April 1829 at Valparaiso

Malacca (ex-*Penang*) built at Penang, launched 1809: broken up 1815

Amphitrite launched 1816: to Coastguard 1857, to contractors at Plymouth 1862, broken up January 1875

Trincomalee launched 1817: hulked 1861

Seringapatam launched 1819: hulked 1847 as coal depot at Cape of Good Hope, broken up 1873-1883

Madagascar launched 1822: hulked 1846 as provision depot at Plymouth, receiving ship at Rio de Janiero 1853-62, sold 1863

Andromeda launched 1829: hulked at Liverpool 1836, sold 24 December 1863

Manilla cancelled 1831

SLOOPS (built at Cochin)

Atholl class

Alligator launched 1821: hulked 1854

Herald (ex-*Termagant*) launched 1822: two major survey commissions 1840s-1850s, hulked 1861

Samarang launched 1822: hulked 1847

BRIGS

Victor launched 1814: foundered in West Indies 1842

Zebra launched 1815: wrecked off Mount Carmel 2 December 1840

Cameleon launched 1816: broken up 1849

Sphinx launched 1815: packet 1825, sold 1835

Nerbudda (ex-*Goshawk*) launched 1848: foundered 1856

Jumna (ex-*Zebra*) launched 1848: sold 1862

26-GUN FRIGATE

Malacca launched at Moulmein 1853: screw fitted Chatham 1854, sold 1869 to Japan and broken up 1906

TANK VESSELS

Cochin built at Cochin in 1820 for Trincomali dockyard: sold 1850

Teazer built at Moulmein in 1851

Appendix 2

Chairmen of the Ship's Committees and Trusts

Implacable Committee

1925–1932	Sir Geoffrey Callender	*Implacable* (ex-FS *Duguay-Trouin*)
1932	Sir Geoffrey Callender	*Implacable* and *Foudroyant* (1)

Implacable Committee of Society for Nautical Research

1933–1940	Vice Admiral Humphrey Hugh Smith DSO (Killed in action 1940, Commodore of Convoys)	*Implacable* and *Foudroyant*
1940–1945	Admiral Sir Aubrey Hugh Smith	do. (2)
	KCVO KCB CVO	do. (2)
1945–1947	Admiral Sir Percy Noble KCB CVO	do. (3)

Foudroyant Committee of Society for Nautical Research

1947–1950	Admiral Sir Percy Noble KCB CVO	*Foudroyant*
1950–1959	Admiral Sir Clement Moody	do.
	KCB	do.

The *Foudroyant* Trust

1959–1967	Frank Carr CB CBE	*Foudroyant*
1967–1975	Admiral Sir Wilfred Woods GBE KCB DSO* (Died 1975)	do.
1975–1978	Captain O M Watts (Acting Chairman)	do.
1979–1992	Captain David T Smith RN (Elder Brother of Trinity House)	do. (4)

The HMS *Trincomalee* Trust

1992–2000	Captain David T Smith RN (Elder Brother of Trinity House)	*Trincomalee*
2000 to present	Colonel Michael Stewart OBE TD DL	do.

Notes:

(1) Sixth Rate ex-*Trincomalee*

(2) 1943 to 1945 both ships mobilised for war service as HMS *Foudroyant*

(3) *Implacable* scuttled in position 9½ miles South East of Owers Light Vessel on 2 December 1947

(4) Reverted to former name *Trincomalee* on formation of new Trust

Appendix 3

Foudroyant Trust (Incorporated 13 May 1959)

Chairmen of the *Foudroyant* Trust

F G G Carr CB CBE	1959 to 1967
Admiral Sir Wilfred Woods GBE KCB DSO*	1967 to 1975
Captain O M Watts ARIN FRAS FRIN (Acting Chairman)	1975 to 1978
Captain D T Smith FNI RN	1979 to 2000
Colonel R M Stewart OBE TD DL BSc	2000 to present

President

Captain D T Smith OBE FNI RN	2000 to present

Vice Presidents and Honorary Members from 1975

Sir Max Aitken Bt DSO DFC	to 1984
Henry Barraclough CVO	to 1982
Vice Admiral Sir Lancelot Bell Davies KBE	2000 to present
Captain R S Clement Brown MBE BA RA	1977 to 1986
John Brown CBE MC	to 1977
F G G Carr CB CBE	to 1991
Sir Harold Danckwerts PC	to 1978
Captain H M Denham CMG RN	to 1993
The Earl of Derby MC	to 1994
Maldwin Drummond OBE DL JP	to 1985
Lord Montagu of Beaulieu	1981 to present
Flag Officer, Portsmouth (Ex Officio)	to 1992
The Lord Mayor of Portsmouth (Ex Officio)	to present
The Mayor of Gosport (Ex Officio)	to present
The Viscount Runciman of Doxford OBE AFC	to 1988
The Lord Wakefield of Kendal	to 1984
Captain O M Watts FRAS FRIN ARIN	1981 to 1984

Trustees from 1975

Captain O M Watts FRAS FRIN ARIN	Acting Chairman from 1975 to 1977, Trustee to 1979
Captain D T Smith FNI RN	Trustee from 1976. Chairman from 1979 to 2000
Colonel R M Stewart OBE TD DL BSc	from 1993. Chairman from 2000
R L Allison BA RD	from 2000 to present
R Atkinson MA	from 1984 to 1988
R Betts	from 1979 to 1990
Captain R S Clement Brown MBE BA RA	from 1978 to 1986
R L de Bunsen MA	to 1977
D Cobb ROI	to 1977
Lady Daley MBE JP	to 1990
Vice Admiral Sir Lancelot Bell Davies KBE	from 1983 to 2000
Maldwin Drummond OBE DL JP	to 1984
T Dulake	from 1987 to 1989
Lieutenant Commander R M Frampton FNI RN	from 1983 to 1997
M J Henley MA	to 1984
N R L Hogg JP MA FICS	from 2000 to present
R Horton	to 1983
M L A Houstoun	from 1979 to 1980
Colonel E H Houstoun OBE	from 1981 to present
B F Hubbard FLAS	to 1978
M J Kearley	from 1981 to 1983
J F Huggett OBE FCIS	from 1988 to 1989
A M C McGinnity	from 1980 to 1990
Admiral Sir Rae McKaig KCB CBE	from 1978 to 1979
W O B Majer	from 1978 to 1985

Mr J O Mennear BSc FMA	from 1992 to present
Lord Montagu of Beaulieu	to 1980
Captain W J Parsons VRD RNR	to 1979
T Pocock	from 1979 to 1989
Douglas R Reeman	to 1990
R J Sale	from 1994 to present
Miss Josepha Aubrey Smith	to 1977
R S Spoor OBE RD DCL DL FCA	from 2000 to present
Commodore P R Sutermeister RN	from 1993 to present
G Symington	to 1980
M J Tapper FRSA	from 2000 to present
R C Thornton	from 1983 to 1992
Colonel W D Tovey MBE TD MSc	from 1993 to present
Captain J R Tyrrell FRIN FBIM	from 1983 to 1998
Commander R L Warren RN	to present
R E Willson	to 1978

Officers of the Trust

Prior to the formation of the *Foudroyant* Trust, the post-war period included a number of Captain Superintendents, of whom Commander K Michel DSO MVO DSC was Superintendent from 1949 to 1950 and Commander M S Spalding in 1955 on behalf of the *Foudroyant* Committee of the Society for Nautical Research.

Lieutenant Commander S S Noble RN	Capt Superintendent 1959–1965
Lieutenant Commander A Langley RN	Capt Superintendent 1966–1972
Lieutenant Commander R Paige MBE RN	Capt Superintendent 1973– 1979
M A Hemmings	Capt Superintendent 1979–1987
Captain R S Clement Brown MBE BA RA	Hon Secretary and Treasurer 1937–1976
M J Kearley	Treasurer 1976–1981
G H Kerr	Treasurer 1982–1984
J E Lee	Treasurer 1984–1987
J F Huggett OBE FCIS	Treasurer 1987–1988
Lieutenant Commander L J Hayward RNR	Hon General Secretary 1976–1978
V G Stamp	Hon General Secretary 1978–1988
Mrs Jill Warren	Appeal Secretary 1982–1984
J Denny	Admin Officer 1984–1987 and Hon General Secretary 1988– 1989
A G Bridgewater	Director 1988–1992

Appendix 4

HMS *Trincomalee* Trust (Incorporated 16 January 1992)

Patron

HRH The Duke of Edinburgh KG KT

President

Captain D T Smith OBE FNI RN from June 2000

Vice Presidents

Vice Admiral Sir Lancelot Bell Davies KBE	from March 2000
Sir Ronald Norman OBE DL	from January 1997
Mr R Thornton	from January 1992

Trustees

Captain D T Smith FNI RN	Chairman from January 1992 until June 2000
Colonel R M Stewart OBE TD DL BSc	from April 1993. Chairman from June 2000

Commodore P R Sutermeister RN	from December 1993. Vice Chairman from June 2000
Mr R L Allison BA RD	from March 2000
Vice Admiral Sir Lancelot Bell Davies KBE	from January 1992 until March 2000
Mr R W H Betts	from January 1992 until October 1997
Councillor S C Close	from December 2000
Councillor D R P Ferriday FRSA AMPA ABIPP	from June 2000 until October 2000
Lt. Commander R M Frampton FNI FRSA RN	from January 1992 until June 1997
Professor D Fraser BA MA PhD FRHist	from December 1998
Councillor Mrs S G Hanson	from December 1998 until June 2000
Mr N R L Hogg JP MA FICS	from May 1998
Colonel E H Houstoun OBE	from January 1992
Mr A M C McGinnity	from January 1992 until July 1997
Air Vice Marshall A F C Hunter CBE AFC DL	from December 2000
Mr J O Mennear BSc FMA	from January 1992
Sir Ronald Norman OBE DL	from January 1992 until January 1997
Mr R J Sale FCIB DL	from October 1994
Mr N A Sloan BSc MPhil CPSA	from December 1998
Mr R C Spoor OBE RD DCL DL FCA	from December 1998
Mr M J Tapper FRSA	from June 1997
Colonel W J Tovey MBE TD MSc	from March 1993
Captain A J R Tyrrell FRIN FBIM MN	from January 1992 until September 1998
Commander R L Warren RN	from January 1992

Company Secretary

Mr A G Bridgewater	from January 1992 until May 1995
Mr R D Wynn	from June 1995 until April 1997
Mr D B Hughes	from February 1998

Appendix 5

Employees of the Trust

A small number of employees began pre-restoration work on the hull from 1989 under the auspices of The *Foudroyant* Trust. Some of these were employed for a short time through Hartlepool Borough Council on a shared basis. This enabled a small team to be mobilised and thereafter expanded as personnel and financial resources became available. With initial preparations completed the restoration commenced on 1 January 1990.

The Trust had, by then, decided to restore the ship to her 1817 configuration whilst maintaining certain in-service improvements. To achieve historical authenticity the ship's name reverted to HMS *Trincomalee* and a new Trust was formed, with the same Trustees and Officers, to reflect the revised objects of the Charity. This was incorporated on 16 January 1992 as The HMS *Trincomalee* Trust, following which the former Trust became dormant, having surrendered all assets to the new Trust.

Administration

		From	*To*
Bryn Hughes	General Manager	1998	Present
Tony Bridgewater	Development Officer	1990	1999
Brenda Forstad	Administration Manager	1997	2001
Robert Day Wynn*	Admin Officer	1992	1997
Jackie Bujnowski	Admin Assistant	1994	1998
Jayne Pounder	Admin Assistant	2001	2001
Christine Robertson	Admin Assistant	2000	Present
Susana Sargeant	Admin Assistant	1998	2000
Eileen Wray*	Admin Assistant	1990	1996
Sandra Young	Admin Assistant	1997	2000

Maximum number of posts during the restoration project = 5

* Denotes the employee died in service

Restoration Workforce

		From	*To*
Bill Stevenson*	Restoration Manager	1991	1999
Keith Johnson	Sen.Tech.Officer/ Draughtsman	1990	2001
Alan Wilson	Project Draughtsman	1990	2000
Jackie Cannon*	Shipwright/ Carpenter (Ch)	1990	1997
Les Gilfoyle	Restoration Ch/Supervisor	1990	1995
Les Gilfoyle	Works Superintendent	1995	Present
Andy Welsh	Shipwright/ Carpenter (Ch)	1990	2001
John Rowntree	Shipwright/ Carpenter (Ch)	1995	2000
Brian Smith	Ships Engineer	1989	2000
Steven Butler	Shipwright/ Carpenter	1997	2001
Leo Dolphin	Shipwright/ Carpenter	1990	Present
Ian Cruikshanks	Shipwright/ Carpenter	1993	2001
Richard Eyre	Shipwright/ Carpenter	1990	1999
Brendon Eyre	Shipwright/ Carpenter	1992	2001
Harry Hall	Shipwright/ Carpenter	1997	2001
Steven Harrison	Shipwright/ Carpenter	1996	2000
John Lowther	Shipwright/ Carpenter	1998	1998
William Percival*	Shipwright/ Carpenter	1992	1994
Ken Pickup	Shipwright/ Carpenter	1992	2000
Norman Readman	Shipwright/ Carpenter	1991	2000
Colin Relton	Shipwright/ Carpenter	1998	2001
Phillip Robinson	Shipwright/ Carpenter	1991	2000
William Robinson	Shipwright/ Carpenter	1992	2000
Thomas Sarginson	Shipwright/ Carpenter	1992	2000
Mark Stevenson	Shipwright/ Carpenter	1996	2000
William Sutheran	Shipwright/ Carpenter	1990	2000
Scott Turnbull	Shipwright/ Carpenter	1997	2001
Robert Thirkell	Shipwright/ Carpenter	1992	2000
Alan Storm	Shipwright/ Carpenter	1992	1999
David West	Shipwright/ Carpenter	1990	2000
Lawrence Winter	Shipwright/ Carpenter	1992	1996
John Gamble	Rigger	1990	2001
Thomas Leck	Rigger	1990	2000
Dave Lilley	Rigger	1995	Present
Robert Monsen	Rigger	1990	2001
Mel Armstrong	Storeman	1996	2000
Robert Bell	Welder	1992	2000
John Winspear	Welder/ Restoration Hand	1993	2000
Robert Chapple	Painter	1990	2000
Ron Turner	Painter	1993	2001
Andrew Emmerson	Electrician	1996	2000
David Mulcahy	Electrician	1990	1993
Peter Filby	Restoration Hand	1993	1995
Martin Griffiths	Driver/ Restoration Hand	1996	2000
David Ablett	Watchman	1994	1995
Robert Davison	Watchman	1994	1995
Leslie Ford	Watchman	1994	1995
Joan Docherty	Cleaner	1990	2000
Francis Nash	Cleaner	2001	2001
Sheila Webster	Cleaner	2001	Present

Maximum number of posts during restoration project = 37
Ch = Chargehand
* denotes died in service

Ship Guides

		From	*To*
Joan Lilley	Chief Guide	1991	Present
Jen Hall	Senior Ships Guide	1992	Present
Katharine Ainger	Guide	2001	Present
Pat Andrews	Guide	1997	Present

		From	*To*
Carol Atkinson	Guide	1994	1997
Kirsty Atkinson	Guide	1997	1997
Richard Banks	Guide	1999	2000
Stuart Burke	Guide	1991	1994
John C Harrison	Guide	2000	Present
Sophie Hogg	Guide	1996	1996
Brian Hopkins	Guide & Security Officer	1990	1999
Ben Kerr	Guide	2001	2001
Liz McCormack	Guide	1993	2000

		From	*To*
Marie Priest	Guide	1991	1995
Ann Simmons	Guide	1993	1997
Pamela Stott	Guide	1992	1997
Bill Waldmeyer	Guide	2001	2001
Jim Waller	Guide	1992	1994
Jackie Ward	Guide	1999	1999
Sheila Willingale	Guide	1992	Present
Kelly Anne Wray	Guide	1994	1995
Ann Parkinson	Guide	1990	1992

All posts are part-time

Appendix 6

Grants, Donations and Gifts to the Trust

The HMS *Trincomalee* Trust acknowledges with grateful thanks the many grants, donations and gifts from institutions, organisations, individuals and well-wishers that have supported the project to date. In addition, the Trust has received valuable help-in-kind, particularly from Teesside Development Corporation, Hartlepool Borough Council and Corus.

The list below identifies the main contributors to the project. The Trust also recognises the many other donations, sometimes anonymously given, that it has received.

Donor	*Date*
James E Atkinson	2001
Barclays Bank	1995
Vice Admiral Sir Lancelot Bell Davies	1999
Hannah Bloom Charitable Trust	1999/2001
British Telecom	1999
E F Blunt	2000
W A Cadbury Charitable Trust	1994
Cleveland Action Team	1990/1992
Cleveland Community Foundation	2001
Clothworkers' Foundation	1992/2001
Cory Towage Limited	1999
Coulthurst Trust	2001
De Claremont Charitable Company Ltd	2001
Dulverton Trust	2001
The Duke of Edinburgh's Trust	2001

Donor	*Date*
English Heritage	1991
European Regional Development Fund	1995/1996 1998/2000
Ernest Cook Trust	2001
Roland Cookson Charitable Trust	2001
Esmee Fairbairn Charitable Trust	1991/1993
Fishmongers' Co. Charitable Trust	2001
Friends of HMS *Trincomalee*	2000
Friends of HMS *Warrior*	1992
Garfield Weston Foundation	1991/1996 1998
Gillham Charitable Trust	2001
Go Ahead Group plc	2001
Gosling Foundation	2001
Alan Green	1992
The Worshipful Company of Grocers	2001
Haberdashers' Company	2001
Hampshire County Council	1987
Hartlepool Borough Council	1989/1992 1999/2001
Hartlepool Safer Cities	1991
Hartlepool Task Force	1990
Percy Hedley Will Trust	1991/2001
Heritage Lottery Fund	1995/1997 1997
P H Holt Charitable Trust	1999
Colonel Euan Houstoun	2001
Major Henry Hugh-Smith	1992
Idelwild Trust	1996

Donor	*Date*
Integrated Development Opportunites Prog.	1991/1992
Inchcape Ltd	1986
Kelly Charitable Trust	2001
John A King	1992
Sir James Knott Trust	1993/1996
L J C Fund Ltd	2001
Andrew G Linsley	2001
Manifold Charitable Trust	1987/2001
R W Mann Trustees Limited	2001
The Marine Society	1986
Sir George Martin Trust	1991
The Hon Company of Master Mariners	2001
Mercers' Charitable Foundation	1994/1996 2001
Mercers' Educational Trust Fund	2001
National Heritage Memorial Fund	1991
Peter Olsen	1999
Orchid Drinks Company Ltd	1999
Peacock Charitable Trust	1991/1993
Pilgrim Trust	1993
Sir John Priestman Charity Trust	2001
Seamen's Hospital Society	1999
P & D Shepherd Charitable Trust	2001
Shipwrights' Company	1991/1994 1996/1999

Donor	*Date*
Captain David Smith	2000
Daphne Smith	2002
W W Spooner Charitable Trust	1999
Roger C Spoor	2000
Colonel Michael Stewart	2001
Peter Stormonth-Darling	2001
Storrow Scott Charitable Trust	2001
Sir Hugh & Ruby Sykes Charitable Trust	2001
Teesside Development Corporation	1989/1992 1996
Tees Valley Training & Enterprise Council	2001
Thornton Foundation	1987/1993 2000
Trinity House Charities	2001
Trinity House London	1986
Tyneside Charitable Trust	2001
Nigel Vinson Charitable Trust	2002
Neville Wadia Charitable Trust	1995
West Hartlepool Steam Navigation Co.	1999
The 1989 Willan Charitable Trust	2001
Woodroffe Benton Foundation	2001
Yorkshire Bank Charitable Trust	2001

Index

Page numbers in *italics* refer to illustrations.